PSYCHE GATE

A ONE STOP SOLUTION FOR GATE PSYCHOLOGY

MR. RAJ SHUKLA

MS. RITU SRIVASTAVA

Contents

Preface

With the rising popularity and competitiveness of the GATE Psychology paper, the need for a structured, concept-driven, and exam-oriented preparation resource has become increasingly important.

Psyche GATE – A One Stop Solution for GATE Examination has been crafted to fulfil this need by offering a comprehensive and detailed analysis of the previous year's questions (PYQs), tailored specifically for aspirants aiming to crack the GATE Psychology exam confidently and clearly.This book is not just a collection of questions and answers—it is a guide to understanding the why behind each correct option and the why not behind the distractors. Through meticulous explanation of every question, this book aims to strengthen conceptual clarity, enhance critical thinking, and provide strategic insights into the nature and structure of the GATE Psychology exam.

Key Highlights of this Book:

- Detailed explanations for all PYQs with conceptual reasoning.
- Mock practice papers.
- Student-friendly language to make complex concepts easy to understand.

Whether you are just starting your preparation or are revising for a second attempt, **Psyche GATE** is designed to serve as your dependable companion throughout the journey. I am confident that this book helps you better understand psychology and equips you to approach the exam clearly and confidently.

Wishing you success, learning, and growth.

Warm regards,

Mr.Raj Shukla

Ms Ritu Srivastava

(Authors – Psyche GATE)

Syllabus Xh-c5 Psychology

C5.1 Research Methods and Statistics

C5.1.1 Approaches to Research: Philosophical worldviews & criteria involved in approach. Research design: quantitative & qualitative, mixed methods.

C5.1.2 Designing Research: Research problems, purpose statement, Variables and Operational Definitions, Hypothesis, Sampling.

C5.1.3 Nature of Quantitative & Qualitative Research: Structured, semi-structured interviewing, self-completion questionnaires (Survey), observation, Experimental, Quasi-experimental, Field studies, Focus group discussions, Narratives, Case studies, Ethnography.

C5.1.4 Ethics in conducting and reporting research.

C5.1.5 Statistics in Psychology: Measures of Central Tendency and Dispersion. Normal Probability Curve. Parametric and Non-parametric tests Effect size and Power analysis.

C5.1.6 Correlational Analysis: Correlation [Product Moment, Rank Order], Partial correlation, multiple correlation. Unique Correlation Methods: Biserial, Point biserial, tetrachoric, phi coefficient. Regression: Simple linear regression, Multiple regression. Factor analysis: Assumptions, Methods, Rotation and Interpretation.

C5.1.7 Experimental Designs: ANOVA [One-way, Factorial], Randomized Block Designs, Repeated Measures Design, Latin Square, Cohort studies, Time series, MANOVA, ANCOVA. Single-subject designs.

C5.2 Psychometrics: Foundations of Psychological measurement; Basic components: scales and items' Construction and analysis of items: Intelligence test items, performance tests, Ability & Aptitude tests, Personality questionnaires. Method of test construction, Standardization of measures: Reliability, Validity, Norms, Application of assessment and measurements in Tests— Applications of psychological testing in various education, counselling and guidance, clinical, organisational and developmental.

C5.3 Biological and Evolutionary Basis of Behaviour: Heredity and behaviour Evolution and natural selection, Nervous system, structures of the brain and their functions, Neurons: Structure, functions, types, neural impulse, synaptic transmission. Neurotransmitters. Hemispheric lateralisation, The endocrine system types and functions, Biological basis of Motivation: Hunger, Thirst, Sleep and Sex. Biological basis of emotion: The Limbic system, Hormonal regulation of behaviour. Methods of Physiological Psychology: Invasive methods – Anatomical methods, degeneration techniques, lesion techniques, chemical methods, microelectrode studies, Non-invasive methods – EEG, Scanning methods, Muscular and Glandular system: Genetics and behaviour: Chromosomal anomalies; NatureNurture controversy [Twin studies and adoption studies]

C5.4 Perception, Learning, Memory and Forgetting: What is sensation, sensory thresholds and sensory adaptations, Vision, hearing, touch and pain, smell and taste, kinesthesis and vestibular sense, Perception: role of attention; organising principles of perception, gestalt perception, depth perception and illusions, Theories of learning: classical conditioning, operant conditioning, social learning theory, cognitive learning, Memory: encoding, storage, retrieval, Information processing theories of memory, Retrieval in Long term memory, reconstructive nature of long-term memory, Forgetting: encoding failure, interference theory, memory trace decay theory, the physical aspects of memory.

C5.5 Cognition: Thinking, Intelligence and Language: Basic elements of thought: Concepts, Propositions, Imagery. Current paradigms of cognitive psychology – Information processing approach, ecological approach, Problem-solving: Methods of problem-solving, Strategies and obstacles, Role of Metacognitive processing, decision-making: choosing among alternatives, Intelligence: Theories of intelligence (Spearman; Thurstone; Jensen; Cattell; Gardner; Stenberg) and Emotional Intelligence; Measuring intelligence, Individual differences in Intelligence; Role of heredity and environment, Difference between Intelligence, Aptitude and Creativity.

C5.6 Personality: Theories of personality: Psychoanalytic, behaviourist, social cognitive view, humanism and trait and type theories, Biology of personality and Assessment of personality.

C5.7 Motivation, Emotion and Stress and Coping: Approaches to understanding motivation: instinct, drive-reduction, arousal, incentive, humanistic, Achievement motivation, Intrinsic motivation, aggression, curiosity and exploration, Emotions: nature of emotions; biological basis of emotions, Theories of emotions: James-Lange, Canon-Bard, Schachter and Singer, Lazarus, Definition of stress; what are stressors; cognitive factors in stress, Factors in stress reaction: General adaptation syndrome; effect of stress, Coping with stress: problem-focused coping; emotion-focused coping, REBT and meditation

C5.8 Social Psychology: Social perception: Attribution; impression formation; social categorisation, implicit personality theory, Social influence: conformity, compliance and obedience, Attitudes, beliefs and values: Evaluating the social world, attitude formation, attitude change and persuasion, cognitive dissonance, Prejudice, discrimination, Aggression, power and prosocial behaviour, Belief systems and value patterns. Group dynamics, leadership style and effectiveness, Theories of intergroup relations and conflicts.

C5.9 Development Across the Life Span: Nature versus nurture in human development, Prenatal development: Chromosomes, Genes and DNA. Physical, cognitive and psychosocial development in infancy, childhood, adolescence and adulthood, Theories of ageing, Moral development.

C5.10 Applications of Psychology: Psychological disorders: Conceptions of mental disorders; Assessment and diagnosis, DSM and Other tools, PTSD and Trauma; Psychotherapies: Psychodynamic, Phenomenological/ Experiential therapy; Behaviour therapy; cognitive therapy; biological therapy, Applications of theories of motivation and learning in School: Factors in educational achievement; counselling & guidance in schools, Application of theories of motivation, learning, emotions, perceptions, group dynamics & leadership to organisational set up, Issues of Personal space, crowding, and territoriality

CHAPTER I

PREVIOUS YEAR QUESTIONS 2025 ANALYSIS

1. Parenting style in which parents are so involved that children are permitted to behave without set limits is termed as__________.

(A) Permissive neglectful parenting
(B) Permissive indulgent parenting
(C) Authoritarian parenting
(D) Willful parenting

Correct Answer (B) Permissive indulgent parenting – This style is characterised by parents who are highly involved in their children's lives but do not enforce rules or discipline. They allow their children to behave freely without setting limits, often to avoid confrontation or because they want to be seen as more of a friend than a parent.

Explanation of other options

(A) Permissive neglectful parenting is a parenting style where parents are uninvolved in their child's life, showing little interest, supervision, or emotional support. They do not set limits but also fail to provide warmth or guidance.

(C) Authoritarian parenting is a strict and controlling parenting style where parents enforce rigid rules and expect obedience without question. There is little warmth or flexibility, and discipline is often harsh.

(D) Willful parenting – This is not a widely recognised psychological term for a parenting style. It may refer to parents who encourage independence and determination but does not explicitly describe a style where children can behave without limits.

Explanation of Keywords: Parenting Style- A parenting style is how parents act, feel, and behave when they spend time with their child.

2.________ in both lobes of the brain are responsible for the coordination and interpretation of information as well as higher mental processing.

(A) Broca's area
(B) Wernicke's area
(C) Parietal area
(D) Association area

Correct Answer: (D) Association area – These areas are found in multiple lobes and are responsible for integrating and interpreting sensory information, coordination, and higher mental functions such as reasoning, problem-solving, and decision-making. Since they exist in both hemispheres, they are crucial in processing information across the brain.

Explanation of other options

(A) Broca's area is a region in the left frontal lobe responsible for speech production and language processing. Damage to Broca's area can result in difficulty forming words (Broca's aphasia), but comprehension remains mostly intact.

(B) Wernicke's area – Located in the left temporal lobe, Wernicke's area is crucial for language comprehension. Damage to this area can cause Wernicke's aphasia, where individuals can speak fluently but with little meaningful content.

(C) Parietal area – The parietal lobe processes sensory information such as touch, spatial awareness, and body position.

Explanation of Keywords: Higher Mental Processing- In psychology, higher mental processing refers to complex cognitive activities that involve thinking, reasoning, problem-solving, decision-making, and understanding

3. If Skinner: Behaviorism, then Howard Gardner: ________________

(A) Sociocultural
(B) Cognitivism

(C) Evolutionary perspective

(D) Humanistic perspective

Correct Answer: (B) Cognitivism

Howard Gardner is best known for his Theory of Multiple Intelligences (MI), which argues that intelligence is not a single general ability (as traditional IQ tests suggest) but consists of multiple distinct types (e.g., linguistic, logical-mathematical, spatial, musical, bodily-kinaesthetic, interpersonal, intrapersonal, and naturalistic intelligence).

His work aligns with Cognitivism, a psychological approach focusing on mental processes such as perception, problem-solving, memory, and learning.

Explanation of other options

(A) Sociocultural Perspective: This theory, proposed by Lev Vygotsky, emphasises how social interactions, culture, and language shape cognitive development.

(C) Evolutionary Perspective: This perspective, championed by figures like David Buss and Leda Cosmides, suggests that human psychological traits have evolved through natural selection. Gardner's theory is not rooted in evolutionary explanations but rather in cognitive psychology and education.

(D) Humanistic Perspective: The Humanistic Perspective, led by theorists such as Carl Rogers and Abraham Maslow, focuses on personal growth, free will, and self-actualisation. While Gardner's work values individual potential, it is primarily a cognitive framework rather than a humanistic one.

Explanation of Keywords: Behaviorism: Behaviorism school focuses on studying observable behaviours rather than internal thoughts or feelings.

4. An experimental set-up where neither the experimenter nor the participants know who is in the experimental or control groups is known as?

(A) Random experimentation

(B) Blind experimentation

(C) Single-blind study

(D) Double-masked study

Correct Answer: (D) Double-Blind Study – In this setup, neither the participants nor the experimenter knows which individuals are in the experimental or control groups. This design is used to eliminate both participant and experimenter bias, making the results more reliable.

Explanation of other options:

(A) Random Experimentation – This refers to an experimental design where participants are randomly assigned to different groups (e.g. experimental or control groups) to minimise bias.

(B) Blind Experimentation – Some information is hidden from the participants or the researchers.

(C) Single Blind Study – In this type of study, only the participants do not know whether they are in the experimental or control group, but the experimenter does. This helps reduce participant bias (e.g., placebo effects) but does not eliminate experimenter bias.

Explanation of Keywords:

Experimental Group: This group receives the treatment or intervention being tested. Researchers observe how this group responds to determine the effect of the treatment.

Control groups: This group does not receive the treatment or Placebo. It compares to the experimental group, helping researchers see if the treatment had any effect.

5. If Cultural Congruence: Social Psychology, then Evoked Culture: _______?

(A) Evolutionary psychology

(B) Cultural psychology

(C) Cross-cultural psychology

(D) Clinical psychology

Correct Answer: (A) Evoked Culture (Evolutionary Psychology): Evoked culture refers to cultural behaviours and traits that emerge due to environmental pressures and evolved psychological mechanisms. This concept is central to evolutionary psychology, which explores how evolutionary processes have shaped human cognition and behaviour.

Explanation of other options

(B)Cultural psychology: Focuses on how culture influences psychological processes but does not explicitly emphasise the evolutionary basis of culture.

(C)Cross-cultural psychology: Compares psychological phenomena across different cultures but does not primarily focus on how evolutionary factors evoke culture.

(D)Clinical psychology: Deals with diagnosing and treating mental disorders and is not directly related to evoked culture.

Explanation of Keywords: Cultural Congruence (Social Psychology): Cultural congruence refers to how well an individual's behaviours, attitudes, or beliefs align with the cultural norms of their society.

Social psychology studies how people's behaviour is influenced by social contexts, making it the relevant field for understanding cultural congruence.

6. Match the following:

Colum I: Perspectives in Psychology.	Column II: Concept of human nature
P. Psychodynamic	(i) Reactors to the environment
Q. Behavioral	(ii) As thinkers
R. Humanistic	(iii) Controlled by inner forces and conflicts
S Cognitive	(iv) Free agent seeking self-realization

(A) P-iv; Q-iii; R-ii; S-i
(B) P-iii; Q-i; R-ii; S-iv
(C) P-iii; Q-i; R-iv; S-ii
(D) P-iv; Q-iii; R-i; S-ii

Correct Answer: (C) P-iii; Q-i; R-iv; S-ii

Explanation of other options

(P) Psychodynamic → (iii) Controlled by inner forces and conflicts

The psychodynamic perspective, founded by Freud, suggests that unconscious conflicts, past experiences, and inner psychological forces drive human behaviour.

(Q) Behavioural → (i) Reactors to the environment

The behavioural perspectives given by Pavlov, Skinner, and Watson emphasize that environmental stimuli, reinforcement, and conditioning shape behaviour.

(R) Humanistic → (iv) Free agent seeking self-realisation

The humanistic approach, given by Rogers and Maslow, sees individuals as autonomous beings with free will, striving for personal growth and self-actualisation.

(S) Cognitive → (ii) As thinkers

The cognitive perspective focuses on mental processes like perception, thinking, memory, and problem-solving, emphasising how people process and interpret information.

7. Which statistical technique is used to analyse patterns of loading of coefficients?

(A) Correlation
(B) Regression
(C) Factor Analysis
(D) Item Analysis

Correct Answer: (C) Factor Analysis: A statistical technique to identify underlying dimensions (factors) in a dataset by grouping related variables. It helps reduce large sets of variables into smaller factors.

Types: Exploratory Factor Analysis (EFA): Identifies possible underlying factors without prior assumptions.

Confirmatory Factor Analysis (CFA): Tests a hypothesised factor structure to see if it fits the data.

Example: In psychological test construction, factor analysis can determine whether a set of test items measures a single psychological trait or multiple dimensions.

Explanation of other options

(A) Correlation: It measures the strength and direction of the relationship between two variables.

Types: Positive correlation (both variables increase together), negative correlation (one variable increases while the other decreases), and zero correlation (no relationship).

Example: If you measure the correlation between self-esteem and academic achievement, a high positive correlation would suggest that students with higher self-esteem tend to perform better academically.

(B) Regression: Regression is a statistical method used to predict the value of one variable based on another. It helps understand the relationship between dependent and independent variables.

Types: Simple Regression: Examines the relationship between one independent variable and one dependent variable.

Multiple Regression: Includes two or more independent variables predicting a dependent variable.

Example: Multiple regression analysis predicts academic achievement based on self-esteem and resilience scores.

(D) Item Analysis: A process used to evaluate the quality and effectiveness of individual test items. It helps refine a test by identifying poorly performing items.

Key Aspects: Item Difficulty: Measures how many test-takers answer an item correctly.

Item Discrimination: Examines how well an item differentiates between high- and low-performing test-takers.

Example: If a test item on an intelligence test is too easy (almost everyone gets it right), it may not help distinguish between different ability levels.

Explanation of Keywords

Loading of coefficiets: In statistical psychology, the term loading of coefficients often refers to factor loadings in factor analysis or principal component analysis (PCA).

Factor Loadings: These numerical values show how strongly each observed variable (e.g., questionnaire items or test scores) is related to a latent factor (an underlying concept that is not directly measured, like intelligence or anxiety). A higher factor loading (closer to +1 or -1) means the variable has a strong relationship with the factor, while a loading near 0 means a weak relationship.

For example, in a study on emotional intelligence, items measuring empathy, self-regulation, and motivation might load highly on an Emotional Intelligence Factor.

8. Match the following:

Column1	Column 2
P. Instinct	i) Environmental motivation triggers
Q. Incentive	ii) Are fixed action patterns
R. Self-actualization	iii) Self-determination theory
S. Intrinsic motivation	iv) Considered by Maslow as the highest need

(A) P:iv, Q: ii, R: iii, S: i

(B) P:ii, Q:i, R: iv, S:iii

(C) P: i, Q: iii, R: ii, S: iv

(D) P: iii, Q: i, R: iv, S: ii

Correct Answer: (B) P: ii, Q: i, R: iv, S: iii

Explanation of other options

P. Instinct → ii) Are fixed action patterns

Instincts are innate, biologically programmed behaviours that occur in response to specific stimuli. They are often referred to as fixed action patterns because they are automatic and unlearned (e.g., birds migrating, infants sucking).

Q. Incentive → i) Environmental motivation triggers

Incentives are external stimuli that motivate behaviour. These can be rewards (e.g., money, praise) or punishments that influence a person's actions, acting as environmental motivation triggers.

R. Self-actualization → iv) Considered by Maslow as the highest need

Self-actualization is at the top of Maslow's hierarchy of needs, representing the fulfilment of personal potential, creativity, and self-growth.

S. Intrinsic motivation→ iii) Self-determination theory

Intrinsic motivation refers to engaging in an activity for its own sake rather than an external reward. This concept is central to Self-Determination Theory (SDT), which emphasises autonomy, competence, and relatedness as key psychological needs.

9. The tendency to observe the behaviours of others in ways that are according to your expectations about them is called:

(A) Schema

(B) Confirmation bias

(C) Social judgment

(D) Anchoring

Correct Answer: (B) Confirmation bias – Confirmation bias is the tendency to interpret, seek, and remember information that supports preexisting beliefs or expectations while ignoring contradictory evidence. This directly applies to the tendency to observe others' behaviours in ways that align with expectations about them.

Explanation of other options

(A) Schema – A schema is a cognitive framework or concept that helps individuals organize and interpret information. Schemas influence how we perceive the world, including people and social situations.

(C) Social judgment – Social judgment refers to forming impressions and evaluating others based on social cues.

(D) Anchoring – Anchoring is a cognitive bias where individuals rely too heavily on an initial piece of information (the "anchor") when making decisions or judgments. This is more about decision-making than observing behaviour in line with prior expectations.

For Example - Price Negotiation: If a car salesman starts with a very high asking price, the buyer might perceive a lower price as a good deal, even if it's still above the car's actual value.

Explanation of Keywords

Behaviour: It refers to any observable action or reaction of an individual, often in response to a specific situation or environment.

10. The tendency to explain other people's behaviour as the result of personal factors is called ________________.

(A) Fundamental attribution error

(B) Stereotypes

(C) Schemas

(D) Actor-observer bias

Correct Answer: (A) Fundamental Attribution Error – This is the tendency to overemphasise personal traits and underestimate situational factors when explaining others' behaviour.

For example, if someone cuts you off in traffic, you might assume they are rude or reckless rather than considering that they might be in an emergency.

Explanation of other options

(B) Stereotypes – These are oversimplified and generalised beliefs about a group of people. They are often based on limited or inaccurate information and can lead to prejudice and discrimination.

Example- The belief generalised that women are bad drivers or that men are naturally aggressive.

(C) Schemas – Schemas are mental structures that help us understand and predict situations, events, and people. They are like mental shortcuts that allow us to process information quickly and efficiently.

Example- A child might develop a schema that females are meant to do all the household tasks, while fathers are meant to punish and provide for the family.

(D) Actor-Observer Bias – This refers to the tendency to attribute one's own actions to external factors (situations) while attributing others' actions to internal factors (personality).

For example, if you fail a test, you might blame the difficulty of the exam, but if someone else fails, you might assume they did not study enough.

11. Ankit was chased by a dog when he was a child. Now, he is afraid of all animals. This is an example of:

(A) Stimulus generalization

(B) Extinction

(C) Conditioned response

(D) Secondary learning

Correct Answer: (A) Stimulus Generalization – This occurs when a learned response to a specific stimulus is extended to similar stimuli. In this case, Ankit initially feared dogs due to an experience, but now his fear has generalized to all animals, not just dogs.

Explanation of other options

(B) Extinction – This refers to a conditioned response's gradual weakening and disappearance when the conditioned stimulus is presented repeatedly without reinforcement. If Ankit's fear gradually disappeared after repeated safe encounters with animals, then extinction would be happening.

(C) Conditioned Response – A conditioned response is a learned reaction to a previously neutral stimulus. In this case, Ankit's fear of dogs (but not all animals) would be a conditioned response.

(D) Secondary Learning – This usually refers to learning that builds on previous knowledge, often in an educational context or through indirect experiences.

Example: Studying grammar rules after learning how to read and write

12. Identify "False" and "True" statements

(P) Little children wearing neon green colour jackets on field trips illustrate the use of exogenous attention

(Q) Scanning the room for green colour because your friend said she would wear a green dress illustrates the use of endogenous attention

(R) Endogenous attention is voluntary – exogenous attention is involuntary

(S) Endogenous attention is a bottom-up process, and exogenous attention is a top down process

(A) P – false, Q – true, R– true, S – true

(B) P – true, Q – false, R – true, S – true

(C) P – true, Q – true, R – true, S – false

(D) P – false, Q – true, R – false, S – false

Correct Answer : (C) P – true, Q – true, R – true, S – false

Explanation of Keywords

Exogenous Attention: Also called bottom-up attention. External stimuli, like sudden sounds, bright lights, or unexpected movements automatically capture it. Example: Turning your head when you hear a loud noise or see a flashing light.

Endogenous Attention: Also known as top-down attention. It is intentionally directed based on goals, interests, or tasks. Example: Focusing on reading a book in a noisy room because you are interested in the story.

Voluntary - Consciously choosing to focus on something,

Involuntary- Stimulus-driven and occurs automatically

13. Specific description of a variable that allows it to be measured is called:

(A) Experimental

(B) Designing a study

(C) Operationalization

(D) Conceptualization

Correct Answer: (C) Operationalization – This is defining a variable in practical, measurable terms. For example, if you study self-esteem, you need to operationalise it by deciding how to measure it (e.g., using a questionnaire like the Rosenberg Self-Esteem Scale).

Explanation of other options

(A) Experimental – This refers to a type of research design where variables are manipulated to determine cause-and-effect relationships.

(B) Designing a study – This is the overall process of planning how a research study will be conducted, including choosing participants, selecting methods, and determining procedures.

(D) Conceptualization – This refers to defining a concept in theoretical terms and explaining what it means abstractly. For example, self-esteem can be conceptually defined as an individual's overall sense of self-worth without specifying how to measure it.

Explanation of Keywords:

Variables are any characteristic, number, or quality that can change or vary. They are essential in research because they help researchers measure and analyze relationships.

14. In which method(s) we gather detailed information of a small number of persons? (MSQ)

(A) Surveys

(B) Depth Interview

(C) Correlational Research

(D) Case Study

Correct Answer: (B) and (D)

(B) Depth Interview – This method involves conducting detailed, open-ended interviews with few participants. It allows researchers to explore personal experiences, opinions, and emotions deeply.

(D) Case Study – A case study is an in-depth investigation of a single person, group, or organization. It provides detailed, qualitative insights and is often used in psychology, education, and social sciences.

Explanation of other options:

(A) Surveys – Surveys are used to collect data from many people using questionnaires or structured interviews. They provide broad, generalised information but usually do not gather in-depth details about individuals.

(C) Correlational Research – Using statistical analysis, this research method examines the relationship between two or more variables. It does not focus on in-depth information about individuals but on patterns across a larger sample.

15. Which of the following option(s) do(es) NOT denote the state of internal physiological equilibrium that the body strives to maintain?

(A) Intrinsic motivation

(B) Homeostasis

(C) Instincts

(D) Drive

Correct Answer: (A), (C), (D)

(A) Intrinsic Motivation – This refers to engaging in a behaviour because it is inherently rewarding or satisfying rather than driven by external rewards or pressures.

(C) Instincts – These are innate, biologically driven behaviors that help an organism survive (e.g., reflexes, parental care). While instincts may contribute to survival, they do not specifically denote internal physiological balance like homeostasis does.

(D) Drive-In psychology, a drive is an internal state of tension that motivates an organism to take action to restore homeostasis (e.g., hunger leading to eating).

Explanation of other options:

(B) Homeostasis – This is the body's ability to maintain a stable internal environment (e.g., regulating body temperature, blood sugar, and hydration levels).

Explanation of Keywords:

Physiology: the study of how the body and its systems function. It focuses on understanding the biological processes that maintain life, including how organs, tissues, and cells work together.

Equilibrium: state of balance within the body. This is often called homeostasis, where the body maintains a stable internal environment despite external changes.

16.Which of the following option(s) refer(s) to secondary appraisal?

(A) Thoughts about what to do in a stressful situation

(B) Thoughts about whether an event is generally threatening

(C) Evaluation of an event's relevance, threat and stressfulness

(D) Evaluation of coping resources and options for dealing with a stressful event

Correct Answer: C and D

Explanation of Keywords:

Secondary appraisal: evaluating one's ability to cope with a stressful situation after recognising it as a potential threat or challenge during the primary appraisal.

For example, if a student fails an exam (primary appraisal: viewing it as a threat or challenge), their secondary appraisal might involve thinking, "Do I have time to study for the next exam?" "Can I ask for help from a teacher or tutor?" "Do I have the emotional strength to try again?"

17. Which of the following is/are included as a basic type of intelligence in Sternberg's Triarchic Theory?

(A) Analytic

(B) Experiential/creative

(C) Crystallization

(D) Synthesis

Correct Answer: A and B

(A) Analytic Intelligence: The ability to analyse, evaluate, compare, and contrast information. It involves problem-solving, logical reasoning, and academic tasks. Often measured by traditional IQ tests and is associated with academic success.

(B) Experiential/Creative Intelligence: Also known as creative intelligence, it involves generating new ideas, solving novel problems, and thinking outside the box. People with strong creative intelligence excel in innovation and artistic thinking.

Explanation of other options:

(C) Crystallization: This term is not part of Sternberg's Triarchic Theory. It is associated with crystallized intelligence in Cattell's theory, referring to the accumulated knowledge and skills gained through experience and education.

(D) Synthesis: Synthesis is not explicitly a part of Sternberg's Triarchic Theory. It generally refers to combining ideas or information to form a coherent whole.

Explanation of Keywords: Sternberg's Triarchic Theory: Sternberg's Triarchic Theory of Intelligence was proposed by Robert J. Sternberg and suggests that intelligence comprises three key components (Analytical, creative, and practical intelligence). Sternberg's theory emphasizes that intelligence is not solely determined by academic abilities but also by creative thinking and practical problem-solving skills.

18. As per the ethical guidelines of American Psychological Association, which of the option(s) depict(s) unacceptable use of 'Deception' in psychology research?

(A) Falsifying the data

(B) Temporary withholding of information about the study from the participants

(C) Not taking informed consent

(D) Use of confederates

Correct Answers A and C

Explanation of Keywords

Deception' Deception in psychology research refers to intentionally misleading or withholding information from participants about the true purpose of a study.

Informed consent - Informed consent is a crucial ethical principle where potential participants are fully informed about the study's purpose, procedures, risks, and benefits.

19. Match the following theories of ageing

P. Cellular-Clock Theory	(i) Oxygen molecule with an unstable electron
Q. Wear-and-Tear Theory	(ii) Elderly persons who remain active in some way adjust more positively to ageing
R. Free-radical Theory	(iii) Cells are limited in the number of times they can reproduce to repair damage
S. Activity Theory	(iv) Body organs and cell tissues wear out with repeated use and abuse

(A) P-ii; Q-iv; R-i; S-iii
(B) P-iv; Q-i; R-iii; S-ii
(C) P-iii; Q-ii; R-i; S-iv
(D) P-iii; Q-iv; R-i; S-ii
Correct Answer (D) P-iii; Q-iv; R-i; S-ii
Explanation of other options:

P. Cellular-Clock Theory → (iii) Cells are limited in the number of times they can reproduce to repair damage

This theory, proposed by Leonard Hayflick, suggests that cells have a biological clock and can only divide a limited number of times (Hayflick limit). As cells reach this limit, ageing occurs because they can no longer effectively repair tissue damage.

Q. Wear-and-Tear Theory → (iv) Body organs and cell tissues wear out with repeated use and abuse

This theory suggests that ageing is caused by the gradual breakdown of the body due to accumulated damage from everyday activities, environmental factors, and stress. Over time, the body's repair mechanisms become less effective, leading to ageing and disease.

R. Free-Radical Theory → (i) Oxygen molecule with an unstable electron

According to this theory, ageing is caused by damage from free radicals—unstable oxygen molecules that steal electrons from other molecules, causing cellular damage. This damage accumulates over time and contributes to ageing, as well as diseases like cancer and Alzheimer's.

S. Activity Theory → (ii) Elderly persons who remain active in some way adjust more positively to ageing

This theory suggests that staying physically, socially, and mentally active leads to better ageing outcomes. Elderly individuals who engage in social and meaningful activities tend to maintain higher levels of well-being and life satisfaction.

Explanation of Keywords: Ageing: Aging refers to the natural and gradual ageing process. It involves biological, psychological, and social changes over time.

20. Match the neurotransmitters with their functions

P. Acetylcholine	(i) Movement and pleasure sensation
Q. Dopamine	(ii) Sleep, anxiety, and appetite
R. Serotonin	(iii) Attention and memory
S. Norepinephrine	(iv) Arousal and mood

(A) P-ii; Q-i; R-iv; S-iii
(B) P-iii; Q-i; R-ii; S-iv
(C) P-iv; Q-ii; R-i; S-iii
(D) P-iv; Q-iii; R-i; S-ii
Correct Answer (B) P-iii; Q-i; R-ii; S-iv
Explanation of other options
(P) Acetylcholine — (iii) Attention and Memory

- Acetylcholine is a neurotransmitter primarily involved in learning, memory, and attention.
- It plays a crucial role in the brain's ability to process information and is linked to memory formation.
- It also affects muscle contractions in the peripheral nervous system.
- Disorders like Alzheimer's disease are associated with reduced acetylcholine levels.

(Q) Dopamine — (i) Movement and Pleasure Sensation

- Dopamine is known as the "feel-good" neurotransmitter.
- It is involved in reward, motivation, and pleasure.
- Additionally, it regulates voluntary movements and motor control.
- Low levels of dopamine are linked to Parkinson's disease, while excess dopamine is associated with schizophrenia.

(R) Serotonin — (ii) Sleep, Anxiety, and Appetite

- Serotonin influences mood regulation, sleep, appetite, and anxiety levels.
- It plays a significant role in emotional well-being and mental health.
- Low levels of serotonin are commonly associated with depression and anxiety disorders.

(S) Norepinephrine — (iv) Arousal and Mood

- Norepinephrine functions as both a neurotransmitter and a hormone.
- It is involved in arousal, attention, and regulating mood.
- It also plays a role in the fight-or-flight response, increasing heart rate and energy levels.
- Imbalances in norepinephrine are linked to conditions like depression and anxiety.

Explanation of Keywords
Neurotransmitters- are chemical messengers in the brain and nervous system. They transmit signals from one nerve cell (neuron) to another across a small gap called the synapse. Neurotransmitters are crucial in regulating various bodily functions, including mood, emotions, memory, and movement.
21.Match the concerned human nervous system with their associated functions.

P. Sympathetic	(i) Carrying messages from Central Nervous System to muscles and glands
Q. Parasympathetic	(ii) Carrying messages from senses to Central Nervous System
R. Afferent	(iii) Maintaining body functions under normal conditions
S. Efferent	(iv) Fight-or-flight system

(A) P-iv; Q-iii; R-ii; S-i
(B) P-iii; Q-i; R-ii; S-iv
(C) P-iv; Q-ii; R-i; S-iii
(D) P-iv; Q-iii; R-i; S-ii
Correct Answer (A) P-iv; Q-iii; R-ii; S-i
Explanation of other options:
P. Sympathetic – (iv) Fight-or-flight system
The sympathetic nervous system activates the body's "fight-or-flight" response in stressful or emergencies. It increases heart rate, dilates pupils, and redirects blood flow to muscles, preparing the body for action.
Q. Parasympathetic – (iii) Maintaining body functions under normal conditions
The parasympathetic nervous system is responsible for the "rest and digest" functions. It helps conserve energy, slows heart rate, and promotes digestion and other routine bodily functions.
R. Afferent – (ii) Carrying messages from senses to the Central Nervous System
Afferent neurons (sensory neurons) carry sensory information (e.g., touch, pain, temperature) from sensory organs to the brain and spinal cord (Central Nervous System - CNS).
S. Efferent – (i) Carrying messages from the Central Nervous System to muscles and glands
Efferent neurons (motor neurons) transmit signals from the brain and spinal cord to muscles and glands, enabling movement and responses to stimuli.
Explanation of Keywords: Nervous system: It is a complex network of nerves and cells that carry messages between the brain, spinal cord, and the rest of the body. It controls and coordinates all voluntary and involuntary activities, including movement, thought, and bodily functions.
22.A researcher plans to study the long-term effect of Covid-19 on human cognitive functions. The plan is summarized below.
STUDY- I (Study conducted in 2022)
Group- A: 10 years old males and females
Group B: 20 years old males and females
Group- C: 30 years old males and females
STUDY- II (Study to be conducted in 2025)
Group D: 13 years old males and females
Group E: 23 years old males and females
Group F: 33 years old males and females
This research design is known as?
(A) Cross-sectional design
(B) Longitudinal design
(C) Cross-sequential design
(D) Long-term design

Correct Answer: (C) Cross-Sequential Design.A combination of cross-sectional and longitudinal designs. Researchers study multiple age groups (like in a cross-sectional design) and follow them over time (like in a longitudinal study). Helps to reduce cohort effects while still providing insights into individual developmental changes.

Explanation of other options:

(A) Cross-Sectional Design. It involves studying different groups of people of various ages at a single point in time. It is a quicker and more cost-effective method for examining age-related differences. A limitation is that it does not track individual development over time, which can lead to cohort effects (differences due to generational influences rather than actual development).

(B) Longitudinal Design. It involves studying the same group of individuals over an extended period, sometimes years or even decades. Allows researchers to observe how individuals change over time. A limitation is that it is time-consuming, expensive, and has the risk of participant dropout (attrition).

(D) Long-Term Design. This is not a commonly recognised research design in psychology. It may refer to longitudinal research, but the term itself is not standard.

Explanation of Keywords: Research design refers to a researcher's overall strategy or plan to conduct a study. It outlines how data will be collected, measured, and analysed to answer research questions.

23.If Central Nervous System = Brain + Spinal Cord, then Peripheral Nervous System = ________?

(A) Sympathetic + Parasympathetic Systems

(B) Forebrain + Hindbrain

(C) Somatic + Autonomic Nervous Systems

(D) Cerebrum + Cerebellum

Correct Answer: (C) Somatic + Autonomic Nervous System

The PNS consists of two main divisions: The Somatic Nervous System (SNS), Which controls voluntary movements and transmits sensory information to the CNS. Autonomic Nervous System (ANS): Regulates involuntary bodily functions, including heart rate, digestion, and respiration. Together, these systems connect the CNS to the rest of the body.

Explanation of other options:

(A) Sympathetic + Parasympathetic Systems

The sympathetic and parasympathetic systems are subdivisions of the autonomic nervous system, part of the Peripheral Nervous System (PNS). While not the entire PNS, they regulate involuntary functions like heart rate, digestion, and breathing. Sympathetic activates the "fight or flight" response, while Parasympathetic promotes "rest and digest."

(B) Forebrain + Hindbrain

The forebrain and hindbrain are significant parts of the Central Nervous System (CNS), not the PNS.The Forebrain includes structures like the cerebrum, thalamus, and hypothalamus.The Hindbrain contains the medulla, pons, and cerebellum, primarily responsible for vital functions and motor control.

(D) Cerebrum + Cerebellum

The Cerebrum and Cerebellum are parts of the brain, specifically the CNS. The Cerebrum handles higher-order functions like thinking, memory, and decision-making. The Cerebellum coordinates movement, balance, and motor control. They are not components of the Peripheral Nervous System.

Explanation of Keywords: CNS includes the Brain and Spinal Cord

PNS includes all nerves except the Brain and spinal cord

24.Match the following:

P. Anima	i) A universal idea, image, or pattern, found in the collective unconscious.
Q. Animus	ii) An unconscious image representing unity, wholesome, completion, and balance.
R. Self-Archetype	iii) An archetype representing the female principles.
S. Archetype	iv) An archetype representing the male principles

(A) P: ii, Q: i, R: iv, S: iii
(B) P: iv, Q: ii, R: iii, S: i
(C) P: iii, Q: iv, R: ii, S: i
(D) P: i, Q: iii, R: ii, S: iv
Correct Answer (C) P: iii, Q: iv, R: ii, S: i
Explanation of other options
P. Anima — (iii) An archetype representing the female principles
The Anima is the feminine aspect of the male psyche. According to Jung, every man has an unconscious feminine side, represented by the Anima. It influences how a man relates to women and feminine qualities such as empathy, nurturing, and intuition.
Q. Animus — (iv) An archetype representing the male principles
The Animus is the masculine aspect of the female psyche. It represents logic, assertiveness, and rational thinking. Jung suggested that every woman has an unconscious masculine side, symbolised by the Animus.
R. Self-Archetype — (ii) An unconscious image representing unity, wholeness, completion, and balance
The Self is the central archetype in Jungian psychology, symbolising the unity of the conscious and unconscious mind. It represents personal integration and realising one's full potential through individuation.
S. Archetype — (i) A universal idea, image, or pattern, found in the collective unconscious
Archetypes are innate, universal symbols and themes found across different cultures and myths. Examples include the Hero, the mother, the Shadow, and the Wise Old Man. They emerge from the collective unconscious, a level of the unconscious mind shared by all humans.
25.Behavior modification programs aimed at extinction of an undesirable behavior typically make use of:
(A) Punishment and stimulus control
(B) Punishment and shaping
(C) Stimulus control and time out
(D) Non- reinforcement and time out
Correct Answer: (D) Non-Reinforcement and Time Out
Non-Reinforcement: This involves ignoring or withholding reinforcement for a specific behaviour, leading to its reduction. It is often used in behaviour management strategies like extinction. Example: Ignoring a child's tantrum instead of giving attention, thereby reducing tantrums over time.
Time Out: It is a disciplinary technique used to reduce unwanted behaviour.
Explanation of other options:
(A)Punishment and Stimulus Control
Punishment: A consequence that decreases the likelihood of a behaviour occurring again. It can be positive punishment (adding something unpleasant) or negative punishment (removing something pleasant). Example: Giving a child a time-out for hitting a sibling.

Stimulus Control: A situation in which a behaviour is influenced by the presence or absence of a specific stimulus. Example: A student studies diligently when in the library (stimulus control) but not at home.

(B) Punishment and Shaping

Punishment: As explained above, punishment reduces undesirable behaviour.

Shaping: A process of gradually reinforcing behaviors that resemble the desired behaviour until the desired behaviour is achieved.

Example: Teaching a child to write by first reinforcing them for holding a pencil correctly, then for scribbling, and eventually for writing letters.

(C) Stimulus Control and Time Out

Stimulus Control: It involves using environmental cues to manage behaviour.

Time Out: A form of negative punishment where a child is temporarily removed from a reinforcing environment to reduce unwanted behaviour. Example: A child misbehaving in class is placed in a designated "time-out" area to remove access to enjoyable activities.

Explanation of Keywords: Behavior modification is a therapeutic approach that uses learning principles to change undesirable behaviors and encourage positive ones. It is based on behaviourist theories, primarily operant conditioning, by B.F. Skinner and classical conditioning by Ivan Pavlov.

26.Match the concept to the correct answer:

P. Confounding	i) We can draw clear causal conclusions from an experiment.
Q. High internal validity	ii) Presence of an uncontrolled variable creates uncertainty as to whether the dependent variable was influenced by the independent variable.
R. High external validity	iii) Participant improves because of the expectation of receiving a treatment, not because of the treatment itself.
S. Placebo effect	iv) The results of a study generalize to other settings and populations.

(A) P: ii, Q: i, R: iv, S: iii
(B) P: iv, Q: ii, R: iii, S: i
(C) P: iii, Q: iv, R: ii, S: i
(D) P: i, Q: iii, R: ii, S: iv
Correct Answer (A) P: ii, Q: i, R: iv, S: iii
Explanation of other options

P. Confounding → (ii) The Presence of an uncontrolled variable creates uncertainty as to whether the dependent variable was influenced by the independent variable.

Explanation: A confounding variable is an uncontrolled factor that can influence the outcome of an experiment, making it difficult to determine the true effect of the independent variable. It creates uncertainty in causal conclusions.

Q. High internal validity → (i) We can draw clear causal conclusions from an experiment.

Explanation: High internal validity means the experiment is well-controlled, with minimal confounding variables. It ensures that changes in the dependent variable are directly due to the manipulation of the independent variable, allowing clear causal conclusions.

R. High external validity → (iv) The results of a study generalize to other settings and populations.

Explanation: High external validity indicates that the study's findings are applicable beyond the experimental conditions. This means the results can be generalized to different environments, populations, or real-world situations.

S. Placebo effect → (iii) Participant improves because of the expectation of receiving a treatment, not because of the treatment itself.

Explanation: The placebo effect occurs when participants experience a perceived or actual improvement simply because they believe they are receiving treatment, even if the treatment has no therapeutic effect.

27. Assertions

P. Factor analysis reduces a large number of measures to a smaller number of clusters.

Q. The measures within each cluster are highly interconnected and reflect the same underlying dimensions.

Which of the following is correct?

(A) Only P is correct

(B) Only Q is correct

(C) Both P and Q are correct

(D) Neither P nor Q is correct

Correct Answer: (C) Both P and Q are correct

Explanation of Keywords: Factor analysis is a statistical method used in psychology and other fields to identify underlying relationships between many variables. It helps in simplifying complex data by grouping correlated variables into smaller, more manageable factors.

28._____________ perspective is considered as the 'first force' in Psychology, whereas _____________ perspective is regarded as the 'third force' in Psychology.

Fill in the blanks using the suitable option given below.

(A) Psychodynamic and Humanistic

(B) Behavioral and Humanistic

(C) Humanistic and Cognitive

(D) Cognitive and Gestalt

Correct Answer: (A) Psychodynamic and Humanistic

The Psychodynamic perspective (founded by Sigmund Freud) is considered the "first force" in psychology. It emphasizes unconscious processes, childhood experiences, and inner conflicts as determinants of behaviour. The Humanistic perspective (developed by Carl Rogers and Abraham Maslow) is considered the "third force" in psychology. It emerged as a response to both the psychodynamic and behavioural perspectives, emphasizing personal growth, free will, and self-actualization.

Explanation of other options:

(B) Behavioural and Humanistic: The Behavioural perspective (pioneered by John B. Watson and B.F. Skinner) is often regarded as the "second force" in psychology. It focuses on observable behaviour and conditioning. The Humanistic perspective is indeed the "third force."

(C) Humanistic and Cognitive

The Humanistic perspective is the "third force, The Cognitive perspective (which focuses on mental processes like perception, memory, and problem-solving) is not considered one of the three main "forces" in psychology.

(D) Cognitive and Gestalt: The Cognitive perspective is not the "first force." The Gestalt perspective focuses on holistic perception and is not classified as the "third force."

Explanation of Keywords: In psychology, "force" refers to significant movements or schools of thought that shaped the understanding of human behaviour and mental processes.

29. In language development, which of the following statement(s) is/are true:

(A) The ability to distinguish speech from non-speech sounds is likely to develop before three months.

(B) The ability to distinguish between words without understanding their meaning is likely to develop before the age of seven months.

(C) Babbling is not likely to develop before the age of six months.

(D) The ability to use single words is not likely to begin before the age of ten months.

Correct Answers: A and D

Explanation of Keywords:

Stages of Language Development:

1. Pre-Linguistic Stage (0-12 months): Babbling, cooing, and making sounds.
2. One-Word Stage (12-18 months): Using single words to express needs (e.g., "milk").
3. Two-Word Stage (18-24 months): Combining two words to form basic sentences (e.g., "want toy").
4. Telegraphic Stage (2-3 years): Forming short sentences using essential words (e.g., "go park now").
5. Complex Sentences (3+ years): Using more advanced grammar and vocabulary.

30. Projective Techniques would NOT interest which type(s) of personality theorists?

(A) Humanistic theorists

(B) Cognitive theorists

(C) Trait theorists

(D) Psychodynamic theorists

Correct Answer A,B and C

A) Humanistic Theorists: Humanistic theorists, like Carl Rogers and Abraham Maslow, focus on conscious experiences, personal growth, self-actualization, and free will. They believe in understanding people through their own perspective rather than relying on unconscious processes. Projective techniques are not of much interest to humanistic theorists because they emphasize self-report methods like interviews and questionnaires that capture conscious experiences.

(B) Cognitive Theorists: Cognitive theorists study how individuals perceive, think, reason, and solve problems. They are interested in understanding cognitive processes through objective and structured assessments. Projective techniques are generally not preferred by cognitive theorists as these methods lack objective measurement and may introduce biases. Instead, they often use experiments, cognitive tasks, and standardized tests.

(C) Trait Theorists: Trait theorists, like Gordon Allport and Raymond Cattell, focus on measuring stable personality traits using objective, quantitative tools. They rely heavily on self-report inventories and factor analysis to study traits. Projective techniques are not useful for trait theorists since they prefer data that is reliable, valid, and quantifiable.

Explanation of other options:

(D) Psychodynamic Theorists: Psychodynamic theorists, like Sigmund Freud and Carl Jung, emphasize the role of unconscious thoughts, desires, and conflicts in shaping behaviour. Projective techniques, such as the Rorschach Inkblot Test and the Thematic Apperception Test (TAT), are widely used by psychodynamic theorists to explore unconscious content. These techniques align with their belief that unconscious motives influence behaviour.

Explanation of Keywords: Projective techniques are psychological assessment methods to uncover unconscious thoughts, feelings, and desires. These techniques present individuals with ambiguous stimuli, such as images or incomplete sentences, and ask them to interpret or respond.

31. Which of the following is/are characteristic(s) of Type A personality:

(A) Ambitious

(B) Competitive

(C) Time conscious

(D) Laid back

Correct Answer A, B and C

(A) Ambitious: Type A individuals are typically very ambitious and driven. They set high goals for themselves and are constantly striving to achieve more. This ambition often leads to stress and pressure.

(B) Competitive: Competitiveness is a key characteristic of Type A personalities. They often view situations as win-lose scenarios and work hard to outperform others. This competitive nature can lead to both success and frustration.

(C) Time Conscious: Type A individuals are extremely time-conscious and often feel a sense of urgency. They dislike delays and tend to multitask to maximize efficiency. This heightened time awareness can lead to stress and anxiety.

Explanation of other options:

(D) Laid Back: Being laid back is not a characteristic of a Type A personality. This is more typical of a Type B personality, who is generally relaxed, patient, and less stressed under pressure. Type B individuals enjoy a slower-paced lifestyle and tend to be more easy-going.

Explanation of Keywords: Type A personality is a behavioural pattern characterized by specific traits and behaviours often linked to high stress levels and competitiveness. The concept was introduced by Friedman and Rosenman in the 1950s during their research on the link between personality traits and heart disease.

32. Which of the following is/are source(s) of variability that contribute(s) to errors in measurement of estimating reliability?

(A) Reactivity carryover actual change over time

(B) Making incorrect predictions or decisions about individuals

(C) Inconsistency of test content non-parallel halves

(D) Consistency of test content

Correct Answers A and C

Explanation of Keywords: Variability refers to how much the data points in a dataset differ from each other and from the average (mean).

Reliability refers to the consistency and stability of a measurement tool over time.

33. The humanistic approach to therapy would be the least effective in treating which of the following condition(s)?

(A) Schizophrenia

(B) Mild depression

(C) Paranoia

(D) Childhood abuse

Correct Answer A and C

(A) Schizophrenia: Humanistic therapy is generally ineffective for schizophrenia, a severe mental disorder characterized by hallucinations, delusions, and disorganized thinking. Schizophrenia typically requires antipsychotic medications and structured therapeutic approaches like Cognitive Behavioural Therapy (CBT) or Psychosocial Rehabilitation.

(C) Paranoia: Humanistic therapy may not be suitable for individuals experiencing paranoia, which often involves extreme distrust and delusional thinking. Conditions like Paranoid Personality Disorder (PPD) or Paranoid Schizophrenia often require CBT or medication.

Explanation of other options:

(B) Mild Depression:Humanistic therapy can be beneficial for mild depression as it encourages self-awareness, emotional expression, and self-acceptance. It helps individuals explore their feelings and develop coping mechanisms in a supportive environment.

(D) Childhood Abuse: Effective with limitations: Humanistic therapy can be helpful for individuals dealing with the emotional aftermath of childhood abuse by providing a safe, non-judgmental space. However, for severe trauma, specialized approaches like Trauma-Focused CBT (TF-CBT) or Eye Movement Desensitization and Reprocessing (EMDR) may be more effective.

Explanation of Keywords: Humanistic approach -The humanistic approach is a psychological perspective that emphasizes the study of the whole person and their potential for personal growth.

34. Characteristic feature(s) of an aptitude test is/are:

(A) Evaluate the effects of an unknown, uncontrolled set of experiences

(B) Rely heavily on the content validation procedure

(C) Evaluate the potential to profit from training

(D) Evaluate the outcome of training

Correct Answers A and C

Explanation of Keywords: Aptitude test - An aptitude test is a standardized assessment used to evaluate a person's natural abilities, talents, or potential to perform specific tasks.

35. From the following options, what is/are illusion(s)?

(A) Erroneous perceptions

(B) Schemas

(C) Perceptual constancies

(D) Incorrect perceptual hypothesis

Correct Answers A and D

(A) Erroneous Perceptions: This is a correct description of illusions. An illusion occurs when our perception does not match physical reality. For example, visual illusions like the Müller-Lyer illusion trick the brain into misjudging the length of lines.

(D) Incorrect Perceptual Hypothesis: This can describe an illusion. When the brain makes an incorrect assumption or hypothesis about the nature of a stimulus, it can lead to an illusion. For instance, the brain may interpret a visual input incorrectly in ambiguous images or optical illusions.

Explanation of other options:

(B) Schemas: Schemas are mental frameworks or thought patterns that help us organize and interpret information. While schemas can influence perception, they are not illusions themselves. They play a role in perception by shaping expectations but do not directly cause perceptual distortions.

(C) Perceptual Constancies: Perceptual constancy refers to the brain's ability to recognise objects as remaining constant despite changes in distance or lighting. Examples include size constancy (perceiving an object as the same size despite its distance) and colour constancy.

Explanation of Keywords: Illusion - An illusion is a false or misleading perception of a real object, situation, or sensory experience. It occurs when the brain misinterprets sensory information, leading to a distorted perception of reality. Illusions can affect any of the senses, but visual and auditory illusions are the most common.

36. Refer to Column I and Column II and mark the statement(s) that is/are "True."

Column I: Class 8, Section A marks	Column II: Class 8, Section B marks
12	18
12	18
11	15
11	15
10	10
10	10
9	5
9	5
8	2
8	2

(A) The mean of Section A is different from that of Section B

(B) The standard deviation of Section A is similar to that of Section B

(C) The mean and the standard deviation of Section A is the same

(D) The mean of Section A and Section B are the same, the standard deviation is different

Correct Answer D

Explanation of Keywords: Standard Deviation - Standard deviation is a measure of how much the individual data points in a dataset deviate from the mean (average).

37. Which of the following is/are valid for conformity:

(A) Size influences conformity only up to a certain level

(B) Size always influences conformity

(C) Group unanimity influences conformity

(D) Status does not have any influence on conformity

Correct Answers A and C

Explanation of Keywords: Conformity -It refers to the tendency of individuals to adjust their thoughts, feelings, or behaviours to match those of a group or social norm.

38. When the probability of Type I error (α) is 0.05 and the maximum acceptable probability of Type II error (β) is 0.20, the researcher is willing to accept that Type I error is ___________ (answer in integer) times more serious than a Type II error.

Correct Answer 4 to 4

Explanation of Keywords: Type 1 error occurs when a researcher rejects a true null hypothesis.

Example - A researcher concludes a new therapy is effective when it has no impact.

Type 2 error happens when a researcher fails to reject a false null hypothesis.

Example - A depression screening test fails to detect depression in a person who is suffering from it.

39. If Soni got an intelligence score of 115, then what percentage of the population (%, as given in the graph) will have intelligence scores higher than the score obtained by Soni? (rounded off to 2 decimal places)

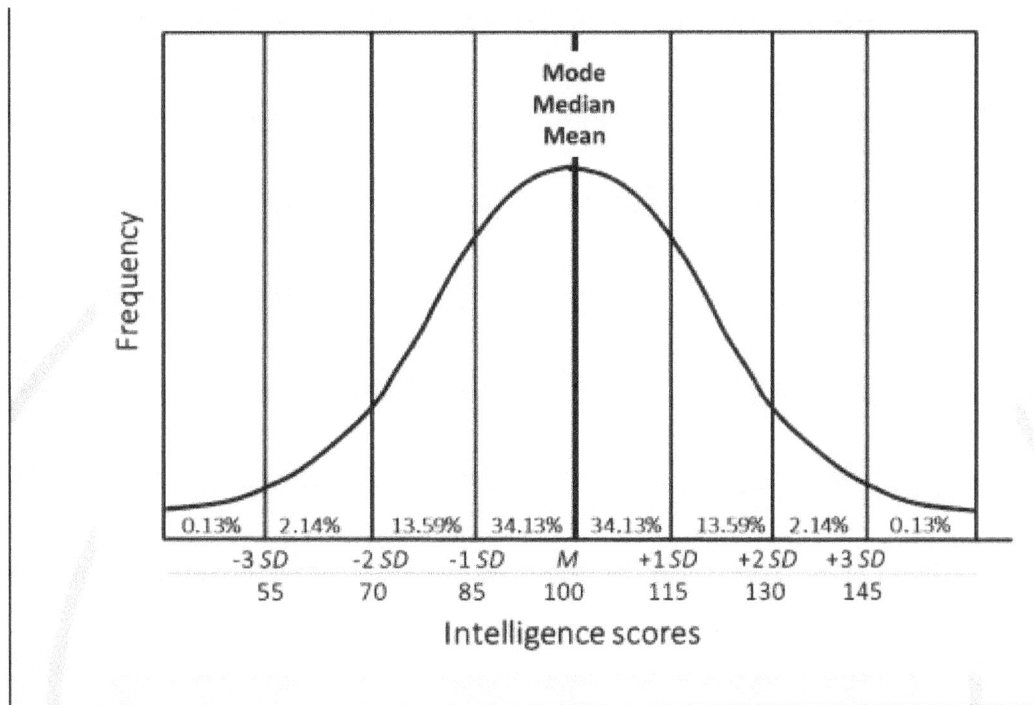

Correct Answer 15.00 to 16.00

Explanation of Keywords: IQ, or Intelligence Quotient, measures a person's cognitive abilities and intellectual potential compared to others of the same age. It is often assessed using standardized tests designed to evaluate various aspects of intelligence.

CHAPTER II

PREVIOUS YEAR QUESTIONS 2024 ANALYSIS

1. In a sampling design, where every Kth case is selected from a random starting point with the value K kept constant throughout, is an example of.

(A) Convenient sampling

(B) Systematic sampling

(C) Stratified sampling

(D) Cluster sampling

Correct Answer- (B) Systematic sampling: A probability sampling technique where every nth individual from a list or population is selected after a random starting point. Example: In a population of 1,000, if a sample of 100 is needed, select every 10th person after randomly choosing the first person.

Explanation of other options:

(A)Convenient sampling: A non-probability sampling technique where samples are selected based on ease of access, availability, or proximity to the researcher. Example: Surveying people at a nearby coffee shop because they are easily accessible.

(C) Stratified sampling: A probability sampling method where the population is divided into homogeneous subgroups (strata) based on specific characteristics and samples are drawn proportionally from each subset. Example: A researcher divides a population by age group (e.g., 18–25, 26–35, etc.) and selects a proportional number of participants from each group

(D)Cluster sampling: A probability sampling technique where the population is divided into groups (clusters) and a random selection of clusters is made. Data is then collected from all or a random sample within those clusters. Example: To study schools in a city, randomly select five schools (clusters) and survey all students in those schools.

Explanation of keywords in questions-

Sampling design is a plan for selecting a sample from a population. It involves choosing a sampling method, determining the sample size, and specifying how to implement the plan. Probability and non-probability sampling are two main methods for selecting a sample from a population.

Probability sampling is when each member of the population has an equal chance of being selected, while non-probability sampling is when the selection is based on other criteria.

2. Which among the following correlation coefficient values represents the most substantial relationship between two variables?

(A) 0.86

(B)+ 0.68

(C) + 0.59

(D) 0.05

Correct Answer- (A)

Explanation of other options:

The strength of the relationship between two variables is determined by the absolute value of the correlation coefficient, denoted as r. – sign in correlation shows direction only, not strength.

The closer the absolute value of r is to 1, the stronger the relationship. r=1 or r=−1 Perfect correlation (most substantial relationship).r=0 No correlation (no relationship). Values close to 0 (e.g., 0.1 or -0.1): Weak correlation. Values close to ±1 (e.g., 0.9 or -0.9): Strong correlation.

Explanation of keywords in questions-

Correlation is a statistical measure that indicates the extent to which two or more variables change in relation to each other.A positive correlation indicates how much those variables increase or decrease in parallel. A negative correlation indicates the extent to which one variable increases as the other decreases.

3. A researcher experiments to learn if room temperature affects the aggression displayed by college students under crowded conditions in a simulated prison environment. In this experiment, the independent variable is:

(A) Aggression

(B) Crowding

(C) Room temperature

(D) Simulated prison

Correct Answer (C): Room temperature, especially outside the comfortable range for humans (around 20-22°C or 68-72°F), can significantly impact mood and behaviour.

Explanation of other options:

(A) Aggression refers to behaviours intended to harm or injure another person, either physically or psychologically. It can be caused by various factors, including biological influences (like genetics or brain chemistry), environmental triggers, and learned behaviours (Social learning).

Types of aggression:

Hostile aggression: Impulsive and emotion-driven, aimed at causing harm (e.g., a fight sparked by anger).

Instrumental aggression: Deliberate and goal-oriented, used to achieve something (e.g., external, like obtaining money, or internal, like bullying, to assert dominance).

(B) Crowding refers to the psychological perception of too many people occupying a space, leading to feelings of discomfort, stress, or frustration. It is not just about the physical number of people but how the space is experienced.

(D) A simulated prison is a controlled experiment designed to replicate a prison environment to study human behaviour under such conditions.

Notable study: The *Stanford Prison Experiment* (1971) by Philip Zimbardo is the most famous example. College students were assigned roles as either prisoners or guards in a mock prison setup. The study demonstrated: *Deindividuation*: Individuals in authority roles (guards) adopted aggressive and abusive behaviours toward prisoners, losing a sense of personal accountability.

The psychological impact of institutional environments, showing how situational factors (rather than inherent personality traits) can lead to extreme behaviours.

Explanation of keywords in questions- An independent variable is exactly what it sounds like. It is a variable that stands alone and is not changed by the other variables you are trying to measure.

4. If the data distribution is skewed to the left, it means:

(A) More scores have low values than have high values

(B) Fewer scores have low values than have high values

(C) Fewer scores have high values than have low values

(D) More scores have high values than have low values

Correct Answer-(B)

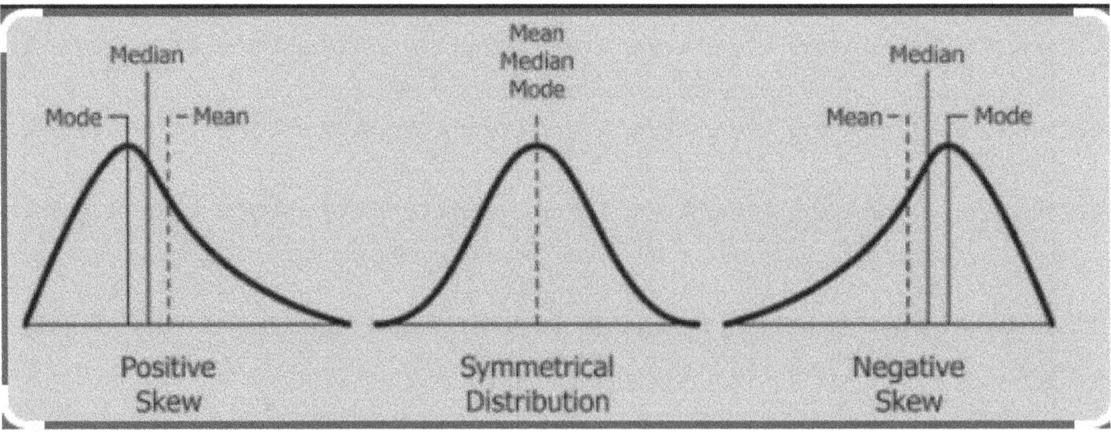

Explanation-

Longer Tail on the Left: The left side of the distribution (lower values) has a longer tail than the right side (higher values). This indicates the presence of outliers or extreme values in the lower range.

Median > Mean: The mean is typically less than the median for a left-skewed distribution. This happens because the lower values "pull" the mean downward, whereas the median remains relatively resistant to extreme values.

Explanation of keywords in questions-

Skewness is a measure of the asymmetry of a distribution. A distribution is asymmetrical when its left and right sides are not mirror images.A distribution can have right (or positive), left (or negative), or zero skewness. A right-skewed distribution is longer on the right side of its peak, and a left-skewed distribution is longer on the left side of its peak.

5. The theory of psychoanalysis is based on method.

(A) Survey

(B) Observation

(C) Case study

(D) Introspection

Correct Answer(C): A **case study** is an in-depth investigation of a single subject, group, event, or organisation over a period. Example: Analyzing the recovery journey of a patient with a rare disease to understand treatment outcomes.

Explanation of other options:

(A) A survey is a research method used to collect information from a pre-defined group of people. This method often employs questionnaires or interviews to gather data. Example: Surveying to measure customer satisfaction after using a product.

(B) Observation is collecting data by watching and analysing behaviour or phenomena as they occur in natural or controlled settings.

Types: Participant Observation: The researcher actively engages in the setting being studied.

Non-Participant Observation: The researcher observes without direct interaction.

Structured Observation: Predefined categories or criteria are observed.

Unstructured Observation: More open-ended and exploratory.

Example: Watching how children interact in a playground to study social behaviours

(D) Introspection is examining one's thoughts, feelings, and mental states to gain insight into inner experiences. Example: A person reflecting on their emotions after a significant life event to understand their coping mechanisms.

Explanation of keywords in questions: Psychoanalysis is a theory of personality and a therapeutic approach developed by Sigmund Freud in the late 19th century. It focuses on understanding the unconscious mind, which Freud believed contains thoughts, memories, and desires that influence behavior.

6. If a court acquits the criminal for lack of evidence and sentences the victim to 2 years of rigorous imprisonment in a case, it is an example of:

(A) Type I error only

(B) Type II error only

(C) Type I and Type II errors, respectively

(D) Type II and Type I errors, respectively

Correct Answer: (D) First, a Type II error: Failing to reject H0 when it is false. Then, a Type I error Rejecting H0 when it is true.

Explanation of other options:

(A) A Type I error occurs when the null hypothesis (H0) is incorrectly rejected when it is true. This is a "false positive" error. Example: Concluding that a new drug is effective when it has no effect. The probability of making a Type I error is denoted by (α)alpha, often called the "significance level."

(B) A Type II error occurs when the null hypothesis (H0) is not rejected when it is false This is a "false negative" error. Example: Failing to detect that a new drug is effective when it works. The probability of making a Type II error is denoted by(β) beta. $1-\beta$ is the power of the test.

(C) First, a Type I error: Rejecting H0 when it is true.Then, a Type II error: Failing to reject H0 when it is false.

7. In the Darwinian sense, _it_ refers to the ability of an organism to survive and produce a large number of fertile offspring.

(A) Selection

(B) Intersexual competition

(C) Evolution

(D) Fitness

Correct Answer- (D) In evolutionary biology, **fitness** refers to an organism's ability to survive, reproduce, and pass on its genes to the next generation.

Absolute Fitness: The total number of offspring an individual produces.

Relative Fitness: How an individual's reproductive success compares to others in the population.

Traits that increase fitness (e.g., adaptability, speed, mating success) are more likely to be passed on.

Explanation of other options:

(A) Selection refers to the process by which certain traits become more or less common in a population due to their effects on the reproductive success of individuals. There are two main types:

Natural Selection: Traits that improve survival or reproduction become more frequent over generations (e.g., better camouflage, resistance to diseases).

Sexual Selection: Traits that improve mating success, even if they don't aid survival, become more common (e.g., elaborate peacock feathers).

(B) This is a form of sexual selection where individuals of one sex (usually females) choose mates based on certain traits. Example: Female birds might prefer males with brighter plumage or more complex songs.

The traits chosen often signal fitness (e.g., health, good genes) and influence reproductive success.

(C) Evolution is the change in the genetic composition of a population over generations.

Key mechanisms of evolution include:

1. Mutation: Random changes in DNA that create genetic diversity.
2. Natural Selection: Differential survival and reproduction based on traits.
3. Genetic Drift: Random changes in trait frequency, especially in small populations.
4. Gene Flow: Movement of genes between populations due to migration.

8.Which theory states that people try to regulate their emotions to minimize the distress caused by a situation?

(A) Problem-focused coping

(B) General Adaptation Syndrome

(C) Cognitive appraisal

(D) Emotion-focused coping

Correct Answer (D) Emotion-focused coping: This strategy involves managing emotions related to a stressful situation rather than addressing the problem itself. It's often used when the stressor is outside one's control. Example: If someone is grieving a loss, they might seek support from friends or engage in activities to distract themselves rather than trying to "solve" the loss.

Explanation of other options:

(A) This is a strategy for dealing with stress by addressing the source of the problem directly. The goal is to eliminate or reduce the stressor. Example: If someone is stressed about an upcoming exam, they might study more, create a timetable, or ask for help to better understand the material.

(B) This is a three-stage physiological response to chronic stress, developed by Hans Selye.

Stages:

Alarm: The body's immediate reaction to a stressor (fight-or-flight response), characterized by the activation of the sympathetic nervous system and release of stress hormones like adrenaline and cortisol.

Resistance: The body attempts to adapt to the stressor, maintaining a heightened state of alertness and resistance to stress.

Exhaustion: Prolonged stress depletes the body's resources, potentially leading to burnout, illness, or other negative effects.

Example: A person facing prolonged workplace pressure may initially feel energized (alarm), adjust their routine to cope (resistance), but over time, may experience fatigue and health issues (exhaustion)

(C) This is the process of evaluating a situation to determine its significance for one's well-being. Introduced by Richard Lazarus, it is central to understanding stress.

Two Stages:

- Primary Appraisal: Assessing whether the situation is a threat, challenge, or irrelevant.
- Secondary Appraisal: Evaluating available resources and options for coping.
- Example: If someone gets a flat tire, they might appraise it as a minor inconvenience (low threat) or a significant problem if they're late for a job interview (high threat).

9. Which of the following is a suitable description of "grounded theory"?

(A) Theoretical ideas and concepts should emerge from the data.

(B) Theory precedes the data.

(C) Integration of data with researchers' interpretations.

(D) Conducting in-depth interviews and focus groups.

Correct Answer (A) Grounded theory is a qualitative research methodology that emphasises the development of theories directly grounded in empirical data. Researchers analyse the data inductively to allow patterns, themes, and theoretical concepts to emerge naturally rather than imposing pre-existing theories on the data.

Explanation of other options

(B) Theory precedes the data

This describes a deductive approach, not grounded theory. In grounded theory, data comes first, and theory is developed inductively.

(C) Integration of data with researchers' interpretations

While researchers do interpret data, grounded theory emphasizes that interpretations should strictly arise from the data, not be pre-shaped by preconceived notions or frameworks.

(D) Conducting in-depth interviews and focus groups

While these methods may be used in grounded theory research, the methodology is not defined by specific data collection methods. It is defined by how the data is analyzed and theory is developed.

Explanation of keywords in questions:

Grounded Theory (GT) is a qualitative research methodology used to develop theories directly from data. Instead of testing an existing theory, researchers using grounded theory aim to generate a new theory that explains a phenomenon based on systematically collected and analyzed data.

10. Percentage of scores between the mean and ± 1 standard deviation in a normal distribution is closest to

(A) 68%

(B) 34%

(C) 95%

(D) 99%

Correct Answer- A

Explanation of keywords in questions: Standard Deviation (SD) is a statistical measure that shows how much the values in a dataset vary or spread out from the mean (average). It helps to understand the degree of variation or dispersion within a set of data points.

11. Which of the following is a binocular cue for depth perception?

(A) Motion parallax

(B) Texture gradient

(C) Linear perception

(D) Convergence

Correct Answer (D) Convergence is a binocular cue where both eyes move inward (converge) when focusing on an object that is close to you. The amount of convergence gives a sense of how close or far away an object is. The brain uses this information to judge depth.

Example: When you focus on a nearby object, such as a pencil held in front of your nose, your eyes turn inward to keep it in focus. The closer the object, the more your eyes converge. This inward movement of the eyes helps your brain estimate the object's distance

Explanation of other options:

(A) Motion parallax is a depth cue that arises when we move our heads or bodies. Objects closer to us appear to move faster across our field of vision than objects farther away. This difference in speed provides a sense of depth and allows us to perceive how far away objects are in relation to one another.

Example: If you're in a car and look out the window, the trees that are close to you seem to zip past, while mountains in the distance move much slower. This difference in speed helps your brain perceive depth.

(B) Texture gradient refers to the way textures appear denser and more tightly packed as they recede into the distance. The change in texture detail gives a sense of depth, making objects farther away appear smaller and more compressed.

Example: If you're looking at a tiled floor, the tiles near you look larger and more distinct, while the ones further away appear smaller and less detailed, indicating they are farther away.

(C) Linear perspective is a geometric illusion that occurs when parallel lines appear to converge as they recede into the distance. This is due to the way our brains interpret the size and distance of objects based on the angle and convergence of lines.

Example: Looking down a long straight road, the two edges of the road seem to come together in the distance. The parallel lines of the road are actually staying the same distance apart, but they appear to converge because of the way our eyes perceive them..

Explanation of keywords in questions:

Binocular cues are visual signals that require the use of both eyes to perceive depth and distance. Since our eyes are separated by a small distance, they view the world from slightly different angles. The brain uses this difference to interpret depth.

Depth perception is the ability to perceive the world in three dimensions and judge the distance of objects. It allows us to navigate our environment effectively.

12. Match the following schedule of reinforcement with their description.

	Schedule of reinforcement		Description
I	Fixed ratio	a	Where a reinforcement is provided after an unpredictable number of responses
II	Fixed interval	b	Varying amount of time passes between two reinforcements
III	Variable ratio	c	Number of responses required for reinforcement is always the same
IV	Variable interval	d	The interval of time that must pass before reinforcement is always the same

(A).I-c, II-d, III-a, IV-b

(B).I-b, II-c, III-d, IV-a

(C).I-a, II-b, III-c, IV-d

(D).I-d, II-c, III-b, IV-a

Correct Answer- A

Explanation of keywords in questions: Reinforcement is a concept from behavioral psychology, specifically from operant conditioning, introduced by B.F. Skinner. It refers to any stimulus or event that strengthens or increases the likelihood of a particular behavior occurring again in the future.

13. While retrieving a long-term memory, bits and pieces of information are gathered from various sources and put back together in a process called

(A) Consolidation

(B) Reintegration

(C) Constructive processing

(D) Automatic processing

Correct Answer (C): Constructive processing is the process by which memories are actively constructed and shaped by our experiences, knowledge, and beliefs. Rather than being perfect recordings of past events, memories are reconstructed and may be influenced by new information or context.

Example: When you remember a vacation, you may "fill in" gaps in your memory with details you've learned or imagined since the trip, potentially altering the way you remember the experience.

Explanation of other options:

(A) Consolidation is the process by which memories become stable and integrated into long-term memory after an initial encoding stage. It often occurs over time as experiences are processed and stored in the brain. Example: When you study for an exam, the information you learn undergoes consolidation, especially while you sleep. This helps the facts become more durable and easier to recall later.

(B) Reintegration refers to the process of recovering or reconstructing a memory from long-term storage. It involves the retrieval of stored memories, which can sometimes involve piecing together various fragments of information. Example: You may not remember every detail of a childhood event, but when prompted by a certain smell or image, you reintegrate the memory and recall more specific details of the experience.

(D) Automatic processing refers to the unconscious encoding of information that occurs without deliberate effort. It typically involves information that is familiar or repetitive, which does not require conscious thought to process. Example: You likely don't consciously think about how to tie your shoes anymore. After practising it many times, this action is encoded automatically, and you can perform it with little conscious effort.

Explanation of keywords :

Long-term memory refers to the part of the memory system responsible for storing information for extended periods — from hours to a lifetime. Unlike short-term memory, which has a limited capacity, long-term memory can store vast amounts of information indefinitely.

14.Which model of decision making relies on simplifying strategies or rules of thumb based on past experiences, fairness, past events and aversion to loss?

(A) Bounded rationality model

(B) Judgment heuristics and biases model

(C) Social model

(D) Economic rationality model

Correct Answer (B) Judgment Heuristics and Biases Model: People rely on mental shortcuts (heuristics) to make decisions, which often lead to systematic errors (biases), such as overestimating probabilities or relying too much on initial information.

Explanation of other options

(A) Bounded Rationality Model: People make decisions within the limits of their cognitive abilities, available information, and time, often settling for a satisfactory solution rather than the optimal one.

(C) Social Model: Human behavior and decisions are influenced by social factors, norms, relationships, and group dynamics.

(D) Economic Rationality Model: People make decisions to maximize their personal benefit or utility, assuming full information, logical consistency, and optimal decision-making processes.

Explanation of keywords in questions:

Decision-making in psychology refers to the cognitive process of choosing between two or more alternatives. It involves evaluating information, considering possible outcomes, and selecting the best course of action.It can range from simple choices, like what to eat for lunch, to complex decisions, like choosing a career path.

15.When Monkey-A sees Monkey-B touching four pictures in a certain order to gain a banana on a screen Monkey-A learns to imitate that order even when shown a different configuration. This process is known as.

(A) Social imitation

(B) Classical imitation

(C) Cognitive arousal

(D) Cognitive imitation

Correct Answer (D) Cognitive Imitation: Imitating the mental processes and cognitive strategies of others, such as problem-solving techniques, rather than just copying physical actions.

Explanation of other options:

(A) Social Imitation: Imitating behaviors, attitudes, or actions learned through social interaction, often in response to societal or cultural norms.

(B) Classical Imitation: An automatic, reflexive form of imitation influenced by repeated exposure to behaviours or actions, often tied to conditioning processes.

(C) Cognitive Arousal: A heightened mental alertness and awareness in response to a stimulus, which can lead to emotional and behavioural reactions.

16. Match the following.

	Theory of Learning		Psychologist
I	Classical conditioning	a	E. L. Thorndike
II	Instrumental conditioning	b	Ivan Pavlov
III	Insightful learning	c	B. F. Skinner
IV	Trial & Error learning	d	W. Kohler

(A).I-b, II-c, III-d, IV-a
(B).I-c, II-a, III-d, IV-b
(C).I-d, II-c, III-a, IV-b
(D).I-a, II-b, III-c, IV-d

Correct Answer- A

Explanation of other options:

1. Classical Conditioning (Pavlovian Conditioning)

Developed by Ivan Pavlov. Involves learning through association. A neutral stimulus becomes associated with an unconditioned stimulus (UCS) that naturally produces a response. Eventually, the neutral stimulus triggers a similar response on its own.

Example: Pavlov's dogs learned to salivate at the sound of a bell (conditioned stimulus) because it was repeatedly paired with food (UCS).

2.Instrumental Conditioning (Operant Conditioning)

Developed by B.F. Skinner (based on Thorndike's Law of Effect). Learning occurs through reinforcements and punishments that follow a behavior. Reinforcement increases the likelihood of a behavior, while punishment decreases it.

Example: A student gets praised (positive reinforcement) for completing homework, increasing the likelihood of future completion.

3. Insightful Learning

Proposed by Wolfgang Köhler through his experiments on chimpanzees. Learning occurs through a sudden realization or aha moment without trial-and-error attempts.It involves cognitive processing where the learner understands how different elements connect to solve a problem.

Example: A chimp uses a stick to reach a banana placed outside its cage after figuring out the solution mentally

4. Trial and Error Learning

Described by Edward Thorndike in his experiments with cats in puzzle boxes. Involves attempting different actions until a desired outcome is achieved. Unsuccessful attempts are gradually eliminated, while successful behaviors are repeated.

Example: A cat eventually finds the lever to escape a cage after several unsuccessful attempts.

17. Match the following.

	Psychologist		Theory of Intelligence
I	Charles Spearman	A	Level-I & Level-II abilities
II	Arthur Jensen	B	Triarchic theory of intelligence
III	L. L. Thurstone	C	Structure of Intelligence
IV	Robert Sternberg	D	Two-factor theory of intelligence
V	J.P. Guilford	E	Primary mental abilities

(A).I-b, II-a, III-c, IV-e, V-d

(B). I-d, II-a, III-e, IV-b, V-c

(C).I-e, II-d, III-c, IV-b, V-a

(D).I-c, II-d, III-a, IV-e, V-b

Correct Answer- B

Explanation of other options:

1. Level-I & Level-II Abilities (J.P. Das, Jack Naglieri, and Kirby)

This concept is based on the Cognitive Assessment System (CAS) and is influenced by Arthur Jensen.

Level-I Ability (Associative Ability): Involves basic memory and rote learning skills, like recall and recognition. Example: Memorizing a phone number.

Level-II Ability (Cognitive Ability): Requires problem-solving, reasoning, and higher-order thinking.

Example: Solving a math problem using logic. Research suggested that Level-II abilities often show a greater variance in performance across different populations.

2. Triarchic Theory of Intelligence (Robert Sternberg)

Sternberg proposed that intelligence has three components:

Componential Intelligence (Analytical): Problem-solving abilities and logical reasoning. Example: Solving puzzles or analyzing data.

Experiential Intelligence (Creative): Ability to use past experiences to generate new ideas or adapt to novel situations. Example: Inventing a new product.

Contextual Intelligence (Practical): Ability to adapt to the environment, solve everyday problems, and manage situations. Example: Resolving a conflict at work.

3. Structure of Intelligence (J.P. Guilford)

Guilford proposed the Structure of Intellect (SI) Model consisting of three dimensions:

Operations: Types of mental processes (e.g., evaluation, memory, and cognition).

Contents: Types of information (e.g., visual, auditory, symbolic).

Products: Forms of information outcomes (e.g., units, classes, relations).

It results in 150 possible factors of intelligence. Example: Evaluating patterns in data using cognitive operations.

4. Two-Factor Theory of Intelligence (Charles Spearman)

Spearman suggested that intelligence consists of:

General Intelligence (g): A core ability influencing performance across all cognitive tasks.

Specific Intelligence (s): Skills unique to particular tasks.

Example: A student with high general intelligence may excel in both math and language, while another may perform better only in music (specific intelligence).

5. Primary Mental Abilities (Louis Thurstone)

<u>Thurstone identified seven primary abilities rather than a single factor of intelligence:</u>

1. Verbal Comprehension – Understanding words and language.
2. Word Fluency – Ability to produce words quickly.
3. Number Facility – Aptitude for mathematical reasoning.
4. Spatial Visualization – Ability to visualize and manipulate objects.
5. Memory – Ability to recall information.
6. Perceptual Speed – Quickly and accurately recognizing details.
7. Reasoning – Logical thinking and problem-solving.

Example: A student good at solving puzzles and understanding vocabulary may have high reasoning and verbal comprehension abilities.

Explanation of keywords : Intelligence

David Wechsler: Intelligence is the global capacity to act purposefully, think rationally, and deal effectively with the environment.

Jean Piaget: Intelligence is the ability to adapt to the environment through continuous learning and problem-solving.

Robert Sternberg: Intelligence involves goal-directed adaptive behavior.

18. Which theory emphasizes individual's subjective frame of reference?

(A) Behaviouristic

(B) Dispositional

(C) Phenomenological

(D) Psychoanalytic

Correct Answer (C) Phenomenological: Examines human experience from the first-person perspective, focusing on how individuals perceive and interpret their world.

Explanation of other options:

(A) Behavioristic: Focuses on observable behaviors and how they are shaped by the environment through conditioning (learning).

(B) Dispositional: Emphasizes internal traits or dispositions (such as personality) that consistently influence behavior across situations.

(D) Psychoanalytic: Highlights the role of unconscious processes, early childhood experiences, and internal conflicts in shaping behavior and personality.

Explanation of keywords in questions:

An individual's subjective frame of reference refers to the personal perspective through which a person views, interprets, and evaluates experiences, events, and situations. It is shaped by their beliefs, values, emotions, past experiences, cultural background, and cognitive processes.

19. Tentative answer(s) to a simple research problem that is/are expressed in the form of a clearly stated relationship between independent and dependent variables is/are called:

(A) Alternate Hypothesis

(B) Null Hypothesis

(C) Phi-Hypothesis

(D) Nil Hypothesis

Correct Answer- A and B

(A) Alternate Hypothesis (H1): The Alternate Hypothesis suggests that there is a significant effect or relationship between variables.It is what the researcher aims to prove or support in a study. If the null hypothesis is rejected, the alternate hypothesis is accepted.

Example: H1: There is a significant difference in self-esteem levels between orphan and non-orphan adolescents.

(B) Null Hypothesis (H0): The Null Hypothesis assumes that there is no effect, no difference, or no relationship between variables. It serves as the default or baseline hypothesis in research. Researchers aim to test and possibly reject the null hypothesis using statistical analysis.

Example: H0: There is no significant difference in resilience between orphan and non-orphan adolescents.

Explanation of other options:

(C) Phi-Hypothesis: The term Phi-Hypothesis is not commonly used in traditional hypothesis testing. However, in some contexts, it may refer to a hypothesis in categorical data analysis, often associated with the Phi Coefficient (φ), which measures the strength of association between two binary variables.

Example: Examining the association between gender (male/female) and preference for a specific counseling style using the Phi coefficient.

(D) Nil Hypothesis: The Nil Hypothesis is essentially a type of Null Hypothesis that specifically states there is no effect or difference (often assumed to be zero effect).

Example:H0: There is no difference in emotional intelligence scores between the two groups.

Explanation of keywords in questions:

1.Research Problem: A research problem is a specific issue, challenge, or question that a researcher aims to investigate. It forms the foundation of a research study and guides the entire research process. A good research problem is clear, focused, and researchable.

Example: *"What is the impact of resilience on the academic achievement of orphan and non-orphan adolescents?"*

2.Dependent Variable (DV): The Dependent Variable is the outcome or effect that is being measured or observed in a study. It depends on or is influenced by the Independent Variable.

Example: In a study on the effect of emotional intelligence on academic achievement.

Dependent Variable is Academic Achievement (e.g., GPA, test scores)

3.Independent Variable (IV): The Independent Variable is the factor that is manipulated or controlled by the researcher to observe its effect on the dependent variable. It is assumed to be the cause in a cause-and-effect relationship. Example: From above example Independent Variable is Emotional Intelligence (e.g., measured using an EI scale).

20. Independent variable(s) is/are also known as:

(A) Explanatory variable

(B) Explainable variable

(C) Exogenous variable

(D) Explicit variable

Correct Answer- A and C

(A) Explanatory Variable: A variable that is used to explain or predict the variation in another variable (often independent).

(C) Exogenous Variable: A variable that is not influenced by other variables in the model; it is external and typically acts as an independent factor influencing other variables.

Explanation of other options:

(B) Explainable Variable: A variable whose behavior can be explained or predicted by other factors, often used in the context of predictive models.

(D) Explicit Variable: A variable whose relationship with other variables is directly stated or clearly defined in a model or analysis.

Explanation of keywords in questions:

Independent Variable (IV): The Independent Variable is the factor that is manipulated or controlled by the researcher to observe its effect on the dependent variable. It is assumed to be the cause in a cause-and-effect relationship.

21. Which of the following is/are not considered as unethical research practice(s)?

(A) Data fabrication

(B) Salami slicing

(C) Data collection

(D) Statistical analysis

Correct Answer- C and D

(C) Data Collection: Gathering data through various methods to support research and test hypotheses.

(D) Statistical Analysis: The use of mathematical methods to analyze data, test hypotheses, and draw conclusions in research, ensuring the results are valid and meaningful.

Explanation of other options:

(A) Data Fabrication: The unethical practice of making up or falsifying data in research to mislead others.

(B) Salami Slicing: The practice of dividing a single study into multiple smaller, separate publications to increase the number of papers, which can mislead the research community.

Explanation of keywords in questions:

Unethical – It refers to actions or practices that violate moral principles, professional standards, or established ethical guidelines.

22. In which of the following methods are variables not actively manipulated?

(A) Observational

(B) Experimental

(C) Correlational

(D) Descriptive

Correct Answer- A;C;D

(A) Observational Method: Variables are not manipulated; researchers observe and record naturally occurring behaviors or phenomena.

(C) Correlational Method: Variables are not manipulated; the relationship between them is studied as they naturally occur.

(D) Descriptive Method: Variables are not manipulated; the goal is to describe or summarize characteristics or behaviors.

Explanation of other options

(B) Experimental Method: Variables are manipulated to test cause-and-effect relationships.

Explanation of keywords in questions: Variable is any characteristic, number, or quantity that can be measured or manipulated in research. It can change or vary across individuals, groups, or situations, making them essential in psychological and scientific research.

23. Which of the following is/are distribution-free test(s)?

(A) Pearson correlation

(B) Spearman's *rho*

(C) Kruskal-Wallis *H* test

(D) Analysis of variance

Correct Answer- B;C

(B) Spearman's Rho: Measures the monotonic relationship between two ranked or ordinal variables, used when data is not normally distributed or not linearly related.

(C) Kruskal-Wallis H Test: A non-parametric test used to compare the distributions of three or more independent groups when the dependent variable is ordinal or non-normally distributed.

Explanation of other options:

(A) Pearson Correlation: Measures the linear relationship between two continuous variables. It requires data to be normally distributed and linearly related.

(D) Analysis of Variance (ANOVA): A parametric test used to compare the means of two or more groups, assuming normality and homogeneity of variances.

Explanation of keywords in questions:

A Distribution-free test is a type of non-parametric statistical test that does not rely on any assumptions about the specific form or parameters of the population distribution (e.g., normal distribution). These tests are often used when:

- The data do not meet the assumptions of parametric tests (such as normality and homogeneity of variances).
- The sample size is small.
- The data are ordinal, ranked, or involve categorical variables.

24. Which of the following hormones do/does not increase hunger?

(A) Leptin

(B) Insulin

(C) Ghrelin

(D) Melanocortin

Correct Answer- A, B, D

(A) Leptin: Produced by fat cells, reduces appetite, promotes energy expenditure, and helps maintain body weight.

(B) Insulin: Produced by the pancreas, regulates blood sugar levels, promotes fat storage, and influences overall metabolism.

(D) Melanocortin: A group of hormones involved in regulating appetite, energy balance, and pigmentation, with α-MSH reducing appetite.

Explanation of other options:

(C) Ghrelin: Produced in the stomach, increases hunger and stimulates food intake by signaling the brain when the body needs energy.

Explanation of keywords in questions: Hunger is a biological and psychological sensation that signals the need for food intake. It is primarily regulated by the body to maintain energy balance and ensure survival.

25. Component(s) of Peripheral Nervous System is/are

(A) Somatic Nervous System

(B) Central Nervous System

(C) Automatic Nervous System

(D) Autonomic Nervous System

Correct Answer- A,D

(A) Somatic Nervous System (SNS): Controls voluntary movements and transmits sensory information to and from the CNS.

(D) Autonomic Nervous System (ANS): Manages involuntary functions such as heart rate, digestion, and breathing. It has two branches: Sympathetic (fight-or-flight) and Parasympathetic (rest-and-digest)

Explanation of other options:

(B) Central Nervous System (CNS): Includes the brain and spinal cord and processes all incoming sensory information and outgoing responses.

(D) Automatic Nervous System: No such type.

Explanation of keywords in questions

The Peripheral Nervous System (PNS) is a part of the nervous system that exists outside the brain and spinal cord. It serves as a communication network between the Central Nervous System (CNS) and the rest of the body.

Main Function: Transmits signals from the CNS to the body (efferent signals). Sends sensory information from the body to the CNS (afferent signals).

26. Which of the following tests are *post hoc*?

(A) Neuman-Keuls test

(*B*) *t*-test

(C) Duncan Multiple Range test

(D) Tukey test

Correct Answer- A;C;D

(A)Neuman-Keuls Test: A post-hoc test used after ANOVA for pairwise comparisons. It is more powerful but more prone to Type I errors compared to other tests like Tukey's HSD.

(C)Duncan's Multiple Range Test: Another post-hoc test used after ANOVA for multiple pairwise comparisons. It is liberal, meaning it has a higher chance of detecting differences, but also of committing Type I errors.

(D)Tukey's HSD Test: A conservative post-hoc test for pairwise comparisons after ANOVA that controls the overall Type I error rate, making it reliable for detecting differences.

Explanation of other options:

(B) t-test: A statistical test used to compare the means of two groups. It can be either independent (two unrelated groups) or paired (same group tested twice).

Explanation of keywords in questions:

A Post Hoc Test is a type of statistical test used to make multiple comparisons between group means after finding a significant result in an ANOVA (Analysis of Variance) or other omnibus test.

Purpose: To identify which specific groups differ from each other.

To prevent false conclusions by adjusting for the increased risk of Type I errors (false positives) that occur with multiple comparisons.

27. The component(s) of a vertebrate motor neuron is/are:

(A) Axon

(B) Myelin sheath

(C) Soma

(D) Cortisol

Correct Answer-A,B,C

(A) Axon: Transmits electrical impulses away from the neuron's soma to other cells.

(B) Myelin Sheath: Fatty insulation that speeds up electrical signal transmission along the axon.

(C) Soma (Cell Body): Contains the nucleus and organelles, integrating signals and maintaining the neuron's function.

Explanation of other options:

(D) Cortisol: A hormone that plays a crucial role in the body's stress response and helps regulate metabolism and immune functions.

Explanation of keywords in questions:

A vertebrate motor neuron is a type of nerve cell responsible for transmitting signals from the central nervous system (CNS) to muscles or glands, resulting in movement or action. It is a crucial component of the somatic nervous system in vertebrates (animals with a backbone

28. Which of the following is/are measure(s) of dispersion?

(A) Variance

(B) ANOVA

(C) Correlation

(D) Range

Correct Answer- A,D

(A) Variance: Measures the spread of data points around the mean.

(D) Range: The difference between the maximum and minimum values in a dataset, showing the data's spread.

Explanation of other options:

(B) ANOVA: Tests if significant differences exist between the means of multiple groups.

(C) Correlation: Measures the strength and direction of the relationship between two variables.

Explanation of keywords: Dispersion refers to the measure of how spread out or scattered the values of a dataset are around the central value (such as the mean or median). It provides insights into the variability or consistency of the data.

29. Jagruti's mother was upset to find that Jagruti used her crayons to draw the picture of an animal on the wall of the drawing room. Her mother took away the crayons from her and made Jagruti wash the drawings off the wall.

Which of the following statements is/are true?

(A) Having her crayons taken away was a form of punishment by removal.

(B) Having her crayons taken away was a form of negative reinforcement.

(C) Being made to wash off the drawing was a form of punishment by application.

(D) Being made to wash off the drawing was a form of punishment by removal.

Correct Answer- A,C

(A) Having her crayons taken away was a form of punishment by removal.

Punishment by removal, also known as negative punishment, involves taking away a desirable stimulus to decrease the likelihood of a behavior recurring. In this case, Jagruti's crayons (a desirable stimulus) were taken away to discourage her from drawing on the wall in the future.

(C) Being made to wash off the drawing was a form of punishment by application.

Punishment by application, also known as positive punishment, involves presenting an unpleasant stimulus following a behavior to decrease its future occurrence. Requiring Jagruti to wash the wall (an unpleasant task) after drawing on it serves as a consequence aimed at reducing the likelihood of her drawing on the wall again.

Explanation of other options

(B) Having her crayons taken away was a form of negative reinforcement.

Negative reinforcement involves the removal of an unpleasant stimulus to increase the likelihood of a behavior occurring. For example, if a child completes homework to stop a parent's nagging, the removal of nagging (unpleasant stimulus) reinforces the behavior of doing homework. In Jagruti's case, removing the crayons serves as a punishment to decrease undesirable behavior, not as reinforcement to increase a desired behavior.

(D) Being made to wash off the drawing was a form of punishment by removal.

Punishment by removal (negative punishment) entails taking away a pleasant stimulus to decrease a behavior. In this instance, Jagruti is given an additional task (washing the wall), which aligns with positive punishment, not the removal of a positive stimulus.

30. Which of the following statements is/are correct regarding memory?

(A) Visual sensory memory last for a fraction of a second.

(B) Selective attention moves the information from short-term memory to long-term memory.

(C) In short-term memory, the information is held for a brief period of time while being used.

(D) Echoic memory capacity is limited to two seconds but smaller than the capacity of iconic memory.

Correct Answer- A,C

(A) Visual sensory memory, also known as iconic memory, retains visual information for a very short time (approximately 250 milliseconds or 1/4 second). This brief retention allows the brain to process the visual input before it fades.

(C) Short-term memory (STM) temporarily stores information for about 20 to 30 seconds. It is the memory system used when information is actively being processed or manipulated, such as when solving a math problem or remembering a phone number before dialing. The capacity of STM is limited, typically around 7±2 items (as per George Miller's research).

Explanation of other options:

(B) Selective attention is the process of focusing on specific information while ignoring other stimuli.

However, it does not directly transfer information to long-term memory. Instead, it moves information into short-term memory (also known as working memory) for temporary processing. For information to move from short-term memory to long-term memory, it requires additional processes like rehearsal, encoding, or meaningful association.

(D) Echoic memory is the auditory form of sensory memory. It lasts longer than iconic memory, generally around 3 to 4 seconds. While it has a smaller capacity compared to iconic memory (which can store more detailed visual information briefly), echoic memory's longer duration helps in processing spoken language and other auditory stimuli.

Explanation of keywords in questions: Memory is the cognitive process by which we encode, store, and retrieve information. It allows us to retain past experiences, learn new information, and apply knowledge in various situations. Memory is a fundamental aspect of human cognition.

31. Which of the following is/are correct regarding the pre-operational stage (2-7 years) of the cognitive development theory of Piaget?

(A) Infants develop a sense of object permanence.

(B) Tendency of a child to focus only on one feature of an object, while ignoring other relevant features.

(C) The inability of the young child to mentally reverse an action.

(D) The child can conserve, reverse their thinking and classifying objects in terms of various characteristics.

Correct Answer- B,C

(B) Centration: Children in the pre-operational stage tend to focus on one aspect of a situation or object, while neglecting other important features. Example: A child may say that a taller glass has more water than a shorter, wider glass, even if both have the same amount of water.

(C) Irreversibility: Children in this stage cannot mentally reverse a series of events or operations.

Example: If a child watches someone flatten a ball of clay, they may not understand that it can be rolled back into its original shape.

Explanation of other options:

(A) Object permanence (understanding that objects continue to exist even when they are out of sight) occurs in the Sensorimotor Stage (0-2 years), not the Pre-operational Stage. In the Sensorimotor Stage, infants learn through direct sensory and motor experiences.

(D) Conservation (understanding that quantity remains the same despite changes in shape or appearance) and reversible thinking develop in the Concrete Operational Stage (7-11 years). In the Pre-operational Stage, children struggle with these concepts.

Explanation of keywords in questions

Four Stages of Cognitive Development

1. Sensorimotor Stage (Birth to 2 years)

Key Features:

- Infants explore the world through their senses (touch, sight, sound) and motor activities.
- Development of object permanence — the understanding that objects continue to exist even when they are not visible.
- Learning through trial and error and imitation.
- Example: A baby who drops a toy and watches it fall repeatedly learns about cause and effect.

2. Pre-operational Stage (2 to 7 years)

Key Features:

- Children develop symbolic thought — using words, images, and drawings to represent objects.
- Egocentrism — difficulty understanding others' perspectives.
- Centration — focusing on only one feature of an object, ignoring others.
- Irreversibility — inability to mentally reverse an action.
- Lack of conservation — not understanding that quantity remains the same despite changes in shape or appearance.
- Example: A child may think that a tall, thin glass has more water than a short, wide glass, even if both contain the same amount.

3. Concrete Operational Stage (7 to 11 years)

Key Features:

- Logical thinking develops, but it is limited to concrete, tangible objects and events.
- Children understand the concepts of conservation, reversibility, and classification.
- Improved problem-solving and ability to consider multiple situation aspects (decentration).
- Example: A child can sort objects by size, shape, or color and understand that the quantity of liquid remains the same even when poured into a different container.

4. Formal Operational Stage (11 years and older)
Key Features:

- Development of abstract and hypothetical thinking.
- Ability to reason logically about concepts that are not directly observable.
- Understanding of cause and effect relationships and formulation of hypotheses.
- Engages in metacognition (thinking about thinking).
- Example: Teenagers can think about philosophical questions or imagine futuristic scenarios.

32. Which of the following statements is/are correct about "*item-response theory*"?
(A) It talks about how items should function based on the knowledge of an ability or trait.
(B) It compares responses to items to determine how well the items function.
(C) It is based on the assumption that many latent traits underlie test performance.
(D) It is a logistic function having, one, two or three parameters.
Correct Answer- A,B,D
Explanation of keywords in questions:
Item Response Theory (IRT) is a modern approach to test theory that examines the relationship between individuals' latent traits (unobservable characteristics like ability, attitude, or personality) and their performance on test items.
33. Which of the following is/are characteristic(s) of groupthink?
(A) There is excessive optimism and risk-taking.
(B) Silence is interpreted as consent.
(C) Members reduce their efforts and performance levels while acting as a part of the group.
(D) People do not know what they are supposed to be doing.
Correct Answer- A, B
(A) There is excessive optimism and risk-taking.
One symptom of groupthink is the illusion of invulnerability, which fosters excessive optimism and encourages taking extreme risks.
(B) Silence is interpreted as consent.
In groupthink scenarios, an illusion of unanimity prevails, where members perceive silence as agreement, discouraging individuals from expressing dissenting opinions.
Explanation of other options:
(C) Members reduce their efforts and performance levels while acting as a part of the group.
This describes social loafing, not groupthink. Social loafing occurs when individuals exert less effort in a group setting than they would individually.
(D) People do not know what they are supposed to be doing.
Groupthink involves a clear, often unchallenged direction, with members conforming to perceived group consensus, even if it leads to poor decisions. Uncertainty about roles is not a characteristic of groupthink.
Explanation of keywords in questions:
Groupthink- Groupthink is a psychological phenomenon that occurs within a group of people where the desire for harmony or conformity in the group results in an irrational or dysfunctional decision-making outcome.
34. Which of the following dimensions is/are related to Fiedler's Contingency Model of Leadership Effectiveness?

(A) Leader-member relationship

(B) Leader's position power

(C) Leader's personal power

(D) Individual consideration

Correct Answer- A,B

(A) Leader-member relationship

Leader-member relations are a core component of Fiedler's model, emphasizing the importance of trust and respect between leaders and their teams.

(B) Leader's position power

A leader's position power is another critical dimension in the model, highlighting the influence a leader wields based on their formal authority within the organization.

Explanation of other options:

(C) Leader's personal power

Fiedler's model focuses on the leader's position power rather than personal power. Personal power, derived from individual characteristics like expertise or charisma, is not explicitly addressed in this model.

(D) Individual consideration

Individual consideration pertains to transformational leadership, where leaders attend to each follower's needs and development. It is not a dimension in Fiedler's Contingency Model.

Explanation of keywords in questions:

Fiedler's Contingency Model of Leadership, developed by psychologist Fred Fiedler in the 1960s, posits that a leader's effectiveness is contingent upon the interplay between their leadership style and the favorableness of the situational context. This model suggests that there is no single best way to lead; instead, success depends on aligning the leader's inherent style with the appropriate situational variables.

35.Which of the following is/are not culture-fair test(s)?

(A) Ravens Progressive Matrices

(B) Dynamic Progressive Matrices

(C) Advanced Progressive Matrices

(D) Millennium Progressive Matrices

Correct Answer- B,D

(B) Dynamic Progressive Matrices (DPM): A version with adjustable difficulty based on the individual's performance, often used for children or those with cognitive impairments.

(D) Millennium Progressive Matrices (MPM): A modernized version of the RPM, updated for contemporary contexts with an emphasis on cultural validity and accessibility.

Explanation of other options

(A) Raven's Progressive Matrices (RPM): Standard version, measuring abstract reasoning and fluid intelligence with progressively harder questions.

(C) Advanced Progressive Matrices (APM): A more difficult version designed for individuals with higher intellectual abilities, requiring advanced cognitive skills.

Explanation of keywords in questions:

A **culture-fair test** is designed to assess intelligence or cognitive abilities while minimizing the influence of cultural, language, or educational backgrounds. By focusing on non-verbal tasks, such tests aim to provide an equitable evaluation across diverse populations.

36.Which of the following is/are related to reliability?

(A) A test is administered to same set of people in two different occasions.

(B) A test administered once is scored by two or more than two evaluators.

(C) A test administered once is scored by splitting it into two equal-halves.

(D) A test measures what it intends to measure.

Correct Answer- A,B,C

(A) A test is administered to the same set of people on two different occasions.

This describes the Test-Retest Reliability method.It assesses the stability of a test over time. If the same individuals take the test twice with a time gap in between, the results should be similar if the test is reliable.

(B) A test administered once is scored by two or more evaluators.

This refers to Inter-Rater Reliability or Inter-Scorer Reliability. It measures the consistency of test scores when different people evaluate or rate the same test. High agreement among raters indicates strong reliability.

(C) A test administered once is scored by splitting it into two equal halves.

This describes the Split-Half Reliability method. It involves dividing a single test into two equal halves (e.g., odd and even questions) and comparing the scores of both halves. High correlation between the two halves indicates good internal consistency.

Explanation of other options:

(D) A test measures what it intends to measure.

This is a measure of Validity, not reliability. Validity refers to whether a test measures what it is designed to measure. While reliability is about consistency, validity is about accuracy.

Explanation of keywords in questions: Reliability refers to the consistency or stability of a test over time, across different evaluators, or across different forms. A reliable test produces consistent results under similar conditions. It is an essential aspect of test construction

37. Which of the following is/are not defense mechanism(s)?

(A) Projection

(B) Frustration

(C) Introspection

(D) Rationalization

Correct Answer- B, C

(B) Frustration: Frustration is an emotional response to obstacles or perceived failures, not a defense mechanism. It may lead to behaviors like aggression or withdrawal, but it is not classified as a defense mechanism itself.

(C) Introspection: Introspection is the process of self-reflection and examining one's own thoughts, feelings, and behaviors. It is a conscious, self-evaluative process rather than an unconscious defense mechanism.

Explanation of other options:

(A) Projection: Projection involves attributing one's own undesirable thoughts, feelings, or impulses to another person. Example: A person feeling angry may accuse others of being angry.

(D)Rationalization: Rationalization involves justifying or explaining away unacceptable thoughts, feelings, or behaviours in a seemingly logical or reasonable manner. Example: After failing a test, a student may claim the teacher was unfair instead of acknowledging a lack of preparation.

Explanation of keywords: Defence mechanisms are unconscious psychological strategies used by individuals to protect themselves from anxiety or uncomfortable thoughts and feelings. Sigmund Freud introduced this concept in psychoanalytic theory.

38. On a standard test, the population is known to have a mean of 500 and a standard deviation of 100. Those receiving an experimental treatment have a mean of 540. The effect size is . (rounded off to two decimal places)

Correct Answer- 0.40 to 0.40

Explanation of keywords:

Standard Deviation (SD) is a measure of how spread out the numbers are from the mean (average) of the dataset. A low standard deviation means the data points are close to the mean, while a high standard deviation means they are spread out over a wider range.

39. The standard deviation for the following scores: 8, 6, 6, 9, 6, 5, 6, 2 is (rounded off to two decimal places)

Correct Answer- 1.92 to 1.94

Explanation of keywords:

Standard Deviation (SD) is a measure of how spread out the numbers are from the mean (average) of the dataset. A low standard deviation means the data points are close to the mean, while a high standard deviation means they are spread out over a wider range.

CHAPTER III

PREVIOUS YEAR QUESTION 2023 ANALYSIS

1. Blind spot in the retina contains.

    (A)only rod cells

    (B)only cone cells

    (C)both rod and cone cells

    (D)neither rod nor cone cells

Correct Answer- (D) Neither rod nor cone cells

Explanation of other options

Rods are specialised for night vision (scotopic vision) and function well in low-light conditions. Approximately 120 million rods in each eye.

Cones are responsible for colour vision and work best in bright light (photopic vision). Approximately 6 million cones in each eye.

Explanation of keywords;

The blind spot (also called the optic disc) is the area of the retina where the optic nerve exits the eye. Unlike other parts of the retina, the blind spot has no photoreceptor cells (no rods or cones), making it insensitive to light.

2. Taking painkillers eliminates pain, increasing the likelihood that the person will take painkillers again. colourThis is an example of.

    (A)negative punishment

    (B)positive reinforcement

    (C)negative reinforcement

    (D)positive punishment

Correct Answer: (C) Negative Reinforcement: Removing something unpleasant (e.g., stopping loud noise).

Explanation of other options

(A) Negative Punishment: Removing something desirable (e.g., taking away TV time).

(B) Positive Reinforcement: Adding something pleasant (e.g., giving praise or rewards).

(D) Positive Punishment: Adding something unpleasant (e.g., giving extra chores)

3. When learning something new impairs the ability to retrieve information learnt earlier, it is known as .

(A) Retroactive interference

(B) Proactive interference

(C) tip-of-the-tongue phenomenon

(D) recency effect

Correct Answer: (A) Retroactive Interference: New information makes it harder to recall old information

Explanation of other options

.(B) Proactive Interference: Old information makes it harder to learn or recall new information.

(C) Tip-of-the-Tongue Phenomenon: The sensation of knowing something but being unable to retrieve it.

(D) Recency Effect: The tendency to better remember the most recent information or items in a sequence.

Explanation of keywords

Retrieval: It refers to the process of accessing and bringing stored information from memory into conscious awareness. It is one of the key stages of memory, along with encoding (the process of storing information) and storage (maintaining information over time).

4. Iconic memory is a type of .

    (A) short term memory

    (B) sensory memory

    (C) semantic memory

(D) working memory

Correct Answer: (B) Sensory Memory: Very brief storage of sensory information (milliseconds to seconds).

Explanation of other options

(A) Short-Term Memory: Holds limited information for a short period (15-30 seconds).

(C) Semantic Memory: Stores general knowledge and facts unrelated to specific experiences.

(D) Working Memory: Active processing and manipulation of information used for tasks like problem-solving or comprehension

Explanation of keywords

Iconic memory is a type of sensory memory that stores visual information for a very brief period, typically lasting about 250 to 500 milliseconds (a quarter to half a second). It acts as a snapshot of the visual environment, capturing a detailed image that allows the brain to process and interpret visual stimuli.

5. Which one of the following components of language has to do with the practical or social aspects of communication with others?

(A) Phonemes

(B) Morphemes

(C) Pragmatics

(D) Syntax

Correct Answer: (C) Pragmatics: The social rules and context that guide language use in different situations.

Explanation of other options

(A) Phonemes: Smallest units of sound in language that distinguish words.

(B) Morphemes: Smallest units of meanina g in language (can be whole words or parts of words).

(D) Syntax: The rules for arranging words into grammatically correct sentences.

Explanation of keywords in questions

Language is a complex system of communication that involves the use of words, symbols, gestures, and rules to convey meaning. It is a uniquely human ability that allows individuals to express thoughts, emotions, ideas, and information.

6. The Yerkes-Dodson law states that.

(A) performance is affected by the level of arousal

(B) frustration leads to aggression

(C) self-concept helps us organize and remember information

(D) changes in behaviour are a result of experiences that have happened frequently or recently

Correct Answer-A

(A) Performance is affected by the level of arousal.

The Yerkes-Dodson Law states that there is an optimal level of arousal for peak performance. Performance improves with increased arousal to a certain point, but too much or too little arousal can decrease performance. For example, moderate anxiety before an exam can enhance focus, but extreme anxiety might impair concentration.

Explanation of other options

(B) Frustration leads to aggression.

This statement is linked to the Frustration-Aggression Hypothesis, which suggests that when people are blocked from achieving a goal, frustration may lead to aggressive behavior.

(C) Self-concept helps us organize and remember information.

This statement is more aligned with theories of self-concept and self-schema, which refer to how we perceive and organize information about ourselves, influencing memory and thought processes.

(D) Changes in behavior are a result of experiences that have happened frequently or recently.

This concept is related to learning theories like classical conditioning or priming, where frequent or recent experiences influence behavior and responses.

Explanation of keywords

The Yerkes-Dodson Law is a psychological principle that describes the relationship between arousal (a state of alertness or mental and physical activation) and performance.

The law suggests that: Performance improves with arousal to a certain point, known as the optimal level of arousal.Beyond this point, too much arousal can lead to a decline in performance. Conversely, low arousal may lead to poor performance due to a lack of motivation or focus.

The relationship is often illustrated as an inverted U-shaped curve:

- Low Arousal: Leads to boredom, low motivation, and poor performance.
- Moderate Arousal: Enhances focus, motivation, and productivity. This is the optimal zone for most tasks.
- High Arousal: Can result in anxiety, stress, and reduced performance, especially for complex tasks.

7. Transduction of mechanical energy into nerve impulses in the auditory system takes place in reponse to bending of the.
(A) Pinna
(B) hair cells
(C) incus
(D) malleus

Correct Answer: (B) Hair Cells

Hair cells are specialised sensory receptors located in the cochlea of the inner ear.

When sound waves travel through the ear, they cause vibrations in the basilar membrane. These vibrations lead to the bending of hair cells within the organ of Corti. This bending opens ion channels, leading to the generation of nerve impulses that are transmitted to the brain via the auditory nerve. This process is called transduction, where mechanical energy (sound waves) is converted into electrical signals.

Explanation of other options

(A) Pinna: The pinna is the visible, outer part of the ear that collects and funnels sound waves into the ear canal. It helps with the localisation of sound but does not play a role in converting sound into nerve impulses.

(C) Incus: The incus (anvil) is one of the three small bones (ossicles) in the middle ear. It transmits vibrations from the malleus to the stapes but is not directly involved in converting mechanical energy to nerve impulses.

(D) Malleus: The malleus (hammer) is the first ossicle that receives sound vibrations from the eardrum and transfers them to the incus. Like the incus, it aids in sound conduction but is not responsible for the transduction of sound into nerve signals.

Explanation of keywords

1. Transduction

Transduction refers to the process of converting one form of energy into another. In the context of the auditory system, it means converting mechanical energy (sound vibrations) into electrical signals (nerve impulses) that the brain can interpret. This process occurs in the cochlea when hair cells bend in response to sound vibrations.

Example: When you hear music, sound waves travel through your ear, and transduction converts those waves into electrical signals that your brain recognises as sound.

2. Nerve Impulse

A nerve impulse is an electrical signal that travels along a neuron (nerve cell) to transmit information. In the auditory system, the nerve impulse carries sound information from the ear to the brain, specifically to the auditory cortex for processing. It involves a series of electrical and chemical reactions, often initiated by the bending of hair cells in the cochlea.

Example: When the hair cells in your ear detect sound vibrations, they generate nerve impulses that allow you to recognize someone's voice or enjoy music.

3. Auditory System: The auditory system is the sensory system responsible for detecting, transmitting, and interpreting sound.

It includes several parts:

- ○ Outer Ear: Captures sound waves and directs them to the eardrum.
- ○ Middle Ear: Contains the ossicles (malleus, incus, and stapes) that amplify sound vibrations.
- ○ Inner Ear: Contains the cochlea, where transduction occurs.
- ○ Auditory Nerve: Carries nerve impulses from the cochlea to the brain.
- ○ Auditory Cortex: Located in the brain, responsible for interpreting sounds.

Example: The auditory system allows you to hear a car horn and react accordingly by stopping or changing direction.

8. Which one of the following theories states that emotion occurs as a result of physical arousal and labeling of the arousal based on cues from the surrounding environment?

(A) Ekman-Friesen theory

(B) Schachter-Singer theory

(C) James-Lange theory

(D) Cannon-Bard theory

Correct Answer: (B) Schachter-Singer Theory: Emotions arise from a combination of physiological arousal and cognitive labeling of that arousal.

Explanation of other options

(A) Ekman-Friesen Theory: Suggests universal facial expressions for basic emotions.

(C) James-Lange Theory: Emotions are the result of physiological reactions to stimuli.

(D) Cannon-Bard Theory: Emotion and physiological response occur simultaneously but independently.

Explanation of keywords

1. Emotion

Emotion is a complex psychological state that involves three main components:

- Subjective Experience: How a person feels internally (e.g., happiness, anger, sadness).
- Physiological Response: Physical changes in the body, such as increased heart rate or sweating, often controlled by the autonomic nervous system.
- Behavioral Response: Observable expressions of emotion, like facial expressions, gestures, or tone of voice.

Example: Feeling excited before a big event, like a performance or exam, is an emotional response that may include a racing heart and smiling.

2. Arousal

Arousal refers to a state of heightened alertness, energy, or physical and mental activation. It is regulated by the reticular activating system (RAS) in the brain and involves the autonomic nervous system. According to the Yerkes-Dodson Law, moderate arousal often results in the best performance, while extremely high or low arousal can negatively affect performance.

Example: Feeling energised and focused before a competition is a state of high arousal, whereas feeling sleepy or calm while reading a book reflects low arousal.

9. Which one of the following is TRUE for the Pain-Gate control theory?

(A) Gate is a physical structure

(B) Activity of gate cannot be closed by non-pain signals

(C) Substance P released into spinal cord does not activate other neurons that send messages through spinal gates

(D) Pain signals must pass through a gate located in the spinal cord

Correct Answer: (D) (Pain signals must pass through a gate located in the spinal cord) .

According to the theory, the gate in the spinal cord (specifically in the dorsal horn) regulates how much pain information reaches the brain. Factors like attention, emotions, and other sensory inputs can influence whether the gate opens or closes, affecting pain perception.

Explanation of other options

(A) Gate is a physical structure.

The gate is not an actual physical structure; it is a functional process within the spinal cord that controls the transmission of pain signals.

(B)Activity of gate cannot be closed by non-pain signals.

The gate can be closed by non-painful signals from sensory neurons, such as when you rub a sore area, which can reduce the sensation of pain. This is why massaging a painful spot often provides relief.

(C)Substance P released into spinal cord does not activate other neurons.

Substance P is a neurotransmitter involved in transmitting pain signals. It does activate neurons in the spinal cord, sending messages to the brain about the presence of pain.

Explanation of keywords

Pain-Gate control theory-The Gate Control Theory of Pain was proposed by Ronald Melzack and Patrick Wall in 1965. It is one of the most influential explanations of how we perceive pain. The theory suggests that pain is not simply the result of signals sent from the body to the brain, but rather a dynamic process regulated by a "gate" mechanism in the spinal cord.

10. Being treated with warmth and consideration by others only when one behaves as expected, is called as.

(A) openness to experience

(B) conditional positive regard

(C) unconditional positive regard

(D) zone of proximal development

Correct Answer: (B) Conditional Positive Regard: Acceptance or approval based on meeting certain conditions or expectations.

Explanation of other options

(A) Openness to Experience: A personality trait characterized by curiosity, creativity, and a willingness to explore new ideas and experiences.

(C) Unconditional Positive Regard: Acceptance or approval given freely, regardless of a person's actions or performance.

(D) Zone of Proximal Development (ZPD): The range of tasks that a learner can perform with help but not yet independently, highlighting the potential for development with support.

11. Which of the following is/are NOT the factor(s) of the Big Five Personality model?

(A) Conscientiousness

(B) Optimism

(C) Humility

(D) Extraversion

Correct Answer- B,C

(B) Optimism: While optimism (having a positive outlook on life) can influence personality, it is not one of the five core dimensions in the Big Five Model. However, it may be associated with low neuroticism or high extraversion.

(C) Humility : Humility refers to a modest view of one's importance. Although it is a valuable personality trait, it is not specifically categorized under the Big Five. Some newer models, like the HEXACO Model, include humility as a distinct factor.

Explanation of other options

(A) Conscientiousness: Conscientiousness refers to being disciplined, organized, and dependable. People who are highly conscientious tend to be reliable and detail-oriented.

(D) Extraversion: Extraversion involves being energetic, talkative, and sociable. People high in extraversion enjoy social interactions and often feel energized in social settings.

Explanation of keywords :

The Big Five Personality Model (also known as the Five-Factor Model) consists of five broad dimensions that describe human personality. These traits are often remembered using the acronym OCEAN:

1. Openness to Experience: Creativity, curiosity, and willingness to try new things.
2. Conscientiousness: Organized, responsible, and goal-oriented.
3. Extraversion: Outgoing, energetic, and sociable.
4. Agreeableness: Kind, cooperative, and empathetic.
5. Neuroticism: Emotional instability, anxiety, and moodiness.

12. Which of the following is/are TRUE for creative individuals?
(A) They are not very good at mental imagery
(B) They are not afraid to be different
(C) They do not value their independence
(D) They are unconventional in their work
Correct Answer-B,D
(B) They are not afraid to be different.

- Creative individuals are often comfortable with thinking outside the box and challenging societal norms.
- They embrace their unique perspectives and are not afraid to express unconventional ideas, even if it means standing out or facing criticism.
- Many innovators and artists have demonstrated this trait, using their distinctiveness to drive new concepts and inventions.

(D) They are unconventional in their work.

- Creativity is often characterized by unconventionality.
- Creative people tend to approach problems from unique angles and experiment with new methods.
- Whether in art, science, or entrepreneurship, they are willing to break traditional rules and explore novel solutions.

Explanation of other options
(A) They are not very good at mental imagery.
Creative individuals often have a strong ability to engage in mental imagery. Mental imagery is the capacity to visualise scenarios, objects, or concepts in the mind, which is essential for artistic creation, problem-solving, and innovative thinking.
For example, an artist may visualize a painting before starting, or a scientist may imagine possible outcomes of an experiment.
(C) They do not value their independence.
Creative individuals typically value independence and prefer having the freedom to explore their ideas without restrictions. Independence allows them to experiment, take risks, and pursue original thoughts without being limited by others' opinions.
Autonomous thinkers like inventors, writers, and artists often excel in environments where they can work freely.
Explanation of keywords : Creativity refers to the ability to generate, develop, and express original, novel, and useful ideas. It involves thinking in new ways, making unique connections between concepts, and finding innovative solutions to problems. Creativity can be expressed in various fields, including art, science, business, technology, and everyday life.
13. Which of the following is/are included under behavioural genetics studies in humans?
(A) Selective breeding studies
(B) Family studies
(C) Twin studie
(D) Adoption studies

Correct Answer: B,C,D

(B) Family Studies: Examine traits or behaviors in family members to understand genetic and environmental influences.

(C) Twin Studies: Compare identical and fraternal twins to determine the genetic contribution to traits or behaviors.

(D) Adoption Studies: Assess the impact of genetics versus the environment by studying adopted children and their biological and adoptive parents.

Explanation of other options

(A) Selective Breeding Studies: Involve breeding organisms with specific traits to study the inheritance of those traits.

Explanation of keywords : Genetics is the branch of biology that studies how traits are passed from parents to offspring through genes. It explores how organisms inherit characteristics such as eye colour, height, and even certain behaviours or diseases. Genetics helps us understand the biological instructions that influence our growth, development, and function.

14. Which of the following statements regarding locus of control is/are CORRECT?

(A) It can be internal and/or external

(B) It is associated with self-esteem

(C) Internal locus of control is positively correlated with success

(D) Regret has no association with locus of control

Correct Answer-A,B,C

(A) It can be internal and/or external.

Locus of control exists on a spectrum, meaning a person may have a predominantly internal or external locus of control, or a mix of both depending on the situation.For example, someone may have an internal locus regarding academic success but an external locus regarding unexpected life events like natural disasters.

(B) It is associated with self-esteem.

Locus of control is closely linked to self-esteem. Individuals with an internal locus of control tend to have higher self-esteem as they believe their actions lead to success. Conversely, those with an external locus of control may experience lower self-esteem, feeling powerless over their circumstances.

(C) Internal locus of control is positively correlated with success.

Research indicates that people with an internal locus of control are more likely to achieve success in academics, careers, and personal goals.They are generally more motivated, resilient, and take responsibility for their actions.

Explanation of other options

(D)Regret has no association with locus of control

Regret is often associated with locus of control.People with an internal locus of control may experience regret because they feel responsible for their choices. On the other hand, individuals with an external locus of control might avoid regret by attributing their failures to external factors like luck or fate.

Explanation of keywords

Locus of Control: The concept of locus of control was introduced by Julian B. Rotter in 1954. It refers to how individuals perceive the control they have over events in their lives.

There are two types of locus of control:

Internal Locus of Control: Individuals believe that their actions and decisions directly influence the outcomes in their lives. Example: "I did well on the exam because I studied hard."

External Locus of Control: Individuals believe that external forces like luck, fate, or other people determine their outcomes. Example: "I failed the exam because the teacher made it too hard."

15. Which of the following is/are TRUE for nonparametric statistics?

(A) It is often called distribution-free statitstics

(B) It is used to analyze interval data

(C) It is used to analyze ordinal data

(D) It compares groups in terms of means

Correct Answer: A, C

(A) It is often called distribution-free statistics.

Nonparametric statistics are often called distribution-free because they do not assume that the data follows a specific distribution (like a normal distribution). Examples include tests like the Mann-Whitney U test or the Wilcoxon Signed-Rank Test.

(C) It is used to analyze ordinal data.

Nonparametric statistics are particularly useful for analyzing ordinal data (data with a meaningful order but unequal intervals, such as rankings or satisfaction ratings).

Examples:

- Mann-Whitney U Test for comparing two independent groups.
- Kruskal-Wallis Test for comparing more than two groups.
- Wilcoxon Signed-Rank Test for paired data.

Explanation of other options

(B) It is used to analyze interval data.

Interval data refers to numerical data with meaningful intervals but no true zero (e.g., temperature in Celsius). Parametric tests like the t-test or ANOVA are generally used to analyze interval data since they rely on assumptions about the data's distribution.

Nonparametric tests are not the preferred choice for interval data unless the data is skewed or violates parametric assumptions.

(D) It compares groups in terms of means.

Nonparametric tests do not typically compare groups using means. Instead, they compare groups using medians or ranked data.This makes them more robust when data is not normally distributed or contains outliers. Example: The Mann-Whitney U Test compares the ranks of data points instead of the means.

Explanation of keywords

Nonparametric statistics refers to a set of statistical methods used when data does not meet the assumptions of parametric tests. Unlike parametric tests, nonparametric methods do not rely on assumptions about the distribution of the data (e.g., normal distribution) or homogeneity of variance. These tests are often called "distribution-free" tests.

Nonparametric tests are generally used in the following situations:

- When data is measured on a nominal or ordinal scale.
- When the sample size is small.
- When data is not normally distributed.
- When data contains outliers or is skewed.

16. According to the review of research on stress and immune system, which of the following statement(s) has/ have substantial evidence?

(A) There is a negative relationship between stress and functional immune measures

(B) There is no measurable impact of stress on functional immune measures

(C) Loneliness impacts the relationship between stress and functional immune measures

(D) There is a positive relationship between long term stressors and functional immune measures

Correct Answer- A,C

(A) There is a negative relationship between stress and functional immune measures.

- Substantial research supports a negative relationship between stress and immune function.

- Chronic stress releases high levels of cortisol (a stress hormone), which can suppress immune responses.
- This results in reduced production of lymphocytes (white blood cells) and weakened immune responses, making individuals more prone to infections.
- Examples:

  - Studies show that individuals under chronic stress, like caregivers or those with demanding jobs, tend to have lower immune function.
  - Students facing exam stress often show temporary immune suppression.

(C) Loneliness impacts the relationship between stress and functional immune measures.

- Loneliness can worsen the effects of stress on the immune system.
- People who experience loneliness or lack social support tend to have a more pronounced negative impact of stress on immune function.
- Social isolation increases stress levels and reduces the immune response, making individuals more vulnerable to illness.
- Example: Elderly individuals who feel socially isolated often experience heightened stress and weakened immune function.

Explanation of other options

(B) There is no measurable impact of stress on functional immune measures.

Research consistently indicates that stress has a measurable and significant impact on immune function. Both acute stress (short-term) and chronic stress (long-term) are linked to measurable changes in immune markers, such as inflammation and antibody production.

(D) There is a positive relationship between long-term stressors and functional immune measures.

Long-term stressors generally have a negative effect on immune function, not a positive one. While short-term (acute) stress may briefly boost immune responses to deal with immediate threats, chronic stress results in immune suppression over time.

Example: Individuals experiencing prolonged workplace stress or financial difficulties often show elevated inflammation and poor immune resilience.

Explanation of keywords

Stress: It is a natural physiological and psychological response to external or internal challenges, known as stressors. It can arise from daily events, significant life changes, or perceived threats. When faced with a stressful situation, the body activates the stress response, also called the "fight or flight" response, to prepare for immediate action. This involves the release of stress hormones like cortisol and adrenaline.

Immune System: The immune system is the body's defence mechanism against harmful pathogens such as viruses, bacteria, and toxins. It is made up of various cells, tissues, and organs that work together to protect the body from infections and diseases.

17. Which of the following influence(s) gender dysphoria?

(A) Prenatal factors

(B) Early childhood experiences

(C) Socialization

(D) Attention Deficit Hyperactivity Disorder

Correct Answer-A,B,C

(A) Prenatal Factors

- Prenatal factors play a significant role in the development of gender identity.

- Hormonal influences during prenatal development, particularly exposure to androgens (male hormones), can affect brain structures associated with gender identity.
- Genetic factors may also contribute to the development of gender dysphoria.
- Research Evidence: Brain imaging studies have shown differences in the brains of transgender individuals that align more closely with their experienced gender rather than their assigned sex at birth.

(B) Early Childhood Experiences

- Early childhood experiences can shape gender identity and may contribute to gender dysphoria.
- Children typically become aware of their gender identity by the age of 2 to 4 years. Experiences related to gender expression (e.g., dressing, toys, social roles) can influence how they perceive their gender.
- Supportive or unsupportive environments can impact the intensity of gender dysphoria.
- Example: A child assigned male at birth who consistently identifies as female may experience distress if their gender expression is not accepted.

(C) Socialization

- Socialization refers to the process of learning cultural norms, including gender roles and expectations.
- Societal norms and pressures regarding gender conformity can increase the distress experienced by individuals with gender dysphoria.
- Example: A transgender individual may experience rejection, discrimination, or stigma in environments that strictly enforce traditional gender norms.

Explanation of other options
(D) Attention Deficit Hyperactivity Disorder (ADHD)

- While ADHD and gender dysphoria can co-occur in some individuals, there is no direct evidence suggesting that ADHD influences the development of gender dysphoria.
- Some studies have found higher rates of ADHD among transgender youth, but this is likely due to shared challenges such as social stigma or mental health concerns rather than a causal relationship.

Explanation of keywords
Gender Dysphoria is a psychological condition characterised by a significant incongruence between an individual's assigned gender at birth and their experienced or expressed gender. This distress can affect emotional well-being and functioning. The exact causes of gender dysphoria are complex and involve a combination of biological, psychological, and social factors.

18. If the variance of a set of scores is 100, the standard deviation is(in integer).

Correct Answer: 10

Explanation of other options

Variance = 100

Standard Deviation=square root of variance =10

Explanation of keywords

Variance: Variance measures the average squared difference between each data point and the mean of the dataset. It provides a general idea of how spread out the values are.

Standard Deviation: Standard Deviation is simply the square root of the variance. It brings the measure back to the original unit of the data, making it easier to interpret.

19. Match the structures of the brain in the first column with their respective functions in the second column of the table given below.

Brain Structures	Functions
P) Cerebellum	i) Orients a person in the environment
Q) Thalamus	ii) Coordinates heart rate, circulation, and respiration
R) Tectum	iii) Controls fine motor skills
S) Medulla	iv) Relays and filters information from the senses and transmits the information to the cerebral cortex

(A) P-(iii), Q-(i), R-(iv), S-(ii)
(B) P-(i), Q-(iv), R-(ii), S-(iii)
(C) P-(iv), Q-(iii), R-(ii), S-(i)
(D) P-(iii), Q-(iv), R-(i), S-(ii)
Correct Answer: (D) P-(iii), Q-(iv), R-(i), S-(ii)
Explanation of other options
(P) Cerebellum - Controls Fine Motor Skills (iii)

- Cerebellum is located at the back of the brain, beneath the occipital lobes.
- It is primarily responsible for coordinating fine motor skills and ensuring smooth, precise movements.
- It also plays a role in balance, posture, and motor learning.
- Example: When you ride a bicycle or play the piano, the cerebellum helps coordinate your movements.

(Q) Thalamus - Relays and Filters Information from the Senses and Transmits to the Cerebral Cortex (iv)

- The thalamus is located near the center of the brain and acts as a relay station for sensory information (except smell).
- It receives signals from the body, processes them, and directs them to the appropriate areas of the cerebral cortex for further interpretation.
- It also plays a role in consciousness, sleep, and alertness.
- Example: When you touch a hot surface, the thalamus relays the sensation to the brain for processing.

(R) Tectum - Orients a Person in the Environment (i)

- The tectum is part of the midbrain and is involved in visual and auditory processing.
- It contains structures like the superior colliculi (responsible for visual reflexes) and the inferior colliculi (responsible for auditory reflexes).
- The tectum helps to orient a person by directing their attention to moving objects or sounds in the environment.
- Example: When you hear a loud noise and instinctively turn your head, your tectum is responsible for that response.

(S) Medulla - Coordinates Heart Rate, Circulation, and Respiration (ii)

- The medulla is located at the base of the brainstem, connecting the brain to the spinal cord.
- It controls vital autonomic functions such as heart rate, blood pressure, and breathing.
- Damage to the medulla can be life-threatening due to its role in maintaining essential bodily functions.
- Example: During sleep, the medulla ensures that your breathing and heart rate remain stable.

20. Which one of the following is established by the replication of research studies?
(A) Validity of the results
(B) Reliability of the results
(C) Interaction effect
(D) Mediation effect
Correct Answer :(B) Reliability of the Results
Reliability refers to the consistency and stability of the results when the study is repeated. If a study is replicated multiple times with similar results, it confirms the reliability of the findings.
Types of Reliability:

- Test-Retest Reliability: Consistent results over time.
- Inter-Rater Reliability: Agreement between different observers.
- Internal Consistency: Consistency within a set of measurements.
- Replication's Role: Establishing reliability is the primary purpose of replication. If results are reproducible, the study is considered reliable.

Explanation of other options
(A) Validity of the Results
Validity refers to whether a study measures what it claims to measure.
Types of Validity:

- Internal Validity: Ensures the observed effect is due to the manipulation of the independent variable, not external factors.
- External Validity: Determines if the results can be generalized to other populations or settings.
- Replication's Role: Although replication can strengthen claims about validity by confirming results in different contexts, it is not primarily used to establish validity.

(C) Interaction Effect
An interaction effect occurs when the effect of one independent variable on the dependent variable depends on the level of another independent variable.This is typically tested using factorial designs in experiments. Example: The effect of a teaching method on student performance might differ based on students' prior knowledge.
(D) Mediation Effect
A mediation effect explains how an independent variable influences a dependent variable through a mediator variable. Example: Stress might lead to poor academic performance, but the effect could be mediated by poor sleep.
Explanation of keywords: Replication in research refers to the process of repeating a study using the same methods but with different participants, settings, or conditions to verify whether the original findings can be reproduced. Replication strengthens the credibility of scientific knowledge by ensuring that results are not due to chance, bias, or specific conditions in a single study.
21. Match the theory/law in the first column with the corresponding explanation in the second column of the table given below.

Theory/law	Explanation
P) Weber's law	i) The detection of change in a stimulus is relative to the magnitude of the stimulus
Q) Steven's Power law	ii) Sensory magnitude grows in proportion to the physical intensity of the stimulus raised to a power
R) Signal detection theory	iii) The magnitude of a sensation is a logarithmic function of the stimulus
S) Fechner's law	iv) The ability to detect a weak stimulus varies from moment to moment as per response bias

(A) P-(ii), Q-(iv), R-(i), S-(iii)
(B) P-(iv), Q-(iii), R-(ii), S-(i)
(C) P-(i), Q-(ii), R-(iv), S-(iii)
(D) P-(iii), Q-(ii), R-(iv), S-(i)
Correct Answer: (C) P-(i), Q-(ii), R-(iv), S-(iii)
Explanation of other options
(P) Weber's Law → i) The detection of change in a stimulus is relative to the magnitude of the stimulus

- Weber's Law states that the just noticeable difference (JND) between two stimuli is proportional to the magnitude of the original stimulus.
- The larger the initial stimulus, the larger the change needed for the difference to be noticeable.
- Formula:

$$\Delta I/I = k$$

ΔI = Change in stimulus, I= Original stimulus, k = Weber's constant (specific to the type of stimulus)
Example: If you're holding a 1 kg weight, adding 0.1 kg may be noticeable. But if you're holding a 10 kg weight, adding 0.1 kg will not be easily detected.
(B) Steven's Power Law → ii) Sensory magnitude grows in proportion to the physical intensity of the stimulus raised to a power

- Steven's Power Law describes how the perceived magnitude of a stimulus relates to its actual physical intensity.
- Unlike Weber's and Fechner's laws, it introduces a more generalized view of how different senses respond to stimuli using a mathematical model.
- Formula:

$$S = kIn$$

S = Perceived magnitude, k = Constant, I= Physical intensity of the stimulus, n = Exponent depending on the type of stimulus

Example: The brightness of a light or the loudness of a sound follows this law, where perceived intensity increases non-linearly.

(C) Signal Detection Theory → iv) The ability to detect a weak stimulus varies from moment to moment as per response bias

- Signal Detection Theory (SDT) explains how and why people detect faint signals amid noise.
- It suggests that detection is influenced not just by the actual stimulus but also by the individual's sensitivity and response bias.
- Factors like motivation, fatigue, and expectations can influence detection.
- Example: A radiologist might detect a faint tumor in an X-ray based on their experience and confidence, even if it is difficult to spot.

(D) Fechner's Law → iii) The magnitude of a sensation is a logarithmic function of the stimulus

- Fechner's Law builds on Weber's Law and suggests that perceived sensation increases logarithmically with the physical intensity of the stimulus.
- This means that as stimulus intensity increases, the perceived change grows smaller.
- Formula:

S=klog I - S= Perceived sensation , k= Constant. I= Physical stimulus intensity

Example: Doubling the brightness of a light may not appear twice as bright because the perception grows slower than the actual increase in intensity.

22. Match the sleep disorders in the first column with the symptoms in the second column of the table giv en below.

	Sleep disorders	Symptoms
P)	Enuresis	i) Excessive daytime sleepiness
Q)	Hypersomnia	ii) Urinating while asleep in bed
R)	Circadian rhythm disorder	iii) A disorder in which the person stops breathing for brief periods while asleep
S)	Sleep apnea	iv) Disturbances of the sleep-wake cycle

(A) P-(ii), Q-(iv), R-(i), S-(iii)
(B) P-(ii), Q-(i), R-(iv), S-(iii)
(C) P-(ii), Q-(i), R-(iii), S-(iv)
(D) P-(iii), Q-(iv), R-(i), S-(ii)

Correct Answer:B

Explanation of other options

(P)Enuresis → ii) Urinating while asleep in bed

- Enuresis refers to involuntary urination during sleep, commonly known as bedwetting.
- It is most often observed in children, though it can occasionally persist into adulthood.
- It is not typically linked to a physical disorder, but can be related to emotional stress or developmental delays.
- Primary Enuresis: When a child has never been consistently dry at night.
- Secondary Enuresis: When bedwetting returns after a period of dryness.

(Q) Hypersomnia → i) Excessive Daytime Sleepiness

- Hypersomnia is characterized by excessive sleepiness during the day despite getting enough sleep at night.
- People with hypersomnia may struggle to stay awake, leading to frequent naps or long sleep durations.
- It can be caused by medical conditions, neurological disorders, or psychological factors.
- Example: Narcolepsy, head trauma, or depression may contribute to hypersomnia.

(R) Circadian Rhythm Disorder → iv) Disturbances of the Sleep-Wake Cycle

- Circadian rhythm disorders occur when a person's internal body clock (circadian rhythm) is misaligned with the external environment, leading to sleep disturbances.
- Causes may include shift work, jet lag, or delayed/advanced sleep phase syndrome.
- Symptoms: Difficulty falling asleep, waking up too early or too late, and experiencing poor-quality sleep.

(D) Sleep Apnea → iii) A Disorder in Which the Person Stops Breathing for Brief Periods While Asleep

- Sleep apnea is a serious sleep disorder where a person's breathing repeatedly stops and starts during sleep.
- The most common type is Obstructive Sleep Apnea (OSA), caused by blocked airways.
- Another type is Central Sleep Apnea, where the brain fails to send signals to the muscles to breathe.
- Symptoms: Loud snoring, gasping for air, and feeling exhausted during the day despite a full night's sleep.
- Complications: Increased risk of heart disease, stroke, and daytime drowsiness.

Explanation of keywords

Sleep Disorder: Sleep disorders are conditions that disrupt a person's normal sleep patterns, leading to poor sleep quality, difficulty falling asleep, staying asleep, or feeling rested during the day. These disorders can impact physical health, mental health, and overall well-being. There are many types of sleep disorders, often caused by factors like stress, medical conditions, mental health issues, or lifestyle choices.

23. Explains aging as a process of mutual withdrawal of individual and society, whereas assumes positive correlation between activity and successful aging.

(A) Decay theory, Engagement theory

(B) Balance theory, Engagement theory

(C) Disengagement theory, Activity theory

(D) Withdrawal theory, Activity theory

Correct Answer-(C)Disengagement Theory, Activity Theory

Disengagement Theory: Proposes that aging involves a gradual withdrawal from social, physical, and emotional activities. Both society and the individual mutually withdraw from each other, believing it is a natural and inevitable process. This theory was one of the first theories of aging, introduced by Elaine Cumming and William E. Henry in 1961.

Example: An elderly person may retire from work, reduce social interactions, and prefer a quieter lifestyle.

Activity Theory: Suggests that successful aging is linked to maintaining high levels of activity and social engagement. Older adults who stay physically, mentally, and socially active tend to experience greater life satisfaction. This theory promotes active participation in hobbies, social relationships, and community involvement.

Example: Seniors who volunteer, join clubs, or learn new skills often have improved well-being.

Explanation of other options

(A) Decay Theory, Engagement Theory

Decay Theory: This is related to memory and cognitive decline, not specifically about aging and social roles. It suggests that memory fades over time if not used.

Engagement Theory: Not a widely recognized theory in aging studies. The correct counterpart here would be Activity Theory.

(B) Balance Theory, Engagement Theory

Balance Theory: Typically used in psychology to explain how individuals seek consistency in their beliefs, values, and behaviors. It is not specifically related to aging.

Engagement Theory: Again, this is not a valid theory in the context of aging.

(D) Withdrawal Theory, Activity Theory

Withdrawal Theory: This is not an established theory. It might be confused with Disengagement Theory, but the term itself is not used in aging research.

Activity Theory: Correctly describes the belief that remaining active leads to successful aging, but since the first theory is incorrect, this answer is also incorrect.

Explanation of keywords

Aging is a natural and inevitable biological process characterized by gradual changes in the body and mind over time. It is a complex, multifaceted experience that includes biological, psychological, and social changes. While some aspects of aging lead to decline, others can foster growth, wisdom, and resilience.

24. Match the biases/effects in the first column with the descriptions in the second column of the table given below.

	Biases/effects		Descriptions
P)	Barnum Effect	i)	Tendency to take credit for one's success but downplaying responsibility for one's failure
Q)	Reference Group Effect	ii)	Tendency to take the blame for failure but downplay one's role in the success
R)	Self-Serving Bias	iii)	Tendency to rate oneself with respect to one's social and cultural group
S)	Self-Effacing Bias	iv)	Tendency to believe in a description of personality that is supposedly descriptive of oneself but could in fact, describe almost anyone

(A) P-(i), Q-(iii), R-(ii), S-(iv)

(B) P-(iv), Q-(iii), R-(i), S-(ii)

(C) P-(iv), Q-(iii), R-(ii), S-(i)

(D) P-(iv), Q-(i), R-(ii), S-(iii)

Correct Answer: (B) P-(iv), Q-(iii), R-(i), S-(ii)

Explanation of other options

(P) Barnum Effect → iv) Tendency to believe in description of personality that is supposedly descriptive of oneself, but could in fact describe almost anyone

- The Barnum Effect refers to people's tendency to accept vague and general statements as being personally meaningful.
- This effect is commonly seen in horoscopes, fortune-telling, and personality tests that provide statements applicable to a wide audience.
- Named after the famous showman P.T. Barnum who used general statements to attract audiences.
- Example: Believing a horoscope that says, "You enjoy time with friends but also value solitude."

(Q) Reference Group Effect → iii) Tendency to rate oneself with respect to one's social and cultural group

- The Reference Group Effect occurs when individuals evaluate themselves in comparison to others within their own social or cultural group.
- People may judge their behavior, abilities, or opinions based on societal norms or peer expectations.
- This effect is particularly influential in self-report surveys and questionnaires.
- Example: A student may view their academic performance as average compared to peers, even if they perform well objectively.

(R) Self-Serving Bias → i) Tendency to take credit for one's success but downplaying responsibility for one's failure

- The Self-Serving Bias is the tendency for individuals to attribute positive outcomes to their own abilities or efforts, while attributing negative outcomes to external factors.
- It serves as a way to protect self-esteem.
- Example: A student who gets a good grade may say, "I studied hard," but if they get a poor grade, they might say, "The exam was unfair."

(S) Self-Effacing Bias → ii) Tendency to take blame for failure but downplay one's role in the success

- The Self-Effacing Bias is the opposite of the self-serving bias, where individuals tend to blame themselves for failures and credit others or external factors for success.
- This is commonly observed in collectivist cultures where humility and modesty are valued.
- Example: A team member may say, "The team's success was due to everyone's effort," but if the team fails, they might say, "I should have done more."

Explanation of keywords

A bias is a tendency or inclination that affects judgment, decision-making, or perception. Biases can be conscious (explicit) or unconscious (implicit) and often lead to irrational thinking or distorted perceptions. While some biases are helpful for making quick decisions, others can result in errors in judgment.

25. Match the theories in the first column with the central themes in the second column of the table given below.

	Theories		Central themes
P)	Drive theory	i)	Our general level of activation leads to optimization
Q)	Arousal theory	ii)	Behavior is determined by desirable outcomes
R)	Expectancy theory	iii)	Setting specific and challenging goals boosts motivation
S)	Goal setting theory	iv)	biological needs push us to action

(A) P-(iv), Q-(i), R-(ii), S-(iii)
(B) P-(iv), Q-(i), R-(iii), S-(ii)
(C) P-(i), Q-(iv), R-(ii), S-(iii)
(D) P-(ii), Q-(iii), R-(i), S-(iv)
Correct Answer: (A) P-(iv), Q-(i), R-(ii), S-(iii)
Explanation of other options
(P) Drive Theory → iv) Biological needs push us to action

- Drive Theory suggests that behavior is motivated by biological needs or drives.
- When an individual experiences a physiological imbalance, like hunger, thirst, or fatigue, it creates a drive that pushes them to act and restore balance (homeostasis).
- Developed by Clark Hull, this theory focuses on internal states that lead to action.

Example: Feeling hungry (biological drive) motivates you to eat.
(Q) Arousal Theory → i) Our general level of activation leads to optimization

- Arousal Theory posits that people are motivated to maintain an optimal level of arousal — not too high and not too low.
- A certain level of arousal can enhance performance, but too much or too little arousal may reduce efficiency.
- Yerkes-Dodson Law is often used to explain this relationship, suggesting that moderate arousal leads to the best performance.

Example: An athlete may perform better with moderate excitement before a game, but excessive anxiety may hinder performance.
(R) Expectancy Theory → ii) Behaviour is determined by desirable outcomes

- Expectancy Theory (by Victor Vroom) states that behavior is influenced by the belief that efforts will lead to desired results.
- People are motivated when they believe that:

1. Effort will lead to good performance.
2. Performance will result in a desired reward.

3. The reward is valuable to them.

Example: An employee works harder when they expect a promotion or bonus for achieving high performance.
(S) Goal Setting Theory → iii) Setting specific and challenging goals boosts motivation

- Goal Setting Theory (by Edwin Locke and Gary Latham) emphasizes that setting clear, specific, and challenging goals leads to higher performance.
- Goals provide direction, encourage persistence, and increase effort.

Example: A student aiming to achieve a top grade may study consistently with well-defined study goals.

26. Which one of the following would resolve the basic dilemma of the social psychologist?

(A) Conducting carefully designed experiments with high internal validity

(B) By replicating experiments and conducting some new experiments that have internal validity and others that have external validity

(C) Conducting research exclusively in the field

(D) Conducting applied rather than basic research

Correct Answer: (B) By replicating experiments and conducting some new experiments that have internal validity and others that have external validity

This is the most balanced and effective solution.By conducting a combination of controlled lab experiments (high internal validity) and field experiments or observational studies (high external validity), psychologists can cross-validate findings. Replication also strengthens the reliability of results, addressing both internal and external validity concerns.

Explanation of other options

(A) Conducting carefully designed experiments with high internal validity

This option focuses solely on achieving high internal validity by carefully controlling variables in a lab setting.While it ensures a strong cause-and-effect relationship, it sacrifices external validity because the controlled environment may not reflect real-world scenarios. Not the best solution to the dilemma.

(C) Conducting research exclusively in the field

Field research generally has high external validity because it takes place in real-world settings.However, it is difficult to control all variables, reducing internal validity. While valuable, relying only on field research does not resolve the dilemma.

(D) Conducting applied rather than basic research

Applied research focuses on solving practical problems, often emphasising external validity. Basic research, on the other hand, aims to develop theories and principles with high internal validity. While applied research has its place, solving the dilemma requires balancing both types. This alone does not resolve the dilemma.

Explanation of keywords: Dilemma: A dilemma is when a person faces a difficult choice between two or more alternatives, often with no straightforward or easy solution. The key characteristic of a dilemma is that each option has both advantages and disadvantages, making the decision challenging.

27. Match the research methods in the first column with their purposes in the second column of the table given below.

	Research Methods		Purposes
P)	Narrative method	i)	Describing a person, event, and experience in detail
Q)	Ethnography	ii)	Collecting data in the form of cohesive stories
R)	Case Study	iii)	Extracting themes from data
S)	Content analysis	iv)	Describing cultural characteristics in detail

(A) P-(i), Q-(iii), R-(ii), S-(iv)
(B) P-(ii), Q-(iii), R-(iv), S-(i)
(C) P-(i), Q-(iv), R-(ii), S-(iii)
(D) P-(ii), Q-(iv), R-(i), S-(iii)
Correct Answer: (D) P-(ii), Q-(iv), R-(i), S-(iii)
Explanation of other options
(P) Narrative Method → ii) Collecting data in the form of cohesive stories

- Narrative Method involves collecting and analyzing data in the form of stories to understand how people make sense of their experiences.
- Participants often share personal experiences, and researchers interpret these stories to uncover themes or patterns.

Example: A psychologist interviewing trauma survivors to understand their coping narratives.
(Q) Ethnography → iv) Describing cultural characteristics in detail

- Ethnography is a qualitative research method where researchers immerse themselves in a particular community or culture to study it firsthand.
- It often involves participant observation and detailed field notes to capture cultural norms, behaviors, and values.

Example: An anthropologist living in a remote village to study traditional customs and rituals.
(R) Case Study → i) Describing a person, event, and experience in detail

- Case Study research involves an in-depth examination of a single individual, group, event, or phenomenon.
- It is often used to explore complex issues that cannot be investigated through experimental methods.

Example: Studying a rare psychological disorder through an in-depth analysis of one patient.
(S) Content Analysis → iii) Extracting themes from data

- Content Analysis is a systematic method used to analyze and interpret text, images, or media to identify themes, patterns, or meanings.
- It is commonly applied to written documents, speeches, social media posts, or interviews.

Example: Analyzing social media comments to understand public opinion on a social issue.

28. Which one of the following statements is TRUE according to Brehm's reactance theory?

(A) A mild sign prohibiting spitting would be more effective in preventing spitting than a strong sign

(B) A strong sign would be more effective in preventing spitting than a mild one

(C) Absence of any sign would be most effective in preventing spitting

(D) Signs are irrelevant to spitting behaviour

Correct Answer (A) A mild sign prohibiting spitting would be more effective in preventing spitting than a strong sign.

A mild sign (e.g., "Please do not spit") is less likely to provoke resistance because it doesn't appear aggressive or controlling. People are more likely to comply with a polite and respectful request.

Explanation of other options

(B) A strong sign would be more effective in preventing spitting than a mild one

A strong sign (e.g., "Do NOT spit. Violators will be fined!") may trigger reactance and lead to defiance. People might feel their freedom is being restricted and may deliberately spit in rebellion.

(C) Absence of any sign would be most effective in preventing spitting

Without any sign, people may act based on their own judgment. However, social norms and behaviors are not always sufficient to prevent undesired actions.

(D) Signs are irrelevant to spitting behaviour.

Signs can significantly influence behaviour by setting expectations and establishing norms. Even though strong signs may provoke resistance, moderate signs are effective in reducing undesirable behaviour.

Explanation of keywords

Brehm's Reactance Theory: Reactance Theory, proposed by Jack Brehm, suggests that when people perceive their freedom of choice is being threatened or restricted, they often oppose it to regain it. This reaction is called psychological reactance.

29. According to the overjustifcation effect, which one of the following consequences would be TRUE for students who freely choose to study psychology, if marks are given for attendance?

(A) Increased interest of students in the subject

(B) Decreased interest of students in the subject

(C) No effect on the interest of students in the subject

(D) Increased interest in other social science subjects

Correct Answer: (B) Decreased interest of students in the subject

When students initially have an interest in psychology and then receive marks for attendance, their motivation might shift from genuine interest to getting rewarded. Once the rewards stop, their interest in the subject may decline. This is a classic example of the overjustification effect.

Explanation of other options

(A) Increased interest of students in the subject

According to the overjustification effect, rewarding students (e.g., giving marks for attendance) can lead to a decrease in their intrinsic motivation. Instead of enjoying the subject itself, they may attend class only for the marks.

(C) No effect on the interest of students in the subject

The overjustification effect suggests that rewards do impact motivation, especially when the behavior was previously intrinsically motivated.

D. Increased interest in other social science subjects

While the effect may reduce interest in psychology, it does not necessarily increase interest in other subjects.The overjustification effect is specific to the activity that is being rewarded.

Explanation of keywords

Overjustification Effect: The overjustification effect is a psychological phenomenon where providing an external reward for a behaviour that an individual already enjoys can lead to a reduction in intrinsic motivation for that behaviour.

Intrinsic motivation: It means doing something because you find it enjoyable or interesting.

Extrinsic motivation: It involves doing something to earn a reward or avoid punishment.

30. Large rewards and severe punishments are examples of justification for behaviour and result inchanges in attitude.

(A) internal; big

(B) external; big

(C) internal; small

(D) external; small

Correct Answer-(B) External; Big

- External justification refers to using external factors (like rewards or punishments) as a reason for one's actions.
- Large rewards or severe punishments provide strong external justification, so individuals feel little need to change their attitudes.
- Example: A student might pretend to enjoy a boring class just to receive extra credit.

Explanation of other options

(A) Internal; Big

- Internal justification occurs when a person changes their attitude to reduce cognitive dissonance.
- However, large rewards or severe punishments do not lead to internal justification.
- Instead, people attribute their behavior to the external factor (reward or punishment) rather than changing their belief.

(C) Internal; Small

- Small rewards or mild punishments are more likely to lead to internal justification.
- When the external incentive is small, people may not feel that the external factor alone justified their behavior.
- To resolve the dissonance, they might convince themselves that they actually believe in what they're doing.

(D) External; Small

- While small rewards can still serve as external justification, they are often insufficient to fully justify the behavior.
- This can lead to attitude change as people try to internally justify why they performed the behavior.

Explanation of keywords

Justification for Behavior: Justification refers to the reasoning or explanation a person uses to justify their behaviour, particularly when it involves actions that conflict with their attitudes or beliefs.

The concept of cognitive dissonance by Leon Festinger explains that when people experience discomfort due to inconsistencies between their actions and beliefs, they try to reduce that discomfort by justifying their behavior.

31. Which of the following therapies is/are based on classical conditioning?

(A) Systematic desensitization

(B) Aversion therapy

(C) Cognitive behaviour therapy

(D) Rational emotive behaviour therapy

Correct Answer:A,B

(A) Systematic Desensitization: Gradually exposes a person to anxiety-provoking stimuli while helping them practice relaxation techniques to reduce anxiety.

(B) Aversion Therapy: Pairs an unwanted behavior with an aversive stimulus to discourage the behavior.

Explanation of other options

(C) Cognitive Behavior Therapy (CBT): Focuses on changing negative thought patterns and behaviors to improve emotional well-being.

(D) Rational Emotive Behavior Therapy (REBT): Helps individuals identify and change irrational beliefs to reduce emotional distress and improve behavior.

Explanation of keywords

Classical Conditioning is a type of learning in which an organism learns to associate two stimuli, leading to a change in behavior. It was first described by Ivan Pavlov, a Russian physiologist, through his experiments on dogs. In classical conditioning, a previously neutral stimulus becomes associated with a stimulus that naturally produces a response. After repeated pairings, the neutral stimulus alone can trigger the same response.

32.Which of the following characterize(s) Wernicke's aphasia?

(A) Inability to comprehend spoken words

(B) Inability to understand the meaning of words

(C) Inability to speak grammatically correct language

(D) Inability to write and understand the symbols that represent speech sounds

Correct Answer- A,B,D

(A) Inability to comprehend spoken words

- A primary characteristic of Wernicke's aphasia is the inability to understand spoken language.
- Although individuals can produce fluent speech, they may struggle to follow conversations or respond appropriately.

(B) Inability to understand the meaning of words

- People with Wernicke's aphasia often suffer from semantic deficits.
- They may hear words clearly but fail to comprehend their meaning.
- This results in speech that may sound fluent but often lacks coherence or meaning, sometimes referred to as "word salad."

(D) Inability to write and understand the symbols that represent speech sounds

- Wernicke's aphasia can also impact reading and writing.
- Individuals may struggle to comprehend written words and may write incoherently, reflecting their spoken language difficulties.
- This condition is sometimes referred to as agraphia or alexia, depending on the specific impairment.

Explanation of other options

(C) Inability to speak grammatically correct language

- Unlike Broca's aphasia, which affects grammatical speech, individuals with Wernicke's aphasia typically produce grammatically correct sentences.
- However, their speech may be nonsensical and contain made-up or incorrect words (neologisms).

Explanation of keywords

Wernicke's aphasia is a language disorder caused by damage to Wernicke's area, located in the left temporal lobe of the brain. This region is primarily responsible for language comprehension. People with Wernicke's aphasia often have difficulty understanding language and producing meaningful speech, even though their speech may be grammatically correct. Unlike Broca's aphasia, where speech production is impaired, Wernicke's aphasia affects language comprehension and meaning.

33.Which of the following is/are the component(s) of Theory of Mind?

(A) Understanding that people can have false beliefs

(B) Distinguishing faces and smells

(C) Recognizing that others have mental states

(D) Having a vast vocabulary to express one's thoughts

Correct Answer-A,C

(A) Understanding that people can have false beliefs

- One of the most significant milestones in ToM development is recognizing that others can hold false beliefs.
- False belief tasks (e.g., the Sally-Anne test) are often used to measure this understanding.
- Example: A child understands that Sally will look for her toy where she last left it, even though the child knows it has been moved.

(C) Recognizing that others have mental states

- A fundamental aspect of ToM is recognizing that others have thoughts, feelings, beliefs, and desires that may differ from one's own.
- This understanding helps in empathizing and responding appropriately in social situations.

Explanation of other options

(B) Distinguishing faces and smells

While recognizing faces and smells involves sensory perception and memory, it is not a component of Theory of Mind. ToM is about understanding mental states rather than processing sensory information.

(D) Having a vast vocabulary to express one's thoughts

- While language development can support Theory of Mind by enabling individuals to express thoughts and understand others, it is not a direct component of ToM.
- People with limited vocabulary or speech impairments can still develop ToM through non-verbal communication.

Explanation of keywords

Theory of Mind (ToM) refers to the ability to understand that others have thoughts, beliefs, desires, and perspectives that may differ from one's own. It is a crucial cognitive skill that typically develops in early childhood, around the age of 4 to 5 years.

34. Which of the following would NOT be effective in minimizing groupthink?

(A) The leader being impartial to all ideas no matter what they are

(B) The leader reminding the team that everyone will be held responsible for the decision of the group

(C) The leader taking all decisions on behalf of the group

(D) The leader arriving at a consensus quickly

Correct Answer- C,D

(C) The leader taking all decisions on behalf of the group

- When a leader makes decisions without input from the group, it discourages discussion and critical thinking.

- This authoritarian approach eliminates the opportunity for different viewpoints and promotes a passive acceptance of decisions.
- This is a characteristic of groupthink.

(D) The leader arriving at a consensus quickly

- Rushing to a consensus without thorough discussion prevents the exploration of alternative perspectives.
- Effective decision-making requires deliberate evaluation of ideas, and quick consensus can result in overconfidence and poor judgment.
- This behavior often promotes groupthink.

Explanation of other options
(A)The leader being impartial to all ideas no matter what they are

- Effective in minimizing groupthink.
- When a leader remains neutral and open-minded, it encourages group members to express their honest opinions without fear of judgment.
- Leaders should avoid signaling their preferences too early to prevent influencing the group.

(B) The leader reminding the team that everyone will be held responsible for the decision of the group

- Effective in minimizing groupthink.
- When members know they are accountable for the outcome, they are more likely to critically evaluate ideas rather than agreeing for the sake of consensus.
- This sense of responsibility encourages independent thinking and careful consideration of alternatives.

Explanation of keywords
Groupthink is a psychological phenomenon that occurs when a group of people prioritise harmony and consensus over critical thinking and realistic decision-making. In a groupthink scenario, individuals suppress dissenting opinions, fail to consider alternative perspectives and ignore potential risks to maintain unity within the group. Social psychologist Irving Janis introduced the term in 1972, who studied the decision-making processes behind historical political failures like the Bay of Pigs invasion

35. Which of the following describe(s) the standard error of the mean?
(A) It is the standard deviation of the sampling distribution of the mean
(B) It reflects the accuracy with which sample means estimate the population mean
(C) It is the difference between mean and standard deviation of a distribution
(D) It is the standard deviation of a stratified sample
Correct Answer-A,B
(A) It is the standard deviation of the sampling distribution of the mean.

- The Standard Error of the Mean (SEM) is indeed the standard deviation of the sampling distribution of the sample mean.
- When multiple samples are drawn from a population, their means will form a distribution called the sampling distribution of the mean, and the SEM measures its spread.

(B) It reflects the accuracy with which sample means estimate the population mean.

- SEM serves as an indicator of the accuracy of the sample mean as an estimate of the population mean.

- A smaller SEM suggests a more accurate estimate, while a larger SEM indicates greater uncertainty.

Explanation of other options
(C) It is the difference between mean and standard deviation of a distribution

- The SEM is not calculated as the difference between the mean and the standard deviation.
- It is derived from the standard deviation and the sample size.

(D) It is the standard deviation of a stratified sample.

- A stratified sample involves dividing a population into subgroups (strata) and sampling from each group.
- The SEM refers to the standard deviation of the sampling distribution of the mean, not the standard deviation within a stratified sample.

Explanation of keywords
The Standard Error of the Mean (SEM) is a measure that indicates how much the sample mean is likely to deviate from the true population mean . It is often used to assess the accuracy and reliability of the sample mean as an estimate of the population mean.

36. Which of the following describe(s) organizational commitment?
(A) A strong desire to remain a member of the organization
(B) Willingness to exert high level of effort on behalf of the organization
(C) A definite belief in and acceptance of values and goals of the organization
(D) High turnover intention of the employees of the organization
Correct Answer-A,B,C
(A) A strong desire to remain a member of the organization.

- This describes Affective Commitment, where employees genuinely want to stay with the organization because they feel emotionally connected.
- Employees with strong affective commitment often enjoy their work, align with company values, and build long-term careers within the organization.

(B) Willingness to exert high level of effort on behalf of the organization.

- Committed employees often go beyond their job descriptions to contribute to the success of the organization.
- This behavior is a reflection of both Affective Commitment (due to their emotional attachment) and Normative Commitment (because they feel a sense of responsibility).

(C) A definite belief in and acceptance of values and goals of the organization.

- When employees believe in and accept the organization's goals and values, it indicates Affective Commitment.
- Such employees are aligned with the mission and vision of the company, leading to enhanced loyalty and productivity.

Explanation of other options
(D) High turnover intention of the employees of the organization.

- High turnover intention refers to the likelihood that employees will leave the organization, which is the opposite of organizational commitment.

- Low commitment often leads to higher turnover rates, job dissatisfaction, and disengagement.

Explanation of keywords

Organizational Commitment refers to the emotional attachment, loyalty, and dedication an employee has toward their organization. It reflects the degree to which employees identify with the organization's values, goals, and mission, and their willingness to remain part of the organization.

37. Prejudice is supported by the human tendency to categorize into in-groups and out-groups. Prejudice is supported by which of the following processes?

(A) The way we think about others

(B) The way we assign meaning to others behaviour

(C) By following intellectual pursuits

(D) By working towards a common goal

Correct Answer-A,B

(A)The way we think about others

- This involves cognitive biases and stereotypes.
- People often rely on social categorization to simplify complex social information.
- Unfortunately, these mental shortcuts can lead to negative judgments and reinforce prejudice.
- Example: Assuming that all members of a particular group behave in a certain way without knowing them individually.

(B)The way we assign meaning to others' behavior

- This is explained by the concept of attribution bias.
- People often attribute the behavior of out-group members to internal (negative) traits rather than external circumstances.
- Example: If an out-group member makes a mistake, it may be attributed to their "personality," whereas the same mistake by an in-group member may be excused as situational.

Explanation of other options

(C) By following intellectual pursuits.

- Intellectual pursuits like education, critical thinking, and exposure to diverse perspectives typically reduce prejudice rather than support it.
- However, simply having knowledge without challenging biases may not eliminate prejudice.

(D) By working towards a common goal

- Cooperative tasks and common goals can actually reduce prejudice, not support it.
- This concept is supported by Sherif's Robbers Cave Experiment, which showed that working together to achieve shared goals reduced hostility between opposing groups.
- The theory behind this is called the Contact Hypothesis or Superordinate Goals.

Explanation of keywords

Prejudice: It is a negative attitude or belief about an individual or group based solely on their membership in a particular social category. It often involves unjustified assumptions and is typically directed toward people based on characteristics like race, ethnicity, religion, gender, sexual orientation, or nationality. Example: Believing that people from a certain country are lazy without any factual basis.

In-Group: An in-group is a social group with which an individual identifies and feels a sense of belonging. Members of an in-group often share common characteristics, beliefs, or experiences. Example: A person who identifies as a football fan may consider other fans of the same team as their in-group.

Out-Group: An out-group is a group that an individual does not identify with and often perceives as different or even inferior. Example: A person who supports one political party may see supporters of the opposing party as an out-group.

38. Which of the following is/are feature(s) of clinical phobia?

(A) The fear must be persistent

(B) The fear must be a source of significant distress

(C) The fear is rational

(D) The fear is usually perceived as unwarranted

Correct Answer: A,B,D

(A) The fear must be persistent

- One of the key features of a clinical phobia is that the fear lasts for at least 6 months or longer.
- It is not a temporary or situational fear but rather a long-lasting and consistent response.
- Example: Someone with arachnophobia (fear of spiders) experiences fear every time they encounter a spider, even in harmless situations.

(B) The fear must be a source of significant distress.

- For a fear to be classified as a clinical phobia, it must cause considerable emotional or psychological distress.
- It may lead to avoidance behaviors that interfere with work, social activities, or daily routines.
- Example: A person with social phobia may avoid social gatherings, leading to isolation and loneliness.

(D) The fear is usually perceived as unwarranted.

- People with phobias often recognize that their fear is irrational or excessive but feel unable to control their reaction.
- This awareness is a defining feature of many anxiety disorders, including phobias.
- Example: A person with claustrophobia (fear of enclosed spaces) might acknowledge that an elevator is safe but still experience overwhelming fear.

Explanation of other options

(C) The fear is rational

- Phobias are characterized by an irrational fear. While some fears may have a logical basis, a clinical phobia involves an exaggerated fear response that does not align with actual danger.
- Example: A person with a fear of flying (aviophobia) may refuse to board a plane despite air travel being statistically safer than other forms of transportation.

Explanation of keywords

Clinical Phobia : A clinical phobia is a type of anxiety disorder characterized by an intense, irrational fear of a specific object, situation, or activity. This fear is disproportionate to the actual danger posed and can significantly interfere with daily life.

39. The value of F calculated from the data given in the table below is (rounded off to one decimal place).

	Sum of Square (SS)	Degree of freedom (df)	Mean Square (MS)
Between	54	3	18
Within	100	20	5

Explanation

1. Sum of Squares (SS)

The Sum of Squares measures the total variability in the data.

It is divided into:

- SS Between (54) → Measures the variability between groups (due to the independent variable).
- SS Within (100) → Measures the variability within groups (due to random error or individual differences).
- Total Sum of Squares (SS Total) = SS Between + SS Within = 54 + 100 = 154.

2. Degrees of Freedom (df)

Degrees of Freedom represent the number of values in a calculation that are free to vary.

- df Between (3) → Calculated as k - 1, where k is the number of groups.
- df Within (20) → Calculated as N - k, where N is the total number of observations and k is the number of groups.
  Total Degrees of Freedom = df Between + df Within = 3 + 20 = 23.

3. Mean Square (MS)

The Mean Square is the average variability (variance) and is calculated using the sum of squares divided by its corresponding degrees of freedom.

- Formula:
  MS=SS/df
- MS Between = 54/3=18

  - MS Within = 10020=5\frac{100}{20} = 520100=5

CHAPTER IV

PREVIOUS YEAR QUESTION 2022 ANALYSIS

1. The construct validity of a test is assessed through _______________.

(A) Convergent and Discriminant validity
(B) Concurrent and Predictive validity
(C) Convergent and Predictive validity
(D) Discriminant and Predictive validity

Correct Answer- (A) Convergent and Discriminant Validity

Convergent Validity: Demonstrates that the test correlates well with other tests that measure the same construct. Example: A new depression scale should correlate highly with an existing, validated depression scale.

Discriminant Validity: Ensures that the test does not correlate strongly with tests measuring unrelated constructs. Example: A depression scale should not correlate highly with an anxiety scale if it is designed to measure only depression.

Explanation of other options:

(B) Concurrent and Predictive Validity:

Concurrent Validity: Assesses how well a test correlates with an existing measure at the same time. Example: A new test for job performance is compared to current supervisor ratings.

Predictive Validity: Evaluates how well a test predicts future outcomes. Example: An entrance exam predicts future academic success.

(C) Convergent and Predictive Validity:

While convergent validity is a part of construct validity, predictive validity is not.Predictive validity is used to measure whether a test predicts future behavior or performance rather than examining the construct itself.

(D) Discriminant and Predictive Validity

Discriminant validity is indeed a component of construct validity, but predictive validity is not.

Using predictive validity would not provide enough evidence to prove that a test measures the intended construct.

Explanation of keywords: Construct validity refers to the extent to which a test or measurement accurately measures the theoretical concept or construct it is intended to measure. Constructs are abstract concepts such as intelligence, anxiety, self-esteem, or resilience that cannot be directly observed but are inferred from behavior or responses.

2. Memory involves three stages. Find out the correct sequence from the following:

(A) Storage, Encoding, Retrieval
(B) Retrieval, Encoding, Storage
(C) Encoding, Storage, Retrieval
(D) Decoding, Encoding, Storage

Correct Answer (C) Encoding, Storage, Retrieval

Encoding: The process of converting information into a form that can be stored in memory. It can be visual (images), acoustic (sounds), or semantic (meaning-based).

Storage: The process of retaining encoded information over time. This includes short-term memory (STM) and long-term memory (LTM).

Retrieval: The process of accessing and bringing stored information into conscious awareness when needed. This is the correct sequence because it follows the natural memory process.

Explanation of other options:

(A) Storage, Encoding, Retrieval

This sequence is incorrect because information cannot be stored before it has been encoded. Encoding must happen first for the brain to process and store information.

(B) Retrieval, Encoding, Storage

Retrieval comes after encoding and storage. You cannot retrieve information that has not been stored yet.

(D) Decoding, Encoding, Storage

Decoding refers to understanding or interpreting information, often in communication or language. It is not a part of the memory process.

Encoding, not decoding, is the first step in memory formation.

3. Erickson's fifth stage of psychosocial development is

(A) Identity vs role confusion

(B) Intimacy vs isolation

(C) Generative vs stagnation

(D) Integrity vs despair

Correct Answer (A) Identity vs. Role Confusion: Adolescents develop a sense of self and personal identity.

Explanation of other options:

(B) Intimacy vs. Isolation: Young adults form deep relationships or face loneliness.

(C) Generativity vs. Stagnation: Middle-aged adults contribute to society or feel unproductive.

(D) Integrity vs. Despair: Older adults reflect on their lives, feeling either content or full of regret.

Explanation of keywords: Erik Erikson's Theory of Psychosocial Development outlines eight stages that an individual goes through across their lifespan, from infancy to old age. Each stage presents a specific psychosocial conflict or crisis that must be resolved for healthy psychological growth. Successful resolution of each conflict results in the development of essential virtues or strengths.

4. Test developers use reverse coding of certain items in a scale to offset the effects of ____________.

(A) Social desirability

(B) Acquiescence

(C) Faking

(D) Random responding

Correct Answer: (B) Acquiescence: A bias in which a respondent tends to agree with statements regardless of their content, leading to overly positive or agreeable responses.

Explanation of other options

(A) Social desirability: Tendency to provide answers that are socially acceptable or favorable, often not reflecting the truth.

(C) Faking: Deliberately providing false answers to present oneself in a better light or to manipulate the results.

(D) Random responding: Providing inconsistent, irrelevant, or random answers without engaging with the content of the survey or test.

Explanation of keywords: Reverse coding, also known as reverse scoring or negative scoring, is a technique used in survey research to ensure that respondents are paying attention to the questions and to counteract response biases like acquiescence bias (always agreeing or disagreeing).

5. According to Kohlberg's theory of Moral development, at which level individuals judge morality in terms of abstract principles?

(A) Pre-conventional

(B) Post-conventional

(C) Conventional

(D) Transcendental

Correct Answer: (B) Post-conventional: Moral reasoning based on universal ethical principles, such as justice and human rights, which may conflict with laws or norms. It's the highest stage of moral development.

Explanation of other options

(A) Pre-conventional: Moral reasoning based on self-interest, avoiding punishment, and seeking rewards. This is common in children.

(C) Conventional: Moral reasoning based on conforming to societal norms and expectations, maintaining relationships, and following rules.

(D) Transcendental: A more advanced, spiritual level of moral reasoning that transcends traditional moral frameworks, focusing on universal compassion or interconnectedness.

Explanation of keywords:

Kohlberg's Theory of Moral Development: According to Lawrence Kohlberg's Theory of Moral Development, individuals progress through three main levels of moral reasoning, each consisting of two stages. The level at which individuals judge morality in terms of abstract principles is called the Post-Conventional Level.

Level 3: Post-Conventional Level

- At this level, morality is defined by abstract principles and values that apply universally.
- Individuals make decisions based on their personal ethical beliefs rather than simply following societal rules or external authority.
- The focus is on justice, equality, human rights, and the greater good.

Stages of Post-Conventional Level:

1. Stage 5 – Social Contract and Individual Rights

   - People recognize that laws and rules exist for the greater good, but they also understand that laws are not absolute.
   - Individuals may challenge laws that are unjust and advocate for change.
   - Example: Supporting civil rights movements or challenging discriminatory laws.

2. Stage 6 – Universal Ethical Principles

   - Decisions are made based on internal moral principles of justice, dignity, and equality.
   - People may act against laws or social norms if they conflict with their personal principles.
   - Example: A person refusing to follow a law that oppresses others, even at personal risk.

6.You had been driving a car with manual-gear for 5 years. Recently, you started driving a new car with an auto-gear. If you are having any trouble, it is most likely due to _____________.

(A) Proactive interference
(B) Retroactive interference
(C) Anterograde interference
(D) Learning Difficulties

Correct Answer: (A) Proactive interference

Definition: Proactive interference occurs when old information interferes with the ability to learn or recall new information. Essentially, previously learned material disrupts the recall of newer material. When you try to learn something new, the old memories or knowledge that you have can make it harder to store or retrieve the new information.

Example: If you change your phone number, you may have difficulty remembering your new number because the old number keeps interfering with the new one. The old phone number is "proactively" interfering with your ability to recall the new one.

Explanation of other options

(B) Retroactive interference : Retroactive interference occurs when new information interferes with the ability to recall older information. This is the opposite of proactive interference. When you learn new information, it can make it harder to remember or retrieve older information that you previously knew.

Example: If you learn a new password for an account, you may forget the old password because the new one interferes with your ability to recall the older one. The new information is "retroactively" interfering with the old.

(C) Anterograde interference : Anterograde interference refers to difficulties in forming new memories after a particular event, such as a brain injury or trauma. This is often associated with anterograde amnesia, where a person cannot form new long-term memories following a certain point in time. After an event (like a traumatic brain injury), a person may have trouble remembering new experiences, facts, or events that occur after the incident, while still being able to recall older memories from before the event.

Example: After a car accident, a person may not be able to remember anything that happened after the accident but can still recall their life before it.

(D) Learning Difficulties : Learning difficulties are a broad category of conditions that affect a person's ability to acquire, process, or use information efficiently. These difficulties may include issues with reading, writing, math, or more generalized problems with attention, memory, or comprehension. Learning difficulties can vary greatly, from specific challenges like dyslexia (difficulty with reading) or dyscalculia (difficulty with math), to broader cognitive challenges like those seen in ADHD (attention deficit hyperactivity disorder), which affects focus and memory.

Example: A person with dyslexia might have difficulty reading words or understanding text, while someone with ADHD might struggle to maintain focus during lessons or tasks.

7.Which of the following is not a behaviour therapy technique?

(A) Flooding

(B) Countertransference

(C) Counterconditioning

(D) Systematic desensitization

Correct Answer:

(B) Countertransference

Definition: Countertransference refers to the emotional reactions or projections a therapist has toward a client, based on the therapist's own personal experiences, unresolved conflicts, or feelings.

How it works: This occurs when a therapist responds to a client based on their own emotions or experiences, which can affect the objectivity of the therapeutic process. Countertransference can influence how a therapist interacts with or understands the client's situation.

Example: A therapist may feel overly protective of a client because the client reminds them of a family member. This might lead the therapist to treat the client in a way that could interfere with therapy.

Explanation of other options

(A) Flooding

Definition: Flooding is a type of exposure therapy used to treat phobias and anxiety disorders. It involves exposing the patient to their feared object or situation in a very intense and prolonged manner until their fear response diminishes.

How it works: The individual is exposed to the feared stimulus at full intensity for an extended period, without any avoidance behavior. The idea is that the anxiety or fear response will naturally decrease over time as the person learns that the feared situation is not as dangerous as they believed.

Example: If someone is afraid of dogs, they might be placed in a room with a dog and stay there until their anxiety reduces.

(B) Countertransference

Definition: Countertransference refers to the emotional reactions or projections a therapist has toward a client, based on the therapist's own personal experiences, unresolved conflicts, or feelings.

How it works: This occurs when a therapist responds to a client based on their own emotions or experiences, which can affect the objectivity of the therapeutic process. Countertransference can influence how a therapist interacts with or understands the client's situation.

Example: A therapist may feel overly protective of a client because the client reminds them of a family member. This might lead the therapist to treat the client in a way that could interfere with therapy.

(C) Counterconditioning

Definition: Counterconditioning is a behavioral therapy technique used to replace an undesirable behavior or emotional response with a more desirable one. It works by pairing the undesirable behavior with a new stimulus that triggers a more positive response.

How it works: It is often used to help individuals change phobic or negative responses. It involves conditioning a new, more adaptive response to a stimulus that previously triggered a negative or unwanted behavior.

Example: A person who fears dogs might be conditioned to associate the presence of dogs with something pleasant, such as receiving a treat or playing a game, rather than feeling fear.

(D) Systematic desensitization

Definition: Systematic desensitization is a type of exposure therapy and a form of counterconditioning. It involves gradually exposing a person to the feared object or situation in a controlled manner, while teaching relaxation techniques to reduce anxiety.

How it works: The person is gradually exposed to their fear (starting with less threatening versions of it) while simultaneously practicing relaxation techniques (like deep breathing). This reduces anxiety over time and helps the individual to gradually become desensitized to the feared stimulus.

Example: If someone is afraid of flying, they might first be shown pictures of airplanes, then progress to imagining a flight, and eventually take short flights while using relaxation techniques to manage anxiety.

Explanation of keywords

Behavior Therapy is a type of psychotherapy that focuses on identifying and changing unhealthy or maladaptive behaviors. It is based on the principles of behaviorism, which emphasizes that all behaviors are learned and can be modified through conditioning.

8.According to Robert Sternberg, "Street Smarts" refers to –

(A) Analytical intelligence

(B) Creative intelligence

(C) Emotional intelligence

(D) Practical intelligence

Correct Answer: (D) Practical intelligence

Definition: Practical intelligence refers to the ability to handle everyday tasks and challenges, often termed "street smarts." It involves applying knowledge and skills in real-world situations.

Key Features:

- The ability to solve problems and make decisions in everyday life, often in situations where conventional logic or theory might not apply.
- It is the ability to adapt to one's environment, learn from experience, and use practical knowledge to deal with day-to-day problems.
- Practical intelligence may not always require deep intellectual knowledge but rather the application of common sense and learned skills.

Example: Someone with high practical intelligence might be good at managing personal finances, negotiating in business, handling conflict in personal relationships, or navigating difficult social situations.

Explanation of other options

(A) Analytical intelligence

Definition: Analytical intelligence refers to the ability to analyze, evaluate, judge, compare, and contrast. It is often associated with academic problem-solving and logical reasoning.

Key Features:

- Involves tasks that require abstract thinking, solving complex problems, and understanding relationships.
- Typically measured through standard intelligence tests that assess reasoning, mathematical abilities, and pattern recognition.
- It is the ability to break down a problem into smaller, manageable parts and solve it through logical thought processes.

Example: A person with strong analytical intelligence might excel in subjects like mathematics, science, or any area requiring logical reasoning, such as solving puzzles or analyzing data.

(B) Creative intelligence

Definition: Creative intelligence refers to the ability to think in novel ways and generate original ideas. It involves imagination, innovation, and the ability to think outside of conventional patterns.

Key Features:

- The ability to come up with new solutions to problems, often in situations where no clear solution exists.
- Creativity is essential in artistic endeavors, inventing new products, and coming up with innovative ideas for businesses or social solutions.
- Creative intelligence involves divergent thinking, which is the capacity to think broadly and generate multiple possibilities or ideas.

Example: A person with high creative intelligence might be skilled in artistic activities, such as painting, writing, or composing music, or might innovate in fields like technology or business.

(C) Emotional intelligence (EQ)

Definition: Emotional intelligence is the ability to recognize, understand, manage, and influence emotions in oneself and others. It involves perceiving emotions accurately, using emotions to facilitate thinking, understanding emotional meanings, and regulating emotions.

Key Features:

- Self-awareness: Recognizing one's emotions and their impact.
- Self-regulation: Managing one's emotions healthily and constructively.
- Motivation: Being driven to achieve goals despite obstacles and maintaining a positive attitude.
- Empathy: Understanding the emotions of others.
- Social skills: Managing relationships and building networks effectively.

Example: A person with high emotional intelligence might be particularly skilled in leadership roles, managing teams, or navigating social situations effectively. They can empathize with others, motivate themselves and others, and respond to emotional cues in a thoughtful way.

Explanation of keywords: "Street Smarts"According to Robert Sternberg, "Street Smarts" refers to Practical Intelligence, which is one of the three components of his Triarchic Theory of Intelligence.

9.Research design in which several age groups of participants are studied at one particular point of time is called:

(A) Cross-sequential design

(B) Functional design

(C) Cross-sectional design

(D) Longitudinal design

Correct Answer: (C) Cross-sectional design

A cross-sectional design is a type of research design where different age groups (or other variables) are studied at one particular point in time. The primary goal is to compare the groups to identify differences or relationships across age groups at that specific moment.

How it works: Researchers collect data from various age groups at the same time, without tracking changes over time. This design is useful for observing developmental differences or trends without having to follow participants for long periods.

Example: A study comparing 5-year-olds, 10-year-olds, and 15-year-olds in terms of cognitive development, assessing each group at the same time.

Explanation of other options

(A) Cross-sequential design

Definition: A cross-sequential design is a research design that combines elements of both cross-sectional and longitudinal designs. In this design, researchers study different age groups (like in cross-sectional design) but follow them over time (like in longitudinal design).

How it works: It allows researchers to examine both differences between age groups and changes within the same group over time. It helps control for some of the disadvantages of using only cross-sectional or longitudinal designs alone.

Example: A study might assess groups of 5-year-olds, 10-year-olds, and 15-year-olds at the start of the study, and then track their progress over several years.

(B) Functional design

Definition: The term functional design is not commonly used in research methodology in the way the other terms are. It typically refers to designing something based on its intended functions or purposes, but it does not refer to a specific research design in the context of studying age groups. Therefore, it's not the correct answer here.

(D) Longitudinal design

Definition: A longitudinal design involves studying the same group of participants over an extended period of time to observe changes or developments in the participants over time.

How it works: Participants are followed over weeks, months, or even years, with data being collected at multiple points in time. This design is particularly useful for studying developmental changes or long-term effects of certain factors.

Example: A study tracking the cognitive development of the same group of children from 5 years old to 15 years old.

Explanation of keywords:

A research design is a framework or blueprint used to conduct a research study. It outlines how data will be collected, measured, and analyzed to address a specific research question or hypothesis. The research design ensures the study is systematic, logical, and objective.

10. Proximo-distal direction of development explains the nature of the development from ______.

(A) Top to bottom

(B) Internal organs to external organs

(C) Centre to periphery

(D) Sensory organ to motor organs

Correct Answer: (C) Centre to periphery

Explanation of keywords

Proximo-distal direction of development refers to the pattern of development in which physical or motor skills progress from the center (proximal) of the body toward the outer (distal) parts. This term is commonly used in developmental psychology to describe the sequence in which motor skills emerge during infancy and early childhood.

11. A cricket player who could not play an easy ball and gets out without scoring any run and blames the pitch, is an expression of ____________________.

(A) Sublimation

(B) Regression

(C) Projection

(D) Rationalization

Correct Answer: (D) Rationalisation: Justifying actions or thoughts with logical but false reasons to avoid true feelings.

Explanation of other options

(A) Sublimation: Channeling unacceptable urges into socially acceptable behaviors.

(B) Regression: Reverting to childlike behaviors in response to stress.

(C) Projection: Attributing one's own undesirable traits or feelings onto others.

12. The process through which we seek to identify the causes of other's behaviour and gain knowledge of their stable traits and dispositions is known as ______________.

(A) Distribution

(B) Dissemination

(C) Retribution

(D) Attribution

Correct Answer: (D) Attribution

Attribution refers to the process by which people explain the causes of their own and others' behavior. In social psychology, this process involves inferring whether behaviors are due to internal factors (such as personality traits, attitudes, or dispositions) or external factors (such as the environment, situational pressures, or other external circumstances).

Explanation of other options

(A) Distribution

Distribution refers to the process of giving out or spreading something, such as goods, resources, or information. In the context of social psychology, it is not related to understanding others' behavior or their internal traits.

(B) Dissemination

Dissemination refers to the process of spreading or circulating information, ideas, or knowledge widely. This could involve the distribution of research findings, news, or educational content.

(C) Retribution

Retribution refers to punishment or revenge, typically in response to an offense or wrongdoing. It focuses on a reactive, justice-oriented process rather than understanding or explaining behavior.

13. Which of the following techniques is used to measure the variations in the activity of Ascending Reticular Activating System (ARAS)?

(A) ECG

(B) PET

(C) Fmri

(D) EEG

Correct Answer: (D) EEG (Electroencephalography)

EEG is a technique that measures the electrical activity of the brain by placing electrodes on the scalp. It records brain waves (e.g., alpha, beta, delta, theta) that correspond to different mental states like alertness, relaxation, deep sleep, and drowsiness.

Explanation of other options

(A) ECG (Electrocardiography)

ECG is used to measure the electrical activity of the heart, not the brain. It records the heart's electrical impulses and is primarily used to detect heart rate, rhythm problems, and other cardiac conditions.

(B) PET (Positron Emission Tomography)

PET is an imaging technique that measures the metabolic activity in different areas of the brain by detecting the emission of positrons. It is typically used to measure brain activity during specific tasks or conditions by tracking blood flow, glucose metabolism, and other indicators.

(C) fMRI (Functional Magnetic Resonance Imaging)

fMRI measures brain activity by detecting changes in blood flow. It identifies which parts of the brain are involved in particular tasks or stimuli by observing blood oxygenation levels (BOLD response).

Explanation of keywords

ARAS stands for the Ascending Reticular Activating System. ARAS is a network of neurons located in the brainstem, specifically within the reticular formation. It plays a crucial role in regulating arousal, consciousness, and wakefulness.

14. The statement "I can do no wrong, but, you can do no right", refers to _______________.

(A) The self-serving bias

(B) The self-other bias

(C) The other-self bias

(D) The other- serving bias

Correct Answer: (A) The Self-Serving Bias

Definition: This is the tendency to attribute positive outcomes to oneself (internal factors) and negative outcomes to external factors.

Example: A student gets a good grade and credits their intelligence, but if they fail, they blame the teacher or the exam difficulty.

Explanation of other options

(B) The Self-Other Bias

Definition: A pattern where people evaluate themselves differently from how they evaluate others.

Example: You might justify your own bad behavior by citing circumstances, but judge others harshly for similar actions.

(C) The Other-Self Bias

Definition: This is not a recognized term in psychology. It may be a misrepresentation of a bias or a theoretical concept.

(D) The Other-Serving Bias

Definition: This is also not a formally established term in psychology. It could imply a bias where others are attributed more positively than oneself, which is not represented in the statement.

15. Which of the following is a qualitative research design where learned experiences of individuals are examined in their life world?

(A) Phenomenology

(B) Ethnography

(C) Focused group discussion

(D) Grounded-theory

Correct Answer: (A) Phenomenology: Focuses on exploring and understanding individuals' lived experiences and the meanings they attach to those experiences.

Explanation of other options

(B) Ethnography: Involves studying cultures and social practices through immersive observation and participation in the community being studied.

(C) Focused-group Discussion: A qualitative method for gathering opinions and insights from a small group of participants discussing a specific topic under the guidance of a moderator.

(D) Grounded Theory: A method for developing theories directly from qualitative data, aiming to explain a phenomenon by building a theory that is grounded in the data.

Explanation of keywords: Qualitative Research refers to a method of inquiry used in social sciences and psychology to understand how people interpret and give meaning to their experiences. It involves collecting non-numerical data through methods like interviews, observations, and text analysis to explore complex concepts, behaviours, and social phenomena.

16. Which part of the brain is responsible for transferring information from STM to LTM?

(A) Amygdala

(B) Hypothalamus

(C) Hippocampus

(D) Cerebellum

Correct Answer: (C) Hippocampus: Memory formation (long-term), spatial navigation, learning.

Explanation of other options

(A) Amygdala: Emotions (fear, anger), emotional memory, threat detection.

(B) Hypothalamus: Homeostasis, hormone regulation, hunger, thirst, sleep.

(D) Cerebellum: Motor coordination, balance, motor learning, and possibly cognitive functions.

Explanation of keywords

Short-Term Memory (STM)

Definition: A temporary storage system that holds a small amount of information for a short period (typically 20-30 seconds). Limited, usually around 7±2 items (as suggested by Miller's Law). Maintains information for immediate use, such as remembering a phone number before dialing it. Primarily acoustic (sound-based) and visual.

Example: Remembering a grocery list for a few minutes without writing it down.

Long-Term Memory (LTM) : A more permanent storage system with an almost unlimited capacity that retains information over extended periods.Virtually unlimited. Can last from a few hours to an entire lifetime. Stores information like personal experiences, knowledge, skills, and facts. Primarily semantic (meaning-based), but can also be visual or auditory.

Example: Remembering your first day of school or facts learned in a history class.

17. The mean of a distribution is 14 and standard deviation is 5. What would be the value of coefficient of variation? (round off to two decimal places)

Correct Answer: 35,71

Explanation of keywords

The Coefficient of Variation (CV) is calculated using the formula:

$CV=(\sigma/\mu)\times100$

Where:

- CV = Coefficient of Variation
- σ= Standard Deviation
- μ= Mean

18. Swami gets a test score of 190, the mean is 150 and SD is 25. Assuming normal distribution, the Z score would be _______________. (round off to one decimal place)

Correct Answer: 1.6

Explanation of other options

To calculate the Z-score using the given information, we apply the formula

Where:

Z= Z-score, X= Test score, μ = Mean, σ= Standard Deviation (SD)

Given: X=190, μ=150, σ=25

Z=190−150/25 =1.6

Explanation of keywords

A Z score is a standard score that indicates how far a data point is from the mean in terms of standard deviations. It provides valuable information for understanding where a particular data point stands within a distribution and allows for comparisons between different datasets. Z scores are widely used in statistical analysis, probability theory, and in fields like psychology, finance, and research.

19. Which of the following statement(s) is/are correct regarding Multiple Analysis of Variance (MANOVA)?

(A) Tests the mean difference of more than two groups on one dependent variable.

(B) Tests the mean difference of more than two groups across several dependent variables.

(C) The independent variable is measured on a nominal scale and dependent variable on an interval or ratio scale.

(D) The dependent variable is measured on nominal scale and independent variable on an interval or ratio scale.

Correct Answer- B,C

(B) Tests the mean difference of more than two groups across several dependent variables.

This is the primary purpose of MANOVA. It examines whether groups differ across multiple dependent variables simultaneously.

Example: Comparing the effect of a training program on employees' productivity, job satisfaction, and motivation.

(C) The independent variable is measured on a nominal scale and dependent variable on an interval or ratio scale.

In MANOVA, the independent variable is typically categorical (measured on a nominal scale), and the dependent variables are continuous (measured on an interval or ratio scale).

Example: Comparing satisfaction, performance, and stress levels across different job roles (nominal independent variable).

Explanation of other options

(A) Tests the mean difference of more than two groups on one dependent variable.

This describes ANOVA (Analysis of Variance), not MANOVA. ANOVA is used when there is one dependent variable and the goal is to compare the means of two or more groups.

Example: Comparing the average exam scores of students from three different schools.

(D) The dependent variable is measured on a nominal scale and independent variable on an interval or ratio scale.

In MANOVA, the dependent variables must be continuous (interval or ratio scale). If the dependent variable is categorical, a different statistical test like Logistic Regression or Chi-square Test would be appropriate.

Explanation of keywords

MANOVA is a powerful statistical technique used to analyze the effects of independent variables on multiple dependent variables simultaneously. It is especially useful in experimental designs where the goal is to understand how different factors influence a set of outcomes, and it can help control for the risk of Type I errors when multiple dependent variables are involved. However, it is important to ensure that the data meet the assumptions of MANOVA to avoid inaccurate results.

20. Which of the following statements is/are related to observational learning?

(A) Remembering the steps to perform a task

(B) A person in a dinner wants to know how to use the utensils by watching others

(C) A person uses chocolate to motivate his son to perform the task

(D) A person is capable of reproducing the action after viewing it

Correct Answer- A,B,D

(A) Remembering the steps to perform a task

This is related to the Retention phase of observational learning. After observing a model perform a task, an individual needs to remember the steps to replicate it later.

Example: Watching a cooking video and remembering how to follow the recipe.

(B) A person in a dinner wants to know how to use the utensils by watching others

This relates to the Attention and Reproduction phases. The person observes others' behavior and learns how to use utensils in a social setting.

Example: A person dining in a formal restaurant for the first time may watch others to figure out which fork or spoon to use.

(D) A person is capable of reproducing the action after viewing it

This is related to the Reproduction phase of observational learning. The person must have the physical and cognitive ability to replicate the observed behavior.

Example: A child learns how to ride a bicycle by observing a sibling and then practicing it themselves.

Explanation of other options

(C) A person uses chocolate to motivate his son to perform the task

This is an example of Operant Conditioning (B.F. Skinner), where behavior is modified using reinforcement (chocolate as a reward). While motivation is part of observational learning, this scenario lacks the aspect of observing and imitating others.

Explanation of keywords

Observational Learning (also known as Social Learning or Modeling) is a type of learning that occurs by watching others and imitating their behaviors, attitudes, or emotional responses. It is a fundamental way humans and animals learn, especially in social contexts, where individuals observe others and learn from their actions without direct experience or reinforcement.

21. Find out the statements which are related to different types of reliability?

(A) The same test is administered to the same people at two points in time

(B) Give the test once and have it scored by two scorers or by two methods

(C) Give the test in one administration and then split the test into two halves for scoring

(D) The extent to which people score on a measure are correlated with other variables

Correct Answer: A,B,C

(A) The same test is administered to the same people at two points in time

Type of Reliability: Test-Retest Reliability

Explanation: This method evaluates the stability of a test over time. If the scores from both administrations are highly correlated, the test is considered reliable. It is suitable for traits that are stable over time.

(B) Give the test once and have it scored by two scorers or by two methods

Type of Reliability: Inter-Rater Reliability or Scorer Reliability

Explanation: This assesses the consistency of scores assigned by different raters or scoring methods. It is especially relevant in subjective assessments like essays, interviews, or projective tests.

(C) Give the test in one administration and then split the test into two halves for scoring

Type of Reliability: Split-Half Reliability

Explanation: This method measures internal consistency by dividing the test into two halves (e.g., odd vs. even items) and comparing the scores. If the two halves correlate well, the test has good reliability. Spearman-Brown correction is often applied to adjust for the split.

Explanation of other options

(D) The extent to which people score on a measure are correlated with other variables

Type of Reliability: This is not related to reliability; it is more about Validity.

Explanation: Correlating test scores with other variables typically assesses Criterion-Related Validity or Construct Validity. Reliability focuses on consistency, while validity measures the accuracy of the test in assessing what it claims to measure.

Explanation of keywords

Reliability refers to the consistency, stability, and dependability of a test or measurement tool. It measures whether a test produces consistent results over time, across different raters, or within the test itself. It is a crucial aspect of test construction to ensure accurate and meaningful interpretations of scores.

22. Which of the following statement(s) regarding test scores and their interpretations is/are correct?

(A) Frequency distribution are graphs to help us understand the distribution of test scores

(B) Normal probability distribution is a theoretical distribution to help us understand the distribution of test scores

(C) Central tendency measures are numerical tools to help us locate the middle of a distribution of a test score

(D) Measurement of variability are numerical tools to help us understand the spread of a distribution of a test score

Correct Answer- A,B,C,D

(A) Frequency distributions are graphs to help us understand the distribution of test scores.

Frequency distribution is a way to organize test scores by displaying how often each score occurs. It can be represented using histograms, bar graphs, or frequency polygons. It provides a clear visual of the distribution and any patterns like skewness or normality.

(B) Normal probability distribution is a theoretical distribution to help us understand the distribution of test scores.

A normal distribution is a symmetrical, bell-shaped curve representing how test scores tend to cluster around the mean. It is theoretical and used in many psychological and educational tests to predict the probability of various outcomes. Standard deviation and z-scores are often used to interpret scores within a normal distribution.

(C) Central tendency measures are numerical tools to help us locate the middle of a distribution of a test score.

Measures of central tendency refer to statistical tools that indicate the central point of a dataset.

The three main measures are:

- Mean (average)
- Median (middle score)
- Mode (most frequent score)
- These measures provide insight into the typical performance on a test.

(D) Measurement of variability are numerical tools to help us understand the spread of a distribution of a test score.

Measures of variability assess how much test scores differ from the average score.

Key measures include:

- Range (difference between the highest and lowest scores)
- Variance (average of squared deviations from the mean)
- Standard Deviation (square root of variance)
- These measures are useful for understanding score dispersion and consistency.

Explanation of keywords:

Frequency Distribution: Graphical representation showing how often each test score occurs. Helps in visualizing score patterns.

Normal Probability Distribution: A theoretical, bell-shaped curve representing how scores are distributed around the mean. Often used for statistical inferences.

Central Tendency: Numerical measures (Mean, Median, Mode) representing the central or typical score in a dataset.

Measurement of Variability: Tools like Range, Variance, and Standard Deviation that describe the spread or dispersion of test scores.

Score Interpretation: Using statistical tools to analyze and understand the meaning of test scores in a given context.

Z-Score: A standardized score indicating how far a particular score is from the mean in a normal distribution.

Skewness and Kurtosis: Indicate the asymmetry and peakedness of a distribution, respectively.

Raw Scores: The actual test results before applying any statistical adjustments.

Percentile Rank: Indicates the percentage of scores that fall below a particular test score.

23. Which of the following statement(s) is/are correct regarding the negative symptoms of schizophrenia?

(A) Auditory hallucination, persecution, and disorganized thinking

(B) Lack of effect in situation, poor motivation, and social withdrawal

(C) Loss of interest in day-to-day activities, lack of will, and difficulty in expressing emotions

(D) Visual hallucination, delusions of grandeur, and delusion of control

Correct Answer- B,C
(B) Lack of affect in situations, poor motivation, and social withdrawal.

- These are negative symptoms of schizophrenia.
- Lack of affect refers to diminished emotional expression, often showing a blank facial expression or monotone speech.
- Poor motivation is referred to as avolition, where the person has difficulty starting or maintaining purposeful activities.
- Social withdrawal is common due to a lack of interest or enjoyment in social interactions (asociality).

(C) Loss of interest in day-to-day activities, lack of will, and difficulty in expressing emotions.

- These are also negative symptoms.
- Loss of interest in activities (anhedonia) is a typical characteristic, where individuals no longer find pleasure in previously enjoyed activities.
- Lack of will (avolition) is present when the person has difficulty initiating tasks or making decisions.
- Difficulty in expressing emotions is known as blunted affect, where emotional responses are reduced or absent.

Explanation of other options
(A) Auditory hallucination, persecution, and disorganized thinking.

- These are positive symptoms of schizophrenia, not negative symptoms.
- Auditory hallucinations involve hearing voices or sounds that aren't real.
- Delusions of persecution involve false beliefs that others are plotting against the individual.
- Disorganized thinking refers to fragmented or illogical thoughts, often seen in speech.
- Negative symptoms do not involve hallucinations or delusions.

(D) Visual hallucination, delusions of grandeur, and delusion of control.

- These are positive symptoms, not negative.
- Visual hallucinations involve seeing things that are not present.
- Delusions of grandeur are false beliefs of possessing exceptional abilities, wealth, or fame.
- Delusions of control involve believing that one's thoughts or actions are being controlled by external forces.

Explanation of keywords:
Negative symptoms of schizophrenia, such as avolition, alogia, anhedonia, affective flattening, and social withdrawal, significantly impact a person's ability to engage in everyday activities, build relationships, and function in society. These symptoms are often more persistent and disabling than positive symptoms (e.g., hallucinations or delusions). Early recognition, comprehensive treatment, and supportive interventions are essential for managing negative symptoms and improving the quality of life for individuals with schizophrenia.

24. Which of the following statement(s) is/are correct about children with ADHD (Attention Deficit Hyperactivity Disorder)?
(A) They have deficit in brain related executive function
(B) They have difficulty to control voluntary movements, verbal expression and problem solving due to frontal lobes
(C) Cerebellum (an area of the brain) does not work properly, which coordinates muscular activity
(D) It is also known as hypokinetic disorder
Correct Answer A,B,C

(A) They have deficit in brain-related executive function.

- Executive functions (e.g., attention control, impulse regulation, working memory) are primarily controlled by the prefrontal cortex.
- Research shows that children with ADHD often have underdeveloped or dysregulated executive functions, leading to difficulties in focusing, planning, and controlling behavior.

Example: A child with ADHD may struggle to complete tasks, frequently forget instructions, or act impulsively.

(B) They have difficulty controlling voluntary movements, verbal expression, and problem-solving due to frontal lobes.

- The frontal lobes (especially the prefrontal cortex) play a key role in controlling voluntary actions, speech, and higher-order thinking (problem-solving, reasoning, decision-making).
- ADHD is linked to dysfunctions in the frontal lobes, leading to impulsivity, disorganized speech, and difficulty in problem-solving.

Example: A child with ADHD may interrupt conversations, have trouble organizing thoughts, or struggle with decision-making.

(C) Cerebellum (an area of the brain) does not work properly, which coordinates muscular activity.

- The cerebellum plays a role in coordinating motor activity, balance, and movement regulation.
- Studies suggest that children with ADHD have abnormalities in the cerebellum, which can lead to clumsiness, poor motor coordination, and difficulty in fine motor tasks (e.g., handwriting, buttoning shirts, playing sports).

Example: A child with ADHD may struggle with handwriting or frequently bump into objects.

Explanation of other options

(D) It is also known as hypokinetic disorder.

- ADHD is NOT known as a hypokinetic disorder.
- Hypokinetic disorders (e.g., Parkinson's disease) involve reduced movement or lack of movement.
- ADHD, on the other hand, is characterized by hyperactivity and impulsivity, making it more of a hyperkinetic disorder (opposite of hypokinetic).

Explanation of keywords

Children with ADHD typically struggle with inattention, hyperactivity, and impulsivity, leading to difficulties in both academic and social environments. The condition requires proper diagnosis and treatment, including behavioral strategies and, in some cases, medication to help manage symptoms and improve quality of life.

25. Which of the following assumptions are correct about equity theory?

(A) Focusses on procedural justice

(B) Motivation is influenced by relative and absolute rewards

(C) Referent is the other-inside

(D) Achieving balance between input-output

Correct Answer- B,C,D

(B) Motivation is influenced by relative and absolute rewards.

- According to Equity Theory, people evaluate their rewards in relative terms by comparing their input-output ratio to others.

- Absolute rewards (e.g., salary, bonuses) are also considered, but motivation is significantly influenced by perceived fairness compared to peers.

  Example: Earning $50,000 may feel fair until someone discovers a colleague with similar duties earns $60,000.
  (C) Referent is the other-inside.

- Referents are the individuals or groups with whom people compare their input-output ratios.
- "Other-inside" refers to comparisons made with someone in the same organization, typically a peer or colleague.

  Example: An employee may compare their promotion prospects with those of a coworker in the same department.
  (D) Achieving balance between input-output.

- Equity Theory assumes that individuals seek to achieve a balance between their inputs (effort, skills, experience) and outputs (rewards like salary, recognition, benefits).
- If people perceive an imbalance, they may experience feelings of distress and try to restore equity through actions like reducing effort, demanding a raise, or even leaving the job.

  Example: If an employee works overtime without additional pay, they may reduce their effort to restore balance.
  Explanation of other options
  (A) Focuses on procedural justice.

- Equity Theory is primarily concerned with distributive justice (fairness in outcomes or rewards).
- Procedural justice refers to the fairness of the processes used to determine outcomes, which is not the primary focus of Equity Theory.

  Example: Feeling underpaid compared to a colleague with similar qualifications is a concern of distributive justice, not procedural justice.
  Explanation of keywords
  Equity Theory emphasizes the importance of fairness and balance in social exchanges, particularly in the workplace. People compare their inputs and rewards to those of others, and any perceived imbalance (either under-rewarded or over-rewarded) can lead to negative emotions and attempts to restore fairness. Understanding equity theory can help organizations manage motivation and job satisfaction by ensuring fair treatment and equitable rewards.

  26. Which of the following statement(s) are related to Bem's theory of self perception?
  (A) It starts with development of one's basic self-concept
  (B) Behaviour is a source of knowledge
  (C) It is related to attitude formation
  (D) It suggests that people change their attitude because of their behaviour
  Correct Answer- B,C,D
  (B) Behaviour is a source of knowledge.

- According to Bem, people learn about themselves by analyzing their own actions.
- When there is no clear internal cue (e.g., strong emotions), behavior serves as a primary source of self-knowledge.

  Example: A person who frequently watches documentaries may infer that they are curious or enjoy learning.
  (C) It is related to attitude formation.

- Self-perception theory explains how attitudes are formed or changed through observation of behavior.

- If a person repeatedly engages in a behavior without external pressure, they may develop a corresponding attitude.

Example: Someone who eats vegetarian meals often may conclude that they have a positive attitude toward vegetarianism.

(D) It suggests that people change their attitude because of their behavior.

- Bem argued that attitudes often follow behavior rather than the other way around.
- When individuals lack strong attitudes, they adjust their beliefs to align with their actions.

Example: A person who publicly supports a cause may start genuinely believing in it, even if they were initially indifferent.

Explanation of other options

(A) It starts with the development of one's basic self-concept.

Self-perception theory does not emphasize the development of a basic self-concept. Instead, it focuses on how people infer their attitudes based on observing their own behavior.

Example: If someone notices they often volunteer, they might infer that they are a generous person.

Explanation of keywords in questions

Bem's Theory of Self-Perception suggests that individuals come to understand their own attitudes, emotions, and internal states by observing their own behavior and the context in which it occurs, rather than by introspection or reflection on internal experiences. This theory is often seen as an alternative to the idea that we access our attitudes directly through self-reflection.

27. Which of the following statements are related to social cognition?

(A) How individuals interpret, analyze, remember and use information about the social world

(B) How people create mental structure to organise knowledge about the social world

(C) How people think about themselves and the social world

(D) It does not allow interaction between people and the environment

Correct Answer- A,B,C

(A) How individuals interpret, analyze, remember, and use information about the social world.

- Social cognition involves understanding and processing social information to guide behavior.
- People interpret social situations, analyze others' actions, remember past social experiences, and use that information in future interactions.

Example: Someone recalling a past argument to predict how a friend might react in a similar situation.

(B) How people create mental structures to organize knowledge about the social world.

- People form schemas (mental frameworks) to structure their understanding of social situations.
- These schemas help individuals quickly interpret new social experiences based on past knowledge.

Example: A person has a schema for "teacher" and expects them to be knowledgeable, disciplined, and authoritative.

(C) How people think about themselves and the social world.

- Social cognition is not just about others but also about self-perception in relation to society.
- Concepts like self-concept, self-esteem, and self-identity are integral to social cognition.

Example: A student believes they are hardworking because of positive feedback from teachers and peers.

Explanation of other options
(D) It does not allow interaction between people and the environment.

- Social cognition is interactive—it involves continuous adaptation based on environmental and social cues.
- It is influenced by culture, social norms, and experiences rather than being a rigid process.

Example: A person adjusts their behavior in a formal office setting versus a casual gathering.
Explanation of keywords
Social cognition is the study of how we understand and interpret the world around us, especially in social contexts. It involves perceiving others, forming impressions, making attributions, and applying social knowledge to navigate social situations effectively.
28. Which of the following theory(ies) is/are related to work motivation?
(A) Motivation-Hygiene Theory
(B) Expectancy Theory
(C) Trait Theory
(D) ERG Theory
Correct Answer:A,B,D
(A) Motivation-Hygiene Theory (Two-Factor Theory)
Developer: Herzberg
Focus: Job Satisfaction and Motivation
Key Idea: Herzberg proposed that there are two types of factors that influence motivation and job satisfaction:

1. Motivators – Factors that lead to job satisfaction and motivate individuals to perform better. These include achievement, recognition, work itself, responsibility, advancement, and growth.
2. Hygiene Factors – Factors that, when absent or inadequate, lead to dissatisfaction but do not necessarily motivate people when present. These include salary, company policies, supervision, interpersonal relationships, and working conditions.

Application: Improving hygiene factors can prevent dissatisfaction, but true motivation comes from enhancing motivators.
Example: A raise (hygiene factor) might prevent dissatisfaction, but a challenging project (motivator) can inspire an employee to perform better.
(B) Expectancy Theory
Developer: Victor Vroom
Focus: Motivation in the workplace
Key Idea: Motivation is determined by the expectation that effort will lead to desired outcomes (performance), and that performance will lead to rewards. This theory is based on three key components:

1. Expectancy – The belief that effort will lead to good performance.
2. Instrumentality – The belief that good performance will lead to a specific outcome or reward.
3. Valence – The value an individual places on the expected reward.

Formula: Motivation = Expectancy × Instrumentality × Valence
Application: Employees are motivated to perform well if they believe that their efforts will lead to positive outcomes and that the rewards are valuable to them.
Example: An employee is more likely to work hard if they believe their effort will lead to a promotion (expectancy), the promotion is attainable (instrumentality), and the promotion is highly valued (valence).
(D) ERG Theory

Developer: Clayton Alderfer

Focus: Motivation in the workplace and personal life

Key Idea: Alderfer's ERG theory is a modification of Maslow's hierarchy of needs, suggesting that needs are categorized into three groups rather than five:

1. Existence Needs – Basic material needs, including physiological and safety needs (similar to Maslow's first two levels).
2. Relatedness Needs – Social and interpersonal relationships (similar to Maslow's social needs).
3. Growth Needs – Personal development, creativity, and self-actualization (similar to Maslow's self-esteem and self-actualization).

Application: ERG theory is more flexible than Maslow's, suggesting that individuals can be motivated by different types of needs at the same time and that unmet needs can lead to frustration and regression to lower-level needs.

Example: An employee may be simultaneously motivated by social connections (relatedness) and personal growth (growth), and may regress to focusing on basic material rewards (existence) if other needs are not met.

Explanation of other options

(C) Trait Theory of Personality

Developers: Gordon Allport, Raymond Cattell, Hans Eysenck

Focus: Understanding Personality

Key Idea: Trait theory focuses on identifying and measuring individual personality traits that define how people behave across different situations. Traits are seen as enduring characteristics that influence behavior.

- Allport's View: Suggested that personality is composed of central traits (key characteristics), secondary traits (less dominant traits), and cardinal traits (rare, dominant traits).
- Cattell's View: Used factor analysis to identify 16 personality factors (e.g., warmth, sensitivity, intelligence).
- Eysenck's View: Proposed that personality is made up of three dimensions: extraversion, neuroticism, and psychoticism.
- Application: Trait theory is used in personality assessments to understand and predict behavior, such as the Big Five Personality Traits (OCEAN): Openness, Conscientiousness, Extraversion, Agreeableness, Neuroticism.

Example: Someone high in extraversion might be more social and energetic, while someone high in neuroticism might experience more anxiety and stress.

Explanation of keywords

Work Motivation refers to the internal and external factors that stimulate employees to take actions that lead to achieving work-related goals. It is a psychological force that drives a person to engage in their job tasks with enthusiasm, persistence, and direction.

29. Which of the following are not part of Thurstone's theory of primary mental abilities?

(A) Numerical Ability

(B) Word Fluency

(C) Analytical Ability

(D) Short-Term Memory

Correct Answer- C,D

(C) Analytical Ability

Analytical Ability refers to the capacity to analyze, evaluate, and solve problems. This concept is more associated with Sternberg's Triarchic Theory of Intelligence, not Thurstone's.

(D) Short-Term Memory

Short-Term Memory refers to the ability to temporarily store and manipulate information. While Memory is a component of Thurstone's theory, the specific concept of Short-Term Memory as we understand it today is more aligned with Cognitive Psychology and models like Baddeley's Working Memory Model.

Explanation of other options

(A) Numerical Ability

Numerical Ability involves solving mathematical problems and working with numbers quickly and accurately. It is one of the seven primary abilities in Thurstone's theory.

(B) Word Fluency

Word Fluency is the ability to quickly produce words, especially in tasks like word association or verbal tasks. This is also included in Thurstone's primary abilities.

Explanation of keywords

Thurstone's Theory of Primary Mental Abilities proposes that intelligence is composed of several distinct, independent abilities rather than a single general intelligence (g factor), as suggested by earlier theorists like Charles Spearman.

Key Points of Thurstone's Theory:

Primary Mental Abilities (PMAs): Thurstone identified seven primary mental abilities that he believed form the foundation of human intelligence. These abilities are:

1. Verbal Comprehension: The ability to understand and use language, including reading comprehension and vocabulary.
2. Word Fluency: The ability to quickly produce words, such as in verbal brainstorming or finding synonyms.
3. Number Facility: The ability to perform mathematical calculations and reason numerically.
4. Spatial Visualization: The ability to visualize objects and manipulate them mentally (e.g., mental rotation of objects).
5. Associative Memory: The ability to remember and recall information, like names or faces.
6. Perceptual Speed: The ability to quickly and accurately identify similarities and differences between visual stimuli.
7. Reasoning: The ability to solve problems and make decisions based on logic and patterns.

30. Which of the following are the competencies of a Bystander?

(A) Deciding how to help a person in need

(B) Deciding how to avoid a person at the time of his/her distress

(C) Deciding to standby with a person at the time of his/her emergency

(D) Too busy to help

Correct Answer-A,C

(A) Deciding How to Help a Person in Need.

This is a primary competency of a responsible bystander.It involves assessing the situation, determining what kind of help is required, and taking appropriate action, like calling emergency services, offering first aid, or supporting the person emotionally.This is often referred to as bystander intervention.

(C) Deciding to Standby with a Person at the Time of His/Her Emergency.

Providing emotional support by simply being present is a valid form of intervention.A bystander may not always have the skills to offer direct assistance, but their presence can offer comfort and reduce feelings of isolation for the victim.

Explanation of other options

(B) Deciding How to Avoid a Person at the Time of His/Her Distress.

Avoidance is not a competency but a negative response.Some bystanders may avoid helping due to fear, uncertainty, or the assumption that someone else will intervene (known as diffusion of responsibility).

(D) Too Busy to Help.

Being "too busy" reflects a lack of engagement rather than a competency.This can be explained by concepts like time pressure or personal priorities, which can prevent people from taking action.

Explanation of keywords

Bystander effect refers to the phenomenon in which individuals are less likely to offer help to a victim when other people are present. The more bystanders there are, the less personal responsibility any one individual feels, and the less likely they are to intervene.

31. Which of the following functions are related to pancreas?

(A) Release of hormones

(B) Converts food we eat into fuel for the body cells

(C) It regulates the level of glucose in the blood

(D) It damages digestive system

Correct Answer- A,B,C

(A) Release of Hormones.

The pancreas contains islets of Langerhans that release hormones into the bloodstream.

Key hormones produced include:

- Insulin: Lowers blood sugar levels.
- Glucagon: Raises blood sugar levels.
- Somatostatin: Regulates the secretion of insulin and glucagon.

(B) Converts Food We Eat into Fuel for the Body Cells.

Through its exocrine function, the pancreas produces digestive enzymes that help break down carbohydrates, proteins, and fats in the small intestine.

The pancreas releases:

- Amylase: Breaks down carbohydrates.
- Lipase: Breaks down fats.
- Proteases: Breaks down proteins.
- These nutrients are then converted into energy used by body cells.

(C) It Regulates the Level of Glucose in the Blood.

The pancreas plays a primary role in blood glucose regulation through the hormones insulin and glucagon. After a meal, insulin helps cells absorb glucose, while glucagon releases stored glucose from the liver when blood sugar levels are low.

Explanation of other options

(D) It Damages Digestive System.

The pancreas does not damage the digestive system under normal conditions. However, diseases like pancreatitis (inflammation of the pancreas) or pancreatic cancer can lead to severe digestive problems. While not a function of the pancreas, damage may occur due to excessive alcohol consumption, gallstones, or infections.

Explanation of keywords

Pancreatic Functions:

- Regulates Blood Sugar (insulin and glucagon).
- Aids Digestion by producing enzymes that break down fats, proteins, and carbs.
- Neutralizes Acidic Chyme from the stomach to protect the intestine.
- Pancreas is essential for digesting food and maintaining glucose balance in the body.

32. Which of the following psychologists do not belong to behaviourism?

(A) Sigmund Freud

(B) B. F. Skinner

(C) William James
(D) J. B. Watson
Correct Answer: A,C
Explanation of keywords
Behaviorism is a psychological approach that focuses on studying observable behaviors rather than internal mental processes. It emphasizes that all behaviors are learned through interaction with the environment, and that external stimuli shape actions through conditioning.

33. Which of the following theories of emotion explains that arousal must occur before experience of emotion?
(A) Schachter & Singer's Theory
(B) Hertzberg's Theory
(C) Cannon-Bard's Theory
(D) Maslow's Theory
Correct Answer: (A) Schachter & Singer's Two-Factor Theory of Emotion
Focus: Emotion
Key Idea: Emotions arise from a combination of physiological arousal and cognitive interpretation.
Process:

1. Arousal – The body experiences physiological changes (e.g., heart racing).
2. Cognition – The brain interprets the arousal based on the situation (e.g., fear if there's a bear, excitement if at a party).
3. Emotion – The label (fear/excitement) is applied to the arousal, creating the emotional experience.

Example: Your heart races when walking in a dark alley, and you interpret the arousal as fear because of the environment.
Explanation of other options

(B) Herzberg's Two-Factor Theory (Motivation-Hygiene Theory)
Focus: Workplace Motivation and Job Satisfaction
Key Idea:

- Motivators – Factors that lead to job satisfaction (e.g., achievement, recognition, growth).
- Hygiene Factors – Factors that prevent dissatisfaction but don't increase satisfaction (e.g., salary, company policies, work conditions).
- Application: Improving hygiene factors prevents unhappiness, but real motivation comes from enhancing motivators.

Example: A raise (hygiene) prevents complaints, but personal growth (motivator) drives passion and engagement.
(C) Cannon-Bard Theory of Emotion
Focus: Emotion
Key Idea: Emotional and physiological responses happen simultaneously and independently.
Process:

- When an emotion-triggering stimulus is perceived, the brain sends signals to trigger both emotional experience and bodily response at the same time.

Example: Seeing a snake triggers both the feeling of fear and physical arousal (e.g., sweating) at the same time, not one after the other.
(D) Maslow's Hierarchy of Needs

Focus: Human Motivation

Key Idea: Human needs are arranged in a hierarchy, and people must satisfy lower-level needs before pursuing higher-level ones.

Hierarchy:

1. Physiological Needs – Food, water, shelter
2. Safety Needs – Security, stability
3. Love and Belonging – Relationships, friendships
4. Esteem Needs – Respect, recognition
5. Self-Actualization – Personal growth, reaching potential

Example: A person struggling to meet basic needs (like food) will focus on survival before seeking personal fulfillment.

Explanation of keywords

Arousal: Refers to the physiological response of the body, such as an increased heart rate, sweating, or rapid breathing.

Experience of Emotion: The conscious feeling of an emotion like happiness, anger, fear, or sadness.

Theories of Emotion: Psychological models that explain how emotions are generated and experienced.

34. Who among the following psychologists do not belong to the domain of emotional intelligence?

(A) David Mayer

(B) Sigmund Freud

(C) William James

(D) Robert R. Baron

Correct Answer: B,C

Explanation of keywords

Emotional Intelligence (EI) refers to the ability to recognize, understand, manage, and influence emotions in oneself and others. It plays a key role in personal and professional success by fostering better relationships, empathy, and decision-making.

35. Which of the followings are the projective tests of personality?

(A) Rorschach Inkblot Test

(B) 16 PF

(C) TAT

(D) WAT

Correct Answer: A,C,D

(A) Rorschach Inkblot Test

- Type: Projective Personality Test
- Description: Individuals are shown 10 inkblot images (some black-and-white, some colored) and asked what they see. Their responses reveal unconscious thoughts, feelings, and personality traits.
- Purpose: To assess emotional functioning, personality structure, and potential psychological disorders.
- Developed By: Hermann Rorschach (1921).

Example: If someone consistently sees threatening images, it may suggest anxiety or paranoia.

(C) TAT (Thematic Apperception Test)

- Type: Projective Personality Test
- Description: Individuals are shown ambiguous pictures of people in various situations and asked to create a story about them.

- Purpose: Reveals unconscious motives, desires, and concerns.
- Developed By: Henry Murray and Christiana Morgan (1930s).

Example: A person's story about a lonely figure may reflect their own feelings of isolation.
(D) WAT (Word Association Test)

- Type: Projective Test
- Description: Participants are given a list of words and asked to respond with the first word that comes to mind.
- Origin: Often linked to Carl Jung's work in psychoanalysis.
- Purpose: To uncover hidden thoughts, conflicts, and personality dynamics.

Example: If the word "mother" prompts a negative association, it may indicate unresolved issues.
Explanation of other options
(B) 16 PF (16 Personality Factors Test)

- Type: Objective Personality Test
- Description: A questionnaire developed to measure 16 basic personality traits (like warmth, reasoning, emotional stability).
- Purpose: Used for career guidance, psychological research, and clinical diagnosis.
- Developed By: Raymond Cattell.

Example: It can indicate if someone is introverted or extroverted, emotionally stable, or reactive.
Explanation of keywords
Projective tests are psychological assessment tools used to evaluate a person's thoughts, feelings, and underlying personality traits. These tests involve presenting ambiguous or vague stimuli to the individual, allowing them to project their unconscious thoughts, emotions, and desires onto the stimulus.

36.Which of the followings are not learning disorders?
(A) Dyslexia
(B) Dystopia
(C) Dysgraphia
(D) Dystonia
Correct Answer: B,D
(B) Dystopia: A fictional or imagined society that is undesirable or frightening, often characterized by oppression, environmental disaster, or extreme inequality.
(D) Dystonia: A movement disorder that causes involuntary muscle contractions, resulting in abnormal postures or repetitive movements.

- Symptoms: Twisting or tremors in specific body parts (e.g., neck, hands) or the whole body.
- Cause: Can be genetic, caused by brain injury, or linked to neurological diseases like Parkinson's.

Example: Someone with cervical dystonia may experience the head tilting uncontrollably.
Explanation of other options
(A) Dyslexia: A learning disorder characterized by difficulty reading.

- Symptoms: Trouble with recognizing words, poor spelling, and difficulty decoding words.
- Cause: It's a neurological condition affecting the brain's ability to process written language, not related to intelligence.

Example: A child may struggle to read aloud or mix up similar letters like "b" and "d."

(C) Dysgraphia: A learning disability that affects writing abilities.

- Symptoms: Poor handwriting, trouble with spelling, and difficulty organizing thoughts on paper.
- Cause: A neurological disorder that impacts fine motor skills and writing coordination.

Example: A student may write letters in reverse or have inconsistent spacing between words.

Explanation of keywords

Learning disorders refer to a group of neurological conditions that affect an individual's ability to acquire, process, or use specific academic skills. These disorders are not due to a lack of intelligence or motivation; rather, they stem from difficulties in how the brain processes information.

37. Which of the following concepts are not related to Piaget's theory of cognitive development?

(A) Imprinting

(B) Attachment

(C) Schemas

(D) Zone of Proximal Development

Correct Answer: A,B,D

(A) Imprinting

Imprinting is a concept from ethology (study of animal behavior), primarily associated with Konrad Lorenz. It refers to the process by which young animals form strong bonds with the first moving object they see, often their mother.

(B) Attachment

Attachment theory was developed by John Bowlby and later expanded by Mary Ainsworth. It describes the emotional bonds between children and their caregivers.

(D) Zone of Proximal Development (ZPD)

The Zone of Proximal Development (ZPD) is a concept introduced by Lev Vygotsky. It describes the difference between what a child can do independently and what they can achieve with guidance.

Explanation of other options

(C) Schemas

Schemas are a core concept in Piaget's theory. A schema is a mental structure that organizes and interprets information. Piaget believed that children build and modify schemas through processes like assimilation and accommodation.

Explanation of keywords

Piaget's Theory of Cognitive Development:

Piaget proposed a stage theory of cognitive development that describes how children's thinking evolves over time. The four stages are:

- Sensorimotor Stage (0-2 years): Learning through sensory experiences and actions.
- Preoperational Stage (2-7 years): Developing symbolic thinking, but with egocentrism and lack of conservation.
- Concrete Operational Stage (7-11 years): Logical thinking about concrete objects; understanding conservation.
- Formal Operational Stage (12+ years): Abstract thinking, problem-solving, and hypothetical reasoning.

38. Which of the following statement(s) is/are correct regarding exploratory factor analysis (EFA) technique?

(A) It helps to reduce large number of variables into few numbers of factors.

(B) It helps researchers to investigate concepts that cannot easily be measured directly.

(C) It extracts maximum common variance from all variables and put them into a common score.

(D) A technique used to verify the factor structure of a set of observed variables.

Correct Answer:A,B,C

Explanation of keywords in questions

Exploratory Factor Analysis (EFA):

EFA is a statistical technique used to uncover the underlying structure of a set of variables. It identifies latent factors (unobservable variables) that explain the patterns of correlstructureations among observed variables.

39. If you want to examine the difference between the work values of employees in public and private sector and the relationship of work values with employee engagement, what would be the appropriate statistics to test the hypotheses?

(A) F-test

(B) t-test

(C) Pearson Product moment correlation

(D) Chi-square

Correct Answer: B,C

(B) t-test: Compares the means of two groups to determine if they are significantly different.Testing the difference in work values between public and private sector employees. Since the goal is to compare work values between two sectors, a t-test is the most appropriate for this part of the hypothesis.

(C) Pearson Product-Moment Correlation: Measures the strength and direction of the linear relationship between two continuous variables. Testing the relationship between work values and employee engagement. This test is perfect for the second part of the hypothesis, which involves evaluating the relationship between work values and employee engagement.

Explanation of other options

(A) F-test: Compares the means of three or more groups to see if there are significant differences. Testing differences across multiple sectors or groups (e.g., public, private, NGO). The question only involves comparing two groups (public vs. private), so an F-test isn't necessary unless there were more than two groups.

(D) Chi-square: Tests the association between categorical variables. Determining if there is a relationship between categorical data (e.g., sector and job satisfaction levels). Since work values and employee engagement are likely measured on continuous scales (rather than categorical), Chi-square is not appropriate.

Explanation of keywords

Examine the Difference: This suggests comparing two groups (public vs. private sector employees) based on their work values.

Work Values: Employees' beliefs, ethics, and attitudes toward their job, such as job security, autonomy, and work-life balance.

Public and Private Sector: Represents two independent groups that are being compared.

Relationship of Work Values with Employee Engagement: Employee engagement refers to an individual's commitment, enthusiasm, and involvement in their job. The phrase "relationship" suggests looking at associations or correlations between variables.

CHAPTER V

PREVIOUS YEAR QUESTIONS 2021 ANALYSIS

1.According to path goal theory of leadership a type of leadership in which the leader consult with subordinates, involving them in decision making process is------------------

(A)Participative

(B) Directive

(C) Supportive

(D) Achievement oriented

Correct Answer-(A)Participative Leadership: In participative leadership, the leader actively involves team members in decision-making and problem-solving. The leader values their input and encourages collaboration.

Key Concept: This approach works well when the team is skilled, motivated, and capable of contributing ideas. It fosters a sense of ownership and empowerment among employees.

Example: A manager asks team members for their opinions on a new project plan and incorporates their suggestions into the final decision.

Explanation of other options:

(B) Directive Leadership: Directive leadership involves providing clear instructions, setting goals, and closely monitoring performance. The leader tells employees exactly what to do and how to do it.

Key Concept: This style is effective when tasks are unstructured or employees need guidance and clarity. It reduces ambiguity and increases task focus.

Example: A project leader outlines each step in a project, assigns specific tasks, and ensures deadlines are met by giving explicit directions.

(C) Supportive Leadership: Supportive leadership emphasizes creating a friendly and caring environment. The leader prioritizes the well-being of employees and offers emotional and psychological support.

Key Concept: This style is beneficial when stressed employees need reassurance. It helps build trust, boost morale, and improve job satisfaction.

Example: A supervisor regularly checks in on employees, listens to their concerns, and provides encouragement when they are struggling.

(D) Achievement-Oriented Leadership: In achievement-oriented leadership, leaders set high standards and encourage employees to excel and reach their full potential. They express confidence in the team's abilities and push them to achieve challenging goals.

Key Concept: This approach is practical when employees are highly competent and motivated, and the leader believes they can perform at a high level.

Example: A sales manager sets ambitious targets for the team and motivates them to exceed them by recognizing top performers.

Explanation of keywords:

The Path-Goal Theory of leadership, developed by Robert House in 1971, focuses on how leaders can motivate followers to achieve goals. The theory suggests that a leader's role is to clear the path for employees, remove obstacles, provide support, and ensure that goals are attainable.

2. A process to test reliability that involves creating a large bank of items and then dividing it into different versions or creating two tests with items of similar difficulty is called ---------

(A). Alternate and parallel form reliability

(B). Measure of test homogeneity

(C). Test-retest

(D). Interrater reliability

Correct Answer-(A) Alternate and Parallel Form Reliability: This method assesses the consistency of test results by creating two equivalent (parallel) forms of the same test and administering them to the same group of people.

Key Concept: Both forms should measure the same construct, and a high correlation between the two indicates strong reliability. This method controls for memory effects (since the questions differ but assess the same thing).

Example: A math test is created in two forms (Form A and Form B), with different but equivalent questions, and both forms are given to the same students at different times.

Explanation of other option

(B) Measure of Test Homogeneity (Internal Consistency)

Definition: This method evaluates how consistently all items on a test measure the same concept or skill. High internal consistency means that all parts of the test contribute to measuring the same construct.

Key Concept: A common way to assess this is through Cronbach's Alpha – a statistical measure where values closer to 1 indicate higher reliability.

Example: In a depression questionnaire, if all items (such as "I feel sad," "I have no energy") are closely related, the test shows high internal consistency.

(C) Test-Retest Reliability

Definition: This method checks how consistent test results are over time by administering the same test to the same group of people at two different points in time.

Key Concept: A high correlation between the two sets of scores indicates strong reliability. This method assesses the stability of the test.

Example: A personality test is given to a group today and again in three months. If the results are similar, the test has high test-retest reliability.

(D). Inter-Rater Reliability: This type of reliability measures the level of agreement between two or more raters or observers who evaluate the same thing.

Key Concept: High inter-rater reliability means that different raters produce similar scores or judgments when observing the same behaviour or performance.

Example: Two teachers independently grade the same set of student essays. If their grades are similar, the test shows high inter-rater reliability.

Explanation of keywords:

Alternate and Parallel Form Reliability

Definition: A method of assessing reliability by generating a large pool of test items and dividing them into two equivalent test forms. These forms are designed to have similar difficulty and measure the same construct.

Purpose: To evaluate the consistency of results between the two forms when administered to the same group.

Example: Two versions of a standardized aptitude test are created to prevent cheating and ensure score reliability.

3.Delusion of " Reference" is a symptom of Schizophrenia in which people -------

(A) Believe that random events or comments are directed on them

(B) Believe that their thoughts are being broadcasted

(C) Believe they have special power

(D) Have sensory experience in absence of stimulus

Correct Answer-(A)Believe that random events or comments are directed at them.

This is called a Delusion of Reference. Individuals believe unrelated events, gestures, or comments have a special personal significance.

Example: A person may believe a TV show host is sending secret messages directly to them.

Explanation of other options

(B). Believe that their thoughts are being broadcasted

This is a Thought Broadcasting Delusion. The individual believes their thoughts are being transmitted and heard by others. Example: They may feel their thoughts are being broadcast on the radio.

(C). Believe they have special powers

This is a Delusion of Grandeur. The person believes they possess extraordinary abilities, talents, or importance. Example: They may claim to be a divine figure or have supernatural powers.

(D). Have sensory experiences in the absence of stimuli

This describes a Hallucination rather than a delusion. Hallucinations are false sensory perceptions without any external stimuli. Example: Hearing voices or seeing things that are not present.

Explanation of keywords:

Delusion of Reference:

Definition: A false belief where a person thinks that neutral or unrelated events, comments, or behaviors of others are directed at them or hold special meaning for them.

Example: Believing that a news anchor on TV is speaking directly to them or sending hidden messages through gestures.

4.A student who has prepared inadequately for an exam attributes his failing grade to an unfair test, cheating by other students or a professor who taught badly, is expressing ________________.

(A) projection

(B) reaction formation

(C) repression

(D) rationalization

Correct Answer-(A) Projection

Definition: Projection involves attributing one's own unacceptable thoughts, feelings, or impulses to someone else. Instead of recognizing these emotions in themselves, individuals project them onto others.

Key Concept: This mechanism protects the ego by shifting blame or responsibility.

Example: A person who feels hostile toward a colleague might accuse the colleague of being hostile toward them.

Explanation of other options

(B). Reaction Formation

Definition: In reaction formation, a person expresses the opposite of their true feelings or desires because the actual feelings are anxiety-provoking or socially unacceptable.

Key Concept: This mechanism allows individuals to hide threatening emotions by overcompensating with the opposite behaviour.

Example: Someone who harbours anger toward a parent may behave excessively affectionately and dotingly toward them.

(C). Repression

Definition: Repression involves unconsciously blocking unpleasant thoughts, memories, or desires from conscious awareness.

Key Concept: This is one of the most basic defence mechanisms and helps individuals avoid anxiety by keeping distressing material buried in the unconscious.

Example: A person who experienced a traumatic accident as a child may have no memory of the event, even though it shaped their fears and behaviours.

(D). Rationalization

Definition: Rationalization is the process of justifying or explaining away unacceptable behaviour, thoughts, or feelings by offering seemingly logical reasons rather than confronting the true underlying causes.

Key Concept: This defence mechanism helps reduce guilt or embarrassment by making excuses.

Example: A student who fails a test might say, "The teacher didn't explain the material well," rather than admitting they didn't study enough.

Explanation of keywords:

Defence Mechanisms are unconscious psychological strategies used to cope with anxiety, stress, or conflict. Sigmund Freud proposes them as part of psychoanalytic theory.

5. Which of the following theories of emotion best fits with the statement that perception of an environmental situation results in emotions and both, felt emotion and bodily reactions in emotions are independent of each other, but triggered simultaneously?

(A) Cannon-Bard Theory

(B) Lazarus's Cognitive Appraisal Theory

(C) Schachter-Singer Theory

(D) James-Lange Theory

Correct Answer-(A) Cannon-Bard Theory

Definition: The Cannon-Bard Theory suggests that emotions and physiological responses occur simultaneously but independently.

Key Concept: When an emotion-provoking event happens, the brain (thalamus) sends signals to the body (resulting in physiological changes) and to the cortex (producing the feeling of emotion) at the same time.

Example: Seeing a bear leads to both feeling fear and experiencing a racing heart simultaneously.

Explanation of other options

(B) Lazarus's Cognitive Appraisal Theory

Definition: Lazarus proposed that cognitive appraisal (thinking and evaluating the situation) must happen before an emotional response occurs.

Key Concept: According to this theory, how we interpret or label an event (appraisal) determines the type and intensity of the emotional response.

Example: If you see a stranger approaching, your brain first assesses if they are a threat (appraisal). If they seem dangerous, you experience fear and your heart races. If they seem friendly, you feel calm.

(C) Schachter-Singer Two-Factor Theory

Definition: The Schachter-Singer Theory (also called the Two-Factor Theory of Emotion) suggests that emotion arises from a combination of physiological and cognitive interpretations of that arousal.

Key Concept: The theory emphasizes that the same physiological response (like a pounding heart) can produce different emotions depending on how we label the situation.

Example: If your heart races after a roller coaster, you interpret the arousal as excitement. But if your heart races after hearing bad news, you interpret it as fear.

(D) James-Lange Theory

Definition: The James-Lange Theory posits that emotions result from physiological reactions to stimuli.

Key Concept: The body reacts first (e.g., increased heart rate), and the brain interprets these physical changes as emotions.

Example: You see a snake, your heart starts pounding, and then you feel fear due to recognizing the physical reaction.

Explanation of keywords: Emotion refers to a complex psychological state that involves three components:

1. Subjective Experience: How a person feels (e.g., joy, fear, anger).
2. Physiological Response: Bodily reactions like heart rate changes and sweating.
3. Behavioural Response: Facial expressions, actions, or verbal responses.

Q.6 The perceived fairness of the distribution of resources and rewards is described as __________________.

(A) distributive justice

(B) procedural justice

(C) interactional justice

(D) informational justice

Correct Answer-(A) Distributive Justice

Definition: Distributive justice refers to the perceived fairness of outcomes or the distribution of resources, rewards, and benefits.

Key Concept: Employees assess whether they receive a fair share compared to others based on effort, contribution, or performance.

Example: Two employees perform the same job, but one receives a higher bonus. If the other employee feels this distribution is unfair, they perceive low distributive justice.

Explanation of other options

(B) Procedural Justice

Definition: Procedural justice focuses on the fairness of the processes used to make decisions rather than the outcomes.

Key Concept: Even if the result is unfavourable, employees value transparent, unbiased, and consistent procedures.

Example: A promotion decision based on clear and standardized evaluation criteria is considered procedurally fair, regardless of who gets promoted.

(C) Interactional Justice

Definition: Interactional justice reflects the fairness in interpersonal treatment during decision-making processes. It emphasises respect, dignity, and proper communication.

Key Concept: Employees expect to be treated with politeness and care during interactions.

Example: A manager delivering negative feedback in a respectful and constructive manner ensures high interactional justice.

(D) Informational Justice

Definition: Informational justice involves the quality and transparency of information provided during decision-making.

Key Concept: Employees value honest, timely, and adequate explanations for decisions that affect them.

Example: If layoffs occur, providing employees with clear reasons and detailed explanations reflects high informational justice.

Explanation of keywords:

Perceived Fairness: It refers to how fair people believe outcomes, procedures, and interpersonal interactions are in each context, often in organizations or social settings.

7.According to Bandura's theory of personality, which one of the following is the most important person variables in determining personality?

(A) Self-efficacy

(B) Self-concept

(C) Self-esteem

(D) Self-determination

Correct Answer-(A) Self-Efficacy

Definition: Self-efficacy is an individual's belief in their ability to successfully perform specific tasks or handle situations.

Key Concept: Coined by Albert Bandura, self-efficacy focuses on confidence in one's capacity to achieve goals through effort and persistence.

Example: A student believes they can pass a difficult math test after practising regularly. High self-efficacy leads to more extraordinary perseverance and motivation.

Explanation of other options

(B) Self-Concept

Definition: Self-concept is a broad perception of oneself, including beliefs, attributes, and identity. It encompasses how individuals view their strengths, weaknesses, and overall self-worth.

Key Concept: Self-concept answers the question, "Who am I?" and reflects an overall self-image across various domains (academic, social, physical, etc.).

Example: A person might see themselves as athletic, intelligent, and kind, forming an overall sense of self-concept.

(C) Self-Esteem

Definition: Self-esteem is the emotional evaluation of one's self-worth or value. It reflects how much individuals appreciate and like themselves.

Key Concept: High self-esteem is associated with positive self-regard and confidence, while low self-esteem can lead to self-doubt and insecurity.

Example: A person who feels proud of their achievements and believes they deserve respect has high self-esteem.

(D) Self-Determination

Definition: Self-determination is choosing and controlling one's life. It reflects an individual's autonomy and motivation to act according to their values and interests.

Key Concept: Central to Self-Determination Theory (Deci & Ryan), it highlights the importance of intrinsic motivation, personal agency, and the fulfilment of psychological needs (competence, autonomy, and relatedness).

Example: A person chooses a career path based on passion rather than external pressure, demonstrating self-determination.

Explanation of keywords:

Bandura's Theory of Personality: Developed by Albert Bandura, this theory is a part of the social cognitive theory. It emphasizes the role of reciprocal determinism where personal factors, environmental factors, and behaviors interact to shape personality.

8.Match the events in the first column with the different categories of stress in the second column.

	Events		Stress
P	A young child who loses his water bottle on the school bus	(i)	Traumatic event
Q	A person who escaped from the Taj hotel on 26th November, 2008 around midnight and has nightmares about the same incident	(ii)	Chronic stressor
R	Someone fearing the loss of one's job	(iii)	Major life event
S	A woman who has her first baby	(iv)	Daily Hassle

(A) P-(iv), Q-(i), R-(ii), S-(iii)
(B) P-(iv), Q-(iii), R-(i), S-(ii)
(C) P-(ii), Q-(i), R-(iii), S-(iv)
(D) P-(i), Q-(iv), R-(ii), S-(iii)
Correct Answer-(A)
Explanation of other options
(P) A young child who loses his water bottle on the school bus

- Stress Type: (iv) Daily Hassle

Explanation: Losing a water bottle is a minor, everyday annoyance or inconvenience. It does not cause significant emotional distress or long-term effects. Daily hassles refer to routine struggles such as misplacing things, traffic jams, or small conflicts.

(Q) A person who escaped from the Taj hotel on 26th November 2008 around midnight and has nightmares about the same incident

• Stress Type: (i) Traumatic Event

Explanation: This refers to a life-threatening or extremely distressing event, like terrorist attacks, natural disasters, or severe accidents.Trauma can lead to post-traumatic stress disorder (PTSD), nightmares, and long-term anxiety.

(R) Someone fearing the loss of one's job

• Stress Type: (ii) Chronic Stressor

Explanation: Chronic stressors are ongoing and persistent stress sources, like financial struggles, job insecurity, or long-term health issues.The fear of losing a job is not a one-time event but a continuous worry, leading to stress over time.

(S) A woman who has her first baby

• Stress Type: (iii) Major Life Event

Explanation: Events such as marriage, childbirth, moving to a new city, or job change are considered major life events.They bring significant changes and can cause stress, even if they are positive experiences.

9. Which of the following types of colour blindness denotes blue-yellow colour deficiency?

(A) Tritanopia

(B) Protanopia

(C) Deuteranopia

(D) Ritalin

Correct Answer-(A) Tritanopia

Definition: Tritanopia is a rare form of colour blindness where individuals cannot distinguish between blue and yellow hues.

Key Concept: It results from a lack of or defective S-cones (short-wavelength cones) for detecting blue light.

Symptoms: Blue may appear green, and yellow may look like light grey or pink.

Cause: Often genetic but can also result from damage to the eye or brain.

Explanation of other options

(B) Protanopia

Definition: Protanopia is a type of red-green color blindness where individuals lack or have defective L-cones (long-wavelength cones), responsible for detecting red light.

Key Concept: Red appears as dark brown or gray, and shades of green, yellow, and orange may look similar.

Symptoms: Difficulty distinguishing reds from greens.

Cause: Genetic (X-linked), more common in males.

(C) Deuteranopia

Definition: Deuteranopia is another form of red-green color blindness where individuals lack or have defective M-cones (medium-wavelength cones) responsible for detecting green light.

Key Concept: Green appears as beige or red, and there is confusion between reds, greens, and yellows.

Symptoms: Difficulty distinguishing greens from reds.

Cause: Genetic (X-linked), also more common in males.

(D)Ritalin

Definition: Ritalin is a stimulant medication used to treat Attention-Deficit/Hyperactivity Disorder (ADHD) and narcolepsy.

Key Concept: Ritalin works by increasing dopamine and norepinephrine levels in the brain, helping to improve focus, attention, and impulse control.

Symptoms Treated: Hyperactivity, inattentiveness, and impulsivity.

Category: Central Nervous System (CNS) stimulant.

Explanation of Keywords

Color Blindness:

- It refers to the inability or decreased ability to see specific colours or distinguish between them.
- It typically occurs due to the malfunction or absence of specific retina cones (colour receptors).
- The three main types of cone cells are sensitive to red, green, and blue light.

Blue-Yellow Color Deficiency:

- This type of color blindness affects the ability to distinguish between blue and yellow hues.
- It is less common than red-green color blindness.

10. Which of the following properties of sound is similar to the hue of light?

(A) Pitch

(B) Timbre

(C) Loudness

(D) Purity

Correct Answer-(A) Pitch

Definition: Pitch refers to the perceived frequency of a sound – how high or low a tone sounds.

Key Concept:

- High-frequency sound waves = high pitch (e.g., a whistle).
- Low-frequency sound waves = low pitch (e.g., a drum).
- Measured In: Hertz (Hz) – the number of vibrations per second.
- Example: A soprano singer hits high notes (high pitch), while a bass singer produces low notes (low pitch).

Explanation of other options

(B) Timbre: Timbre (pronounced "tam-ber") is the quality or color of a sound that makes it unique, even if pitch and loudness are the same.

Key Concept: Timbre is influenced by the complexity of sound waves and the combination of overtones. It helps differentiate between instruments or voices.

Example: A piano and a violin can play the same note at the same loudness, but they sound different because of their unique timbre.

(C) Loudness

Definition: Loudness refers to a sound's perceived intensity or strength – how soft or loud it is.

Key Concept:

- Larger amplitude of sound waves = louder sound.
- Smaller amplitude = softer sound.
- Measured In: Decibels (dB).
- Example: A whisper is soft (low loudness), while a rock concert is loud (high loudness).

(D) Purity

Definition: Purity describes how uniform or complex a sound wave is. It relates to the clarity and tone of the sound.

Key Concept:

- Pure tones consist of a single frequency (simple waveform).
- Complex tones consist of multiple frequencies blending together.
- Example: A tuning fork produces a pure tone, while the sound of a guitar or human voice has complex frequencies, affecting its purity.

Explanation of Keywords

Properties of Sound:

Sound has various properties, such as pitch, loudness, timbre, and purity, which determine how we perceive it. Similar to how light has characteristics like hue, brightness, and saturation, sound also has perceptual qualities.

Hue of Light: Hue refers to the colour of light, determined by its wavelength. In sound, the equivalent concept relates to the frequency of the sound waves.

11. _______________________ is a reinforcement schedule, where a person or animal receives the reinforcement based on varying amount of time.

(A) Variable-interval

(B) Fixed-ratio

(C) Fixed-interval

(D) Variable-ratio

Correct Answer-(A) Variable-Interval (VI)

Definition: Reinforcement is given after varying, unpredictable amounts of time.

Key Concept: The behaviour is rewarded randomly, but the average time remains consistent.

Effect on Behaviour: Produces slow, steady, and resistant-to-extinction behaviour.

Example: Checking for emails – you don't know when they will arrive, but checking consistently may result in a reward (new message).

Explanation of other options:

(B) Fixed-Ratio (FR)

Definition: Reinforcement occurs after a set number of responses.

Key Concept: The behaviour must be repeated a specific number of times to receive a reward.

Effect on Behavior: Produces high response rates with a short pause after reinforcement.

Example: A factory worker receives payment after every 10 products produced.

(C) Fixed-Interval (FI)

Definition: Reinforcement is given after a fixed amount of time as long as the behavior occurs at least once.

Key Concept: Responses increase as the time for reward approaches but slow down after reinforcement.

Effect on Behavior: Produces a scalloped response pattern (low early, faster closer to reward time).

Example: Receiving a pay check every two weeks.

(D)Variable-Ratio (VR)

Definition: Reinforcement happens after a variable, unpredictable number of responses.

Key Concept: The reward is based on the average number of responses, but the exact number varies.

Effect on Behaviour: Produces high and steady response rates and is most resistant to extinction.

Example: Slot machines – you never know when you will win, but the more you play, the better the chances.

Explanation of Keywords

Reinforcement Schedule:

- A rule or plan determining when and how reinforcement (reward) is delivered in operant conditioning.

- Reinforcement strengthens the behaviour and increases the likelihood of it occurring again.
- Varying Amount of Time:

  - The question specifies reinforcement based on a changing or unpredictable time.
  - This means the individual is rewarded after a random amount of time passes, not based on the number of responses.

12.______________________ is a loss of memory of events that occurred prior to the trauma.

(A) Retrograde amnesia

(B) Anterograde amnesia

(C) Infantile amnesia

(D) Posthypnotic amnesia

Correct Answer (A) Retrograde Amnesia

Definition: Retrograde amnesia is when an individual loses memories of events before a specific time, usually after an injury or trauma.

Key Concept: It primarily affects old memories, while the ability to form new memories remains intact.

Common Causes: Brain injury, stroke, or trauma.

Example: After a car accident, someone may forget everything that happened in the last 5 years but still be able to remember events from their childhood.

Explanation of other options

(B) Anterograde Amnesia

Definition: Anterograde amnesia is when an individual cannot form new long-term memories after a particular event or injury. However, memories before the event remain intact.

Key Concept: It affects new memory formation (e.g., the inability to remember things that happened after the injury), but old memories remain unchanged.

Common Causes: Brain damage to the hippocampus, often due to injury, illness, or surgeries.

Example: A person with anterograde amnesia may meet someone and have a conversation, but minutes later, they will not remember that person or the conversation.

(C) Infantile Amnesia

Definition: Infantile amnesia refers to the inability of most people to recall memories from early childhood, typically before the age of 3 or 4.

Key Concept: It is a normal phenomenon, likely due to the underdevelopment of the brain regions responsible for memory formation (such as the hippocampus) in early childhood.

Example: Most adults cannot remember events that happened when they were infants or toddlers, even though they may have been significant at the time.

(D) Posthypnotic Amnesia

Definition: Posthypnotic amnesia is when an individual fails to recall specific information or events after being hypnotized.

Key Concept: This amnesia is often induced during a hypnosis session, and the person may not remember the suggestions or experiences from the session after coming out of the hypnotic state.

Common Causes: Hypnosis used for therapy or relaxation.

Example: A person might be hypnotized to forget an unpleasant memory or feeling and will not be able to recall it until triggered under hypnosis again.

Explanation of Keywords

Amnesia:

- A condition involving partial or complete memory loss.
- It can result from brain injury, trauma, illness, or psychological stress.

Loss of Memory:

- Memory loss can refer to an inability to recall past events or difficulty forming new memories.

Prior to the Trauma:

- The term "prior to the trauma" refers explicitly to events before the traumatic incident.

13. Phobias and Obsessive Compulsive Disorder fall in the category of _______________________.
(A) anxiety disorders
(B) mood disorders
(C) somatoform disorders
(D) psychotic disorders
Correct Answer-(A) Anxiety Disorders
Definition: Anxiety disorders involve excessive fear, worry, or nervousness that affects daily functioning. Specific situations may trigger the anxiety or can be generalized across many areas of life.
Key Concept: These disorders often lead to physical symptoms like a racing heart, sweating, or trembling and can significantly impair a person's ability to live their daily life.
Examples:

- Generalized Anxiety Disorder (GAD): Chronic worry about a wide range of events.
- Panic Disorder: Recurrent and unexpected panic attacks.
- Social Anxiety Disorder: Intense fear of social situations.
- Phobias: Irrational fear of specific objects or situations (e.g., heights, spiders).
- Treatment: Cognitive Behavioural Therapy (CBT), medication (e.g., SSRIs, benzodiazepines)

Explanation of other options

(B) Mood Disorders
Definition: Mood disorders primarily involve disturbances in a person's emotional state, resulting in periods of extreme sadness or euphoria. These disorders significantly impact behaviour, thoughts, and overall functioning.
Key Concept: Mood disorders include episodes of depression and mania or alternating between both.
Examples:

- Major Depressive Disorder (MDD): Persistent feelings of sadness, hopelessness, and a lack of interest or pleasure in life.
- Bipolar Disorder: Characterized by alternating periods of mania (elevated mood, hyperactivity) and depression.
- Treatment: Therapy (e.g., CBT, psychotherapy), medications (e.g., antidepressants, mood stabilizers).

(C) Somatoform Disorders
Definition: Somatoform disorders involve physical symptoms that suggest a medical condition, but no identifiable medical cause can be found. The symptoms are not intentionally produced and are often tied to psychological factors.
Key Concept: The focus is on physical symptoms that are either unexplained or disproportionate to any physical illness.
Examples:

- Somatic Symptom Disorder: The presence of one or more physical symptoms that cause distress or disruption to daily life without an identifiable medical cause.

- Illness Anxiety Disorder (formerly Hypochondria): Preoccupation with the fear of having a serious illness despite medical reassurance.
- Conversion Disorder: Neurological symptoms (e.g., paralysis, blindness) that medical tests cannot explain.
- Treatment: Psychotherapy (e.g., cognitive behavioural therapy), stress management, and sometimes medications for anxiety or depression.

(D) Psychotic Disorders

Definition: Psychotic disorders involve a loss of touch with reality, including symptoms like hallucinations, delusions, and disorganized thinking. Individuals with these disorders may have difficulty distinguishing what is real from what is not.

Key Concept: Psychotic disorders often cause severe impairments in thought processes, behaviours, and the ability to function in everyday life.

Examples:

- Schizophrenia: A chronic condition characterized by delusions, hallucinations, disorganized speech and behavior.
- Schizoaffective Disorder: A combination of symptoms of both schizophrenia and mood disorders, like depression or bipolar disorder.
- Delusional Disorder: Persistent, false beliefs (delusions) that are not in line with reality, such as believing one has special powers or is being persecuted.
- Treatment: Antipsychotic medications, therapy (e.g., CBT), and rehabilitation programs.

Explanation of Keywords
Phobias:

- Intense, irrational fear of specific objects, situations, or activities.
- Causes significant distress and may lead to avoidance behaviour.
- Example: Fear of heights (Acrophobia), Fear of spiders (Arachnophobia).
- Obsessive-Compulsive Disorder (OCD):

  - Characterized by obsessions (persistent, unwanted thoughts) and compulsions (repetitive behaviours or rituals).
  - Example: Excessive handwashing due to fear of contamination.

Anxiety Disorders:

- A category of mental health disorders marked by excessive fear, worry, or anxiety.
- Phobias and OCD are part of this category.
- Other examples include Generalized Anxiety Disorder (GAD) and panic disorder.

14. The smallest unit of speech perception that has meaning is ________________.
(A) morpheme
(B) syntax
(C) semantics
(D) phoneme
Correct Answer (A) Morpheme
Definition: A morpheme is a language's smallest unit of meaning. It can be a word or part of a word that carries meaning, including prefixes, suffixes, and roots.
Key Concept: Morphemes are the building blocks of words. A single word can consist of one or more morphemes.

Examples:

- The word "unhappiness" has three morphemes: "un-" (prefix, meaning "not"), "happy" (root, the primary meaning), and "-ness" (suffix, meaning "state or quality of").
- The word "cats" has two morphemes: "cat" (the animal) and "s" (plural marker).

Explanation of other options

(B) Syntax

Definition: Syntax refers to the rules and structure governing word arrangement in sentences. It dictates how words should be combined to form meaningful phrases and sentences in a given language.

Key Concept: Syntax focuses on sentence structure and ensures that the order of words follows specific grammatical rules.

Examples:

- In English, the typical sentence structure is subject + verb + object (e.g., "The cat (subject) chased (verb) the mouse (object)").
- "The cat chased the mouse" follows the correct syntax, but "Chased the mouse the cat" does not.

(C) Semantics

Definition: Semantics is the study of the meaning of words and phrases in a language. It is concerned with how words, sentences, and phrases are used to convey meaning.

Key Concept: Semantics is about interpreting meaning, whether it's the meaning of individual words or the meaning derived from a whole sentence.

Examples:

- The word "dog" semantically refers to a specific type of animal.
- The sentence "She is on cloud nine" semantically means that someone is very happy, not that they are literally in the sky.

(D) Phoneme

Definition: A phoneme is the smallest sound unit in a language that can distinguish one word from another. Phonemes do not have meaning alone, but their combination forms meaningful words.

Key Concept: Phonemes are the essential sound elements that makeup words. Different languages have different sets of phonemes.

Examples:

- The words "bat" and "pat" differ only in the first phoneme (b and p), which changes the meaning of the word.
- In English, the sound /k/ in "cat" and "kite" is a phoneme, as changing it can result in a different word.

Explanation of Keywords

Speech Perception: It refers to the process by which the brain interprets and understands the sounds of spoken language. It involves recognizing phonemes (basic sound units), words, and sentences.

15. In adolescence, with the development of the stage of 'formal operations', we are likely to see the development of ________________________.

    (A) post-conventional morality

    (B) pre-conventional morality

    (C) bodily-kinesthetic intelligence

    (D) transference

Correct Answer (A) Post-Conventional Morality

Definition: Post-conventional morality is a stage in Lawrence Kohlberg's theory of moral development where individuals base their moral decisions on abstract principles and the greater good rather than following societal rules or authority.

Key Concept: People in this stage follow self-chosen ethical principles, emphasising justice, rights, and fairness. If they conflict with these higher ethical principles, they may question societal norms and laws.

Examples:

- A person might break the law (e.g., civil disobedience) to promote a more significant moral principle, such as justice or equality, even if it goes against the established legal norms.
- "The social contract" or universal ethical principles such as the right to life and liberty may influence their actions, as seen in figures like Martin Luther King Jr. or Mahatma Gandhi.

Explanation of other options

(B) Pre-Conventional Morality

Definition: Pre-conventional morality is the earliest stage of moral development (according to Kohlberg), where decisions are primarily driven by self-interest and the desire to avoid punishment or gain rewards.

Key Concept: At this stage, individuals make moral choices based on immediate consequences, such as avoiding punishment or obtaining rewards, rather than internalized moral principles.

Examples:

- Children may not steal cookies because they fear getting caught and punished (avoiding punishment).
- A child may only share a toy because they expect to get a reward or avoid getting scolded.

(C)Bodily-Kinesthetics Intelligence

Definition: Bodily-kinesthetic intelligence is one of Howard Gardner's multiple intelligences, referring to the ability to control bodily movements and handle objects skilfully.

Key Concept: This type of intelligence involves using one's body effectively to solve problems or create products, such as athletes, dancers, surgeons, or craftsmen. It emphasizes physical coordination, dexterity, and the ability to express oneself through physical activities.

Examples:

- A dancer who excels at expressing emotions through movement or an athlete who has exceptional coordination and muscle memory.
- Surgeons who perform precise movements during surgery or artisans who work skilfully with tools and materials.

(D)Transference

Definition: Transference is a concept from psychoanalytic theory (primarily introduced by Sigmund Freud), where a person projects or transfers feelings or emotions they have toward a significant person (like a parent or partner) onto another person, often the therapist.

Key Concept: Transference can occur during therapy sessions, where a patient might unconsciously redirect feelings or attitudes from earlier relationships to the therapist. This can be helpful in therapy, as it brings unconscious material to the surface, but it may also distort the patient's perceptions and interactions.

Examples:

- A patient may start feeling anger or affection toward their therapist, reflecting unresolved feelings from their childhood or other past relationships.

◦ A person in therapy might treat the therapist like a parental figure, projecting old frustrations or attachment patterns.

Explanation of keywords

Adolescence: Refers to the developmental period between childhood and adulthood, typically ages 12 to 18.

Formal Operations:This is the fourth and final stage in Piaget's Theory of Cognitive Development, occurring during adolescence (approximately from age 11 onwards).It is characterized by the ability to think abstractly, logically, and hypothetically.

16. Which technique allows researchers to conduct an integrative statistical analysis of multiple independent studies addressing the same question?

(A) Meta-analysis

(B) Correlational analysis

(C) Regression analysis

(D) Bootstrapping

Correct Answer-(A) Meta-Analysis

Definition: Meta-analysis is a statistical technique used to combine and analyze data from multiple independent studies on the same topic to identify patterns, common findings, and overall effect sizes. It provides a comprehensive and more powerful conclusion by synthesizing evidence across studies.

Key Concept: The goal of meta-analysis is to increase statistical power and accuracy by pooling results from various studies, often addressing inconsistencies or contradictions in individual studies.

Example:

◦ A researcher wants to understand the effectiveness of a particular medication in treating depression. By conducting a meta-analysis of various clinical trials, they combine data from multiple studies to get an overall effect size and a clearer picture of the medication's impact.

Explanation of other options

(B) Correlational Analysis

Definition: Correlational analysis is a statistical method used to examine the relationship between two or more variables. It helps to determine whether a change in one variable is associated with a change in another variable, but it does not imply causation.

Key Concept: The relationship between variables is measured using a correlation coefficient, such as Pearson's r, which ranges from -1 to +1. A positive value indicates a direct relationship, while a negative value indicates an inverse relationship. A value close to 0 means little or no relationship.

Example: A study may examine the relationship between exercise and mental health. A positive correlation would suggest that increased physical activity is associated with improved mental well-being, but it does not mean exercise causes better mental health.

(D) Regression Analysis

Definition: Regression analysis is a statistical method used to predict the value of a dependent variable based on one or more independent variables. It helps to determine the strength and nature of relationships between variables and is often used for prediction.

Key Concept: The simplest form, linear regression, involves a straight-line relationship between the independent (predictor) and dependent (outcome) variables. More complex forms (e.g., multiple regression) include multiple predictors.

Example: A researcher might use regression analysis to predict a person's future income (dependent variable) based on their years of education and years of work experience (independent variables).

(D) Bootstrapping

Definition: Bootstrapping is a resampling technique that involves repeatedly sampling with replacement from a single dataset to estimate the sampling distribution of a statistic (e.g., mean, median, standard error). This technique is used to make inferences about a population, especially when the underlying distribution is unknown or the sample size is small.

Key Concept: Bootstrapping allows researchers to estimate the variance or confidence intervals of statistical estimates without needing to make strong assumptions about the population distribution.

Example: A researcher might want to estimate the confidence interval for the mean income in a population. By resampling the dataset with replacement, the researcher creates multiple samples and calculates the mean for each. These means can then be used to construct a confidence interval for the population mean.

Explanation of Keywords:

Integrative Statistical Analysis: Combining and analyzing results from multiple studies to arrive at a comprehensive understanding.

Multiple Independent Studies: Independent research studies that address the same question, often with varying sample sizes, populations, or methods.

17. The role of culture and 'scaffolding' are emphasized in ________________________.

(A) Vygotsky's theory of cognitive development

(B) Piaget's theory of cognitive development

(C) Atkinson-Shiffrin's information-processing model

(D) Kamiloff-Smith's theory of cognitive development

Correct Answer- (A)Vygotsky's Theory of Cognitive Development

Definition: Lev Vygotsky's theory emphasizes the role of social interaction and cultural context in cognitive development. According to Vygotsky, cognitive abilities develop through social interactions with more knowledgeable others (e.g., parents, teachers, peers) and through the use of culturally specific tools, language, and practices.

Key Concepts:

- Zone of Proximal Development (ZPD): The difference between what a child can do alone and what they can achieve with help from a more capable person.
- Scaffolding: The support provided by a teacher or peer that helps a child complete a task within their ZPD.
- Private Speech: Children often talk to themselves when solving problems, which helps them regulate their thinking and actions.

Example: A teacher providing guidance to a child on a math problem by offering hints or suggestions. Over time, as the child becomes more proficient, the teacher reduces the support, allowing the child to complete the task independently.

Explanation of other options

(B) Piaget's Theory of Cognitive Development

Definition: Jean Piaget's theory is based on the idea that children actively construct their understanding of the world through stages of cognitive development. Piaget proposed that cognitive development occurs in four universal stages: Sensorimotor, Preoperational, Concrete Operational, and Formal Operational.

Key Concepts:

- Schemas: Mental structures or frameworks that help individuals organize and interpret information.
- Assimilation and Accommodation: Processes by which children incorporate new information into existing schemas (assimilation) or modify their schemas to accommodate new information (accommodation).
- Stages of Development: Piaget identified four stages (Sensorimotor, Preoperational, Concrete Operational, and Formal Operational) that represent the evolving capacities for thinking, reasoning, and problem-solving.

Example: A child in the Sensorimotor stage learns about object permanence (the understanding that objects continue to exist even when they cannot be seen), while a child in the Concrete Operational stage understands conservation (the understanding that quantity remains the same despite changes in shape).

(C) Atkinson-Shiffrin's Information-Processing Model

Definition: The Atkinson-Shiffrin model, often referred to as the multi-store model of memory, suggests that human memory operates through a series of stages: sensory memory, short-term memory, and long-term memory.

Key Concepts:

- Sensory Memory: Briefly holds sensory information (visual, auditory, etc.) for a very short period of time.
- Short-Term Memory: Holds information for a short duration (a few seconds to a minute) and has limited capacity.
- Long-Term Memory: Stores information indefinitely with a potentially vast capacity, including both explicit (conscious) and implicit (unconscious) memory.
- Encoding, Storage, and Retrieval: The processes by which information moves from sensory input to long-term storage and can be retrieved when needed.

Example:

- When you are presented with a phone number, it first enters your sensory memory, then it is encoded into short-term memory, and if rehearsed, it is transferred to long-term memory for later retrieval.

(D) Kamiloff-Smith's Theory of Cognitive Development

Definition: Annette Kamiloff-Smith's theory emphasizes the role of language and cognitive processes in shaping a child's cognitive development, particularly through the interaction between biological and environmental factors. She proposed a dynamic approach to cognitive development, focusing on the importance of internal representations and how children construct and refine mental models of the world.

Key Concepts:

- Internal Representations: Cognitive models or mental structures that children form through their experiences, which help in organizing their understanding of the world.
- Developmental Stages: Kamiloff-Smith focused on how children shift between different cognitive systems or models as they mature, especially in relation to language development.
- Constructivist Approach: Emphasizes the idea that children build their understanding of the world through active engagement with their environment.

Example:

- A child may first use simple words or phrases to express their thoughts, but as they grow, they refine and expand their understanding of language, using more complex syntax and structures to express more sophisticated ideas.

Explanation of Keywords

Role of Culture: This refers to how social and cultural interactions influence cognitive development.

Scaffolding: A process where a more knowledgeable individual (e.g., parent, teacher) provides temporary support to help a learner achieve a task they couldn't do alone.

Cognitive Development: The process of how thinking, reasoning, and problem-solving abilities grow over time.

18. Most people tend NOT to consider situational factors while judging others' behaviour because ____.

    (A) people are inclined to commit the fundamental attribution error

    (B) of the frustration-aggression relationship

(C) people are influenced by the laws of reinforcement

(D) of the over justification effect

Correct Answer- (A) People are inclined to commit the fundamental attribution error

The fundamental attribution error (FAE) refers to the tendency to overestimate personal traits and underestimate situational factors when explaining others' behavior. People are more likely to blame a person's internal characteristics (like personality or intelligence) rather than considering external factors (like stress or difficult circumstances).

Example: If someone is rude at a store, people might assume they are a "mean" person rather than considering that they may be having a bad day.

Explanation of other options

(B) Because of the frustration-aggression relationship

The frustration-aggression hypothesis suggests that frustration leads to aggressive behavior. While it explains how frustration can result in aggression, it does not directly relate to why people ignore situational factors when judging others.

Example: A person stuck in traffic may become aggressive due to frustration, but this does not explain misjudgment of others' behavior.

(C) People are influenced by the laws of reinforcement

The laws of reinforcement are concepts from behaviourism that describe how behaviour is shaped through rewards and punishments. This concept applies to learning and behavior modification rather than to the attribution of behavior in social situations.

Example: A child may study harder if rewarded with praise, but this does not explain why people misjudge others' motives.

(D) Because of the overjustification effect

The overjustification effect occurs when a person's intrinsic motivation diminishes because they receive external rewards for a behavior. This concept is more relevant to motivation and learning rather than social judgment.

Example: A child who loves drawing might lose interest if they are excessively rewarded for it.

Explanation of Keywords

Judging Others' Behavior: When people judge others, they often neglect situational factors and instead attribute behavior to the individual's personality or characteristics. This is a common cognitive bias studied in social psychology.

19. Using archival analysis, scientists describe a culture by ____.

(A) examining documents like magazines, diaries and newspapers

(B) surveying a representative sample of members of the society

(C) observing the behaviour of members of the society

(D) comparing the direct observations of behaviour from different culture

Correct Answer (A) Examining documents like magazines, diaries, and newspapers

Archival analysis typically involves analyzing pre-existing documents such as newspapers, diaries, letters, photographs, or government reports. It helps researchers understand cultural beliefs, societal norms, and historical perspectives.

Example: Studying newspaper articles to analyze public reactions to a political event.

Explanation of other options

(B) Surveying a representative sample of members of the society

This describes survey research, not archival analysis. Surveys involve directly questioning participants using structured questionnaires or interviews.

Example: Conducting a national poll to gather opinions on social issues.

(C) Observing the behavior of members of the society

Observing behavior directly is a characteristic of naturalistic observation or ethnographic studies, not archival analysis. Researchers in this method watch participants in real-life settings to study behavior.

Example: Observing how people interact in a crowded marketplace.

(D) Comparing the direct observations of behavior from different cultures

This method refers to cross-cultural research or comparative studies rather than archival analysis. Researchers compare behaviors across different cultures to identify similarities or differences.

Example: Studying cultural differences in greeting customs.

Explanation of Keywords: Archival Analysis refers to a research method in which scientists examine existing records or documents to gather data without directly interacting with participants. It is often used in psychology, sociology, and anthropology to study human behavior, cultural norms, and historical trends.

20. Which is/are the component(s) of Gardner's theory of multiple intelligences?

(A) Logical-Mathematical intelligence

(B) Linguistic intelligence

(C) Spatial intelligence

(D) Insight

Correct Answer- A,B,C

(A) Logical-Mathematical Intelligence

Definition: Logical-mathematical intelligence is one of the types of intelligence proposed by Howard Gardner in his Theory of Multiple Intelligences. It refers to the ability to think logically, reason abstractly, and work with numbers and mathematical concepts. People with strong logical-mathematical intelligence excel in problem-solving, pattern recognition, and scientific thinking.

Key Characteristics:

- Strong skills in mathematics, logic, and reasoning.
- Ability to perform complex calculations and understand abstract concepts.
- Preference for problem-solving and working with numbers, patterns, and systems.

Example: A person who is excellent at solving mathematical puzzles, developing algorithms, or analyzing data sets would have strong logical-mathematical intelligence.

(B) Linguistic Intelligence

Definition: Linguistic intelligence is another of Howard Gardner's multiple intelligences, involving the ability to use language effectively. This includes skills in reading, writing, listening, and speaking. People with high linguistic intelligence are often good at storytelling, writing, and explaining concepts clearly through words.

Key Characteristics:

- Strong vocabulary, reading, writing, and verbal communication skills.
- Ability to understand and use language for various purposes (e.g., storytelling, persuading, explaining).
- Sensitivity to the nuances of language, including syntax, sounds, and meanings.

Example:A skilled writer, poet, journalist, or public speaker demonstrates high linguistic intelligence.These individuals may excel in fields such as writing, law, education, journalism, and communications.

(C) Spatial Intelligence

Definition: Spatial intelligence refers to the ability to visualize and manipulate objects or concepts mentally. People with strong spatial intelligence can think in three dimensions and often excel in fields that require visualizing or manipulating objects, such as art, architecture, or engineering.

Key Characteristics:

- Ability to mentally visualize objects, patterns, and spaces.

- Strong skills in drawing, constructing, or navigating physical spaces.
- Good at solving puzzles, interpreting maps, or understanding how parts fit together.

Example: An architect who can envision a building's design and layout in their mind, or an artist who can create complex visual art, demonstrates high spatial intelligence. Careers in architecture, engineering, sculpture, and design often rely on spatial intelligence.

Explanation of other options

(D)Insight

Definition: Insight refers to a sudden realization or understanding of the solution to a problem, often referred to as the "Aha!" moment. It's not considered a distinct type of intelligence, but rather a cognitive process where a person grasps the underlying nature of a problem and arrives at a solution in an intuitive or creative manner.

Key Characteristics:

- Sudden clarity or breakthrough in understanding a complex problem.
- Often occurs after a period of contemplation or when a person approaches a problem from a new perspective.
- Insight is related to creative problem-solving, where a solution becomes apparent after a shift in thinking.

Example: An inventor who, after weeks of failed attempts, suddenly realizes the key innovation needed for their invention demonstrates insight. Insight can also be seen in everyday problem-solving, such as solving a riddle or figuring out a tricky puzzle.

Explanation of Keywords:

Gardner's Theory of Multiple Intelligences: Proposed by Howard Gardner in 1983.Emphasizes that intelligence is not a single entity (like IQ) but consists of multiple independent intelligences.Each type of intelligence represents a different way of processing information.

21. Match the neurotransmitter in the first column with its effect in the second column.

	Neurotransmitter		Effect
P	Acetylcholine	(i)	Primarily involved in control or alertness and wakefulness.
Q	Norepinephrine	(ii)	Plays a role in the regulation of mood, eating, sleeping and arousal.
R	Serotonin	(iii)	Major inhibitory neurotransmitter in the brain.
S	Gamma-aminobutyric acid (GABA)	(iv)	Involved in muscle action, learning and memory.
		(v)	Involved in Parkinson's disease.

(A) P-(iv), Q-(i), R-(ii), S-(iii)

(B) P-(iii), Q-(i), R-(ii), S-(v)

(C) P-(i), Q-(ii), R-(iv), S-(iii)

(D) P-(iv), Q-(i), R-(v), S-(iii)

Correct Answer- (A)

Explanation of other options

(P)Acetylcholine

Explanation: Acetylcholine is a neurotransmitter involved in muscle action, learning, memory, and other cognitive functions. It is essential for neuromuscular junctions and is associated with Alzheimer's disease when levels are low.

Correct Match: (iv) Involved in muscle action, learning, and memory.

(Q) Norepinephrine

Explanation: Norepinephrine functions as both a neurotransmitter and a hormone. It plays a key role in arousal, alertness, and the fight-or-flight response. It also influences mood regulation, sleep, and appetite.

Correct Match: (i) Primarily involved in control or alertness and wakefulness.

(R) Serotonin

Explanation: Serotonin is a neurotransmitter that regulates mood, appetite, sleep, and emotional states. Low serotonin levels are often linked to depression and anxiety.

Correct Match: (ii) Plays a role in the regulation of mood, eating, sleeping, and arousal.

(S) Gamma-Aminobutyric Acid (GABA)

Explanation: GABA is the primary inhibitory neurotransmitter in the brain. It reduces neuronal excitability and plays a crucial role in controlling anxiety, stress, and muscle tone.

Correct Match: (iii) Major inhibitory neurotransmitter in the brain.

22. Match the depth cues in the first column with their description in the second column.

	Cues		**Description**
P	**Aerial perspective**	**(i)**	**The inward turning of the eyes that occurs when you look at an object that is closer to you.**
Q	**Motion Parallax**	**(ii)**	**The distant mountain appears fuzzy.**
R	**Convergence**	**(iii)**	**Parallel lines appear to converge at the horizon.**
S	**Linear perspective**	**(iv)**	**When we travel in a vehicle, objects that are close appear to move in the opposite direction.**

(A) P-(ii), Q-(iv), R-(i), S-(iii)

(B) P-(ii), Q-(iii), R-(iv), S-(i)

(C) P-(iv), Q-(i), R-(ii), S-(iii)

(D) P-(iii), Q-(iv), R-(i), S-(ii)

Correct Answer- (A)

Explanation of other options:

(P) Aerial Perspective

Explanation: Aerial perspective is a monocular depth cue where distant objects appear hazy or blurry due to the scattering of light in the atmosphere. This effect is often seen with mountains or landscapes.

Correct Match: (ii) The distant mountain appears fuzzy.

(Q) Motion Parallax

Explanation: Motion parallax is another monocular depth cue where objects closer to the viewer appear to move faster in the opposite direction when the observer moves, while distant objects seem to move slower.

Correct Match: (iv) When we travel in a vehicle, objects that are close appear to move in the opposite direction.

(R) Convergence

Explanation: Convergence is a binocular depth cue where the eyes turn inward to focus on an object that is nearby. The closer the object, the more the eyes converge.

Correct Match: (i) The inward turning of the eyes that occurs when you look at an object that is closer to you.

(S) Linear Perspective

Explanation: Linear perspective is a monocular cue where parallel lines appear to converge as they recede into the distance, often observed in roads or railway tracks.

Correct Match: (iii) Parallel lines appear to converge at the horizon.

23.Match the concepts in the first column with the description in the second column.

	Concept		Description
P	Transience	(i)	Source of memory is confused
Q	Misattribution	(ii)	Inability to forget undesirable memories
R	Absentmindedness	(iii)	Accessibility of memory decreases over time
S	Persistence	(iv)	Forgetting caused by lapses in attention

(A) P-(iii), Q-(i), R-(iv), S-(ii)

(B) P-(i), Q-(ii), R-(iii), S-(iv)

(C) P-(ii), Q-(i), R-(iv), S-(iii)

(D) P-(iii), Q-(iv), R-(i), S-(ii)

Correct Answer- (A)

Explanation of other options:

(P) Transience

Explanation: Transience refers to the gradual fading or loss of memory over time. It is a normal part of memory decay.

Correct Match: (iii) Accessibility of memory decreases over time.

(Q) Misattribution

Explanation: Misattribution occurs when a person remembers information but attributes it to the wrong source. It is a type of memory distortion.

Correct Match: (i) Source of memory is confused.

(R) Absentmindedness

Explanation: Absentmindedness involves memory failure due to lapses in attention, often caused by distraction or lack of focus at the time of encoding or retrieval.

Correct Match: (iv) Forgetting caused by lapses in attention.

(S) Persistence

Explanation: Persistence refers to the inability to forget unpleasant or intrusive memories, which is common in conditions like PTSD.

Correct Match: (ii) Inability to forget undesirable memories

24. Which of the following will hold true for a learning acquisition curve drawn for a classical conditioning experiment on eye blinking as conditioned response that plots the learning over a number of trials?

(A) The rate of learning on earlier trials is more than that on later trials.

(B) The learning curve is negatively accelerated.

(C) The rate of learning in later trials will be more than that on earlier trials.

(D) The rate of learning is proportionally increasing with increasing number of trials.

Correct Answer- A,B

(A) The rate of learning on earlier trials is more than that on later trials.

In classical conditioning, the initial trials result in faster learning as the subject quickly picks up the association between stimuli. However, as the subject becomes conditioned, learning slows down and approaches a plateau.

(B) The learning curve is negatively accelerated.

A negatively accelerated learning curve is a characteristic feature of classical conditioning. It shows rapid learning initially and then a slowdown as the subject nears complete conditioning.

Explanation of other options

(C) The rate of learning in later trials will be more than that on earlier trials.

This statement describes a positively accelerated learning curve, which is not characteristic of classical conditioning. In classical conditioning, the rate of learning decreases over time instead of increasing.

(D) The rate of learning is proportionally increasing with the increasing number of trials.

A linear or proportional increase in learning with the number of trials would imply consistent learning at the same rate. However, classical conditioning does not follow this pattern; it slows down after a rapid initial phase.

Explanation of Keywords

1. Learning Acquisition Curve

A learning acquisition curve graphically represents the progress of learning over time (with repeated trials). It typically plots learning performance (e.g., the number of successful conditioned responses) on the Y-axis and the number of trials on the X-axis.

2. Classical Conditioning

Developed by Ivan Pavlov, it involves associating a neutral stimulus (e.g., a tone) with an unconditioned stimulus (e.g., a puff of air to the eye). The result is a conditioned response (e.g., eye blinking in anticipation of the air puff).

3. Negatively Accelerated Curve

A negatively accelerated learning curve means that the rate of learning is fast in the initial trials but slows down as trials progress. This is typical in classical conditioning, where most learning happens in the beginning and reaches a plateau.

25. In the situation where 'A teenager who hates studying science but is also not able to tell his parents fearing their reaction', what is the conflict he is facing and which of these may be his way of dealing with this situation?

(A) Avoidance-Avoidance conflict, he will keep vacillating between telling his parents and continuing to study science.

(B) Avoidance-Avoidance conflict, he may contemplate running away from his home.

(C) Approach-Avoidance conflict, he will experience some emotional turmoil.

(D) Multiple Approach-Avoidance conflict, he will be guided by internal values.

Correct Answer- A,B

(A) Avoidance-Avoidance Conflict, he will keep vacillating between telling his parents and continuing to study science.

The teenager is stuck between two undesirable options:

- Continue studying science despite hating it.
- Tell his parents and risk facing their disapproval.
- Vacillating (going back and forth) is a common behavior in avoidance-avoidance conflict.

(B) Avoidance-Avoidance Conflict, he may contemplate running away from his home.

- While this is still an Avoidance-Avoidance Conflict, contemplating running away is an extreme reaction. However, people in severe psychological distress may consider escape as a way to avoid both undesirable options.

Explanation of other options

(C) Approach-Avoidance Conflict, he will experience some emotional turmoil.

Approach-Avoidance Conflict would apply if studying science had some enjoyable aspects along with its difficulties. However, in this case, the teenager seems to dislike science entirely, making this a pure avoidance conflict.

(D) Multiple Approach-Avoidance Conflict, he will be guided by internal values.

A Multiple Approach-Avoidance Conflict would be applicable if the teenager had several alternatives, like choosing between science, arts, or commerce, each with different pros and cons. The scenario here focuses on a simple, single conflict involving fear and dislike.

Explanation of Keywords

1. Conflict: It refers to a psychological struggle that occurs when a person faces two or more incompatible demands, goals, or impulses.

In this scenario, the teenager is experiencing an internal struggle — he dislikes studying science but fears his parents' reaction if he expresses his feelings.

2. Types of Conflict

Avoidance-Avoidance Conflict: Occurs when a person has to choose between two unpleasant options. Example: The teenager dislikes studying science but also dreads confronting his parents.

Approach-Avoidance Conflict: Involves a situation with both positive and negative outcomes. Example: Continuing to study science may gain parental approval (positive), but it makes him unhappy (negative).

Multiple Approach-Avoidance Conflict: Occurs when a person faces multiple choices, each with both positive and negative aspects. Example: The teenager might be considering different academic options while also worrying about his parents' reaction.

26. Which of these is true about individuals high on n-achievement motivation?

(A) High n-achievement individuals like to work on situations where they have control and can get feedback.

(B) High n-achievement individuals persistently work on tasks they perceive as, either reflecting their personal characteristics like intelligence or are careerrelated.

(C) High n-achievement individuals prefer working on extremely challenging tasks for bigger gains.

(D) High n-achievement individuals avoid changing their aspiration levels.

Correct Answer- A,B

Explanation of other options

(A) High n-achievement individuals like to work on situations where they have control and can get feedback.

Individuals with high n-achievement prefer tasks where their success is based on their own efforts rather than external factors.They also seek feedback to gauge their progress and improve their performance.

(B) High n-achievement individuals persistently work on tasks they perceive as, either reflecting their personal characteristics like intelligence or are career-related.

High n-achievement individuals are often motivated by tasks that are personally meaningful and are seen as a reflection of their abilities.They are likely to persist on tasks that contribute to their career goals and demonstrate their competence.

(C) High n-achievement individuals prefer working on extremely challenging tasks for bigger gains.

While they enjoy challenges, they avoid tasks that are too difficult because the risk of failure is high. Instead, they prefer moderately challenging tasks where success is achievable with effort.

(D) High n-achievement individuals avoid changing their aspiration levels.

High n-achievement individuals are often adaptive and willing to adjust their goals based on feedback. If they encounter challenges or setbacks, they are likely to re-evaluate and modify their aspirations rather than sticking rigidly to unrealistic goals.

Explanation of Keywords

1. n-Achievement (Need for Achievement)

n-Achievement is a concept introduced by David McClelland. It refers to an individual's drive to excel, achieve in relation to a set of standards, and strive to succeed.

People with high n-achievement are often motivated by personal accomplishment, competence, and feedback.

2. Characteristics of High n-Achievement Individuals

- Prefer tasks where they can control the outcome.
- Seek constructive feedback to improve their performance.
- Avoid tasks that are too easy (no challenge) or too difficult (risk of failure).
- Maintain realistic but challenging goals.
- They are generally persistent and goal-oriented.

27. Which of the following is/are Allport's basic assumption(s) concerning human nature?

(A) Human growth as an active process of "becoming".

(B) Personality cannot be fully understood by examining each trait separately, though some system of conceptual schemata are essential for personality study and a trait must be related to the total pattern of personality.

(C) Personality is organized in a topographical model.

(D) All human events are determined by powerful instinctual forces.

Correct Answer- A,B

(A) Human growth as an active process of "becoming".

Allport believed that human beings are constantly in the process of becoming — growing, evolving, and pursuing self-fulfillment.This perspective views personality as a dynamic and evolving process, rather than a fixed or static entity. The term "becoming" reflects his belief in continuous self-development.

(B) Personality cannot be fully understood by examining each trait separately, though some system of conceptual schemata are essential for personality study and a trait must be related to the total pattern of personality.

Allport emphasized a holistic view of personality. He argued that studying traits in isolation is insufficient; traits must be understood within the context of the whole personality. He introduced the concept of cardinal traits, central traits, and secondary traits to describe the complexity of personality.

Explanation of other options

(C) Personality is organized in a topographical model.

The topographical model is associated with Sigmund Freud's psychoanalytic theory, which divides the mind into the conscious, preconscious, and unconscious. Allport did not adopt a topographical model; instead, he viewed personality as a unified and evolving structure.

(D) All human events are determined by powerful instinctual forces.

This view is characteristic of psychoanalytic theory (Freud) and the deterministic perspective. Allport rejected the idea that human behavior is solely driven by instincts or unconscious forces. He believed in conscious motivation and the capacity for personal growth and change.

Explanation of Keywords

1. Allport's Theory of Personality

Gordon Allport was a prominent psychologist known for his trait theory of personality.

He emphasized the uniqueness of the individual and believed that personality is shaped by a combination of traits. Allport focused on human growth and conscious motivations, unlike psychoanalytic theories which emphasized unconscious drives.

2. Human Nature According to Allport

Allport believed in the active nature of human beings and their tendency toward growth and self-improvement. He introduced the concept of functional autonomy, suggesting that adult motives are independent of early childhood experiences.

28. Which of the following aspects are characteristics of the group structure in an organizational context?

(A) Task-oriented role (the activities of an individual that involve helping the group reach the goal).

(B) Socio-emotional role (the activities of an individual that involve being supportive and nurturing of other group members).

(C) Prescriptive norms (expectations within groups regarding what has to be done).

(D) Monitoring (observing work performance).

Correct Answer- A,B,C

(A) Task-Oriented Role

A task-oriented role involves activities that directly contribute to achieving the group's goals.

Examples include:

- Leading discussions
- Problem-solving
- Delegating tasks
- Task-oriented members ensure the group stays focused and productive.

(B) Socio-Emotional Role

A socio-emotional role involves actions that provide emotional support, encourage cooperation, and maintain group harmony. Such individuals are often empathetic and nurturing, helping to resolve conflicts or maintain morale.

Examples include:

- Mediating conflicts
- Encouraging participation
- Providing emotional support

(C) Prescriptive Norms

- Prescriptive norms are the unwritten or written expectations that dictate how group members should behave.
- They provide guidance on what is acceptable or required within the group.
- Examples include:

  - Meeting deadlines
  - Communicating respectfully
  - Adhering to professional standards

Explanation of other options

(D) Monitoring : It refers to the act of observing and evaluating employee or group performance. While it is essential for management or supervisors, it is not typically considered a characteristic of group structure. Monitoring is more of a management function than a structural aspect of a group.

Explanation of Keywords

1. Group Structure: Refers to how a group is organized within an organization. It includes roles, norms, relationships, and patterns of communication that define how members interact.

2. Organizational Context: This refers to the setting where formal and informal groups exist within a business or workplace. Groups are typically formed to achieve specific goals, solve problems, or complete tasks.

29. Which of the following needs/motives are proposed by Abraham Maslow?

(A) Deficit needs.

(B) Meta needs.

(C) Self-actualization needs.

(D) Need-achievement.

Correct Answer- A,B,C

(A)Deficit Needs

Definition: Deficit needs refer to the basic needs that arise due to a lack or deficiency of something essential for survival or well-being. These needs must be met before higher-level psychological needs can be pursued. This concept is rooted in Abraham Maslow's Hierarchy of Needs, where the lower levels (physiological, safety, social, and esteem needs) are considered deficit needs.

Key Characteristics:

- Basic needs that, when unmet, lead to discomfort or a deficiency in functioning.
- These needs must be fulfilled first before individuals can focus on higher-order needs.
- Examples include physiological needs (food, water, shelter), safety needs (security, stability), love and belonging (relationships), and esteem needs (self-esteem, respect).

Example: If a person is hungry or lacks shelter, they will prioritize food and safety over higher-level goals such as self-improvement or creativity. These are deficit needs that drive immediate behavior.

(B) Meta Needs

Definition: Meta needs refer to the needs that arise after the basic (deficit) needs are fulfilled, primarily related to personal growth, self-fulfillment, and the pursuit of higher, more abstract goals. These needs are linked to self-actualization and the desire for personal meaning, creativity, and transcendence. Maslow identified these as needs related to the growth of the individual, beyond mere survival.

Key Characteristics:

- Meta needs are linked to self-actualization, meaning achieving one's full potential.
- These needs are less urgent but are essential for personal fulfillment and well-being.

Example: A person who has met their basic needs may pursue artistic expression, self-discovery, or a meaningful life that goes beyond material comfort. These needs often relate to growth, creativity, and contributing to society in a way that aligns with personal values.

(C) Self-Actualization Needs

Definition: Self-actualization needs refer to the need to realize one's full potential and to become the best version of oneself. This is the highest level in Maslow's Hierarchy of Needs, representing the desire for personal growth, creativity, and self-fulfillment once basic and psychological needs are met.

Key Characteristics:

- Self-actualization is about fulfilling one's true potential and being the person one is capable of becoming.
- This need is more abstract and relates to qualities such as creativity, autonomy, moral integrity, and meaning in life.
- People self-actualize through creativity, problem-solving, authenticity, and expressing individuality.

Example:A person might engage in activities such as writing a novel, starting a business that reflects their passion, or dedicating their life to helping others—all with the goal of becoming their most authentic self and making a meaningful contribution to the world.

Explanation oF Other Options

(D) Need-Achievement (Need for Achievement)

Definition: The need for achievement (often referred to as nAch) is a motivational need that drives individuals to pursue success and excellence in their endeavors. People with a high need for achievement are motivated to set challenging goals, overcome obstacles, and measure their success against high standards. This need was popularized by David McClelland as part of his theory of motivation.

Key Characteristics:

- Individuals with a high need for achievement tend to be driven, goal-oriented, and competitive.
- They are motivated by personal accomplishment and the desire to master tasks and demonstrate competence.
- These individuals prefer tasks that provide a moderate level of difficulty, where they can exert effort and achieve results.

Example: An entrepreneur who constantly strives to innovate, a student who aims for top grades, or an athlete who pushes themselves to set new records all exemplify individuals with a high need for achievement.

Explanation of Keywords

1. Needs/Motives: Needs or motives are internal states that drive individuals to act in a certain way to fulfill a specific goal. Maslow proposed a hierarchy of needs that explains human motivation, starting from basic needs and moving towards higher-level growth needs.

2. Abraham Maslow: Abraham Maslow was a psychologist who developed the Hierarchy of Needs theory in 1943. His theory suggests that people are motivated to fulfill basic needs before they can move on to higher-level growth needs.

The hierarchy consists of five levels, often visualized as a pyramid:

1. Physiological Needs – Basic survival needs (e.g., food, water, shelter)
2. Safety Needs – Security and safety (e.g., financial stability, health)
3. Love and Belongingness Needs – Social connections (e.g., friendships, family)
4. Esteem Needs – Respect, recognition, and self-confidence
5. Self-Actualization Needs – Fulfilling one's potential and personal growth

3. Deficit Needs (D-Needs)

Deficit needs are the first four levels of Maslow's hierarchy (Physiological, Safety, Love/Belongingness, and Esteem needs). They are called deficit needs because they arise from a lack of something and motivate behavior to reduce that lack.

4. Meta Needs (B-Needs)

Meta needs (also called Being needs) refer to the desire for personal growth and self-actualization. Unlike deficit needs, these are not driven by a lack but by the urge for personal fulfillment and growth.

5. Self-Actualization Needs

Self-actualization is the highest level in Maslow's hierarchy, representing the realization of one's potential and growth. It involves creativity, self-expression, and achieving personal goals.

6. Need-Achievement

Need-achievement is a concept proposed by David McClelland, not Maslow. It refers to a person's desire to accomplish challenging goals, gain recognition, and achieve success.

30. A researcher is conducting a study involving two independent variables. Which of the following Analysis of Variance (ANOVA) is/are available to him/her?

A) 2 × 2 ANOVA.

(B) 4 × 3 ANOVA.

(C) 3 × 2 × 2 ANOVA.

(D) One-way ANOVA.

Correct Answer- A,B

(A) 2 × 2 ANOVA (Two-way ANOVA with 2 levels in each factor)

Definition: A 2 × 2 ANOVA is a type of two-way ANOVA design that involves two independent variables (factors), each with 2 levels. This design is used to examine the interaction between two independent variables and their individual effects on a dependent variable.

Key Characteristics:

- It involves two factors, each with two levels (e.g., Gender: Male, Female and Treatment: Control, Experimental).
- This type of ANOVA allows for analysis of main effects (the independent effects of each factor) and the interaction effect (how the factors work together).
- It is a factorial design, meaning the combination of all levels of the two factors is considered.

Example:

- If you are testing the effect of type of diet (Low-fat, High-fat) and exercise regimen (No Exercise, Regular Exercise) on weight loss, you would have a 2 × 2 ANOVA with two factors: diet (2 levels) and exercise regimen (2 levels).
- You could then test for the main effects of diet and exercise, as well as their interaction (whether the combination of a specific diet and exercise regimen is more effective).

(B) 4 × 3 ANOVA (Two-way ANOVA with 4 levels for one factor and 3 levels for another factor)

Definition: A 4 × 3 ANOVA is another form of two-way ANOVA, but this time with 4 levels for one independent variable and 3 levels for the other. This design helps assess the effects of two independent variables (with more than two levels per factor) and their potential interaction on a dependent variable.

Key Characteristics:

- It involves two factors, one with 4 levels and the other with 3 levels (e.g., Treatment: No treatment, Low dose, Medium dose, High dose and Time: 1 week, 2 weeks, 3 weeks).
- The design tests for main effects of both factors and the interaction effect between them.

Example: You could test the effects of different drug dosages (No dose, Low dose, Medium dose, High dose) and treatment durations (1 week, 2 weeks, 3 weeks) on the effectiveness of the drug. This design will allow you to examine the main effects of the drug dosage and treatment duration, as well as their interaction (e.g., the impact of drug dosage may depend on the treatment duration).

Explanation of other options

(C) 3 × 2 × 2 ANOVA (Three-way ANOVA with 3 factors, each with 2 or 3 levels)

Definition: A 3 × 2 × 2 ANOVA is a three-way ANOVA design that involves three factors. One factor has 3 levels, while the other two factors each have 2 levels. This design is used to explore the effects of three independent variables and their possible interactions on the dependent variable.

Key Characteristics:

- This design involves three independent variables with different levels (3 levels for one factor, 2 levels for the others).
- It allows you to test for main effects of each factor, as well as all possible two-way interactions and a three-way interaction between the factors.
- A three-way ANOVA is useful for more complex experiments where multiple factors are at play.

Example: Consider an experiment to study the effects of diet (3 levels: Low-carb, High-carb, No-carb), exercise type (2 levels: Aerobic, Strength training), and age group (2 levels: Young, Old) on body fat percentage. The 3 × 2 × 2 ANOVA allows you to explore the main effects of each factor, as well as interactions such as whether the effect of diet on body fat differs by age group or exercise type.

(D) One-way ANOVA (Single factor ANOVA)

Definition: A one-way ANOVA is a simpler design used when you want to test the effect of a single factor with multiple levels on a dependent variable. It is used to determine whether there are any statistically significant differences between the means of more than two groups or treatments.

Key Characteristics:

- There is only one factor (independent variable) with multiple levels (e.g., three or more groups).
- One-way ANOVA tests for differences between the means of the groups and assumes that the groups are independent of each other.
- This is the most basic form of ANOVA and is often used for experiments with a single independent variable.

Example: If you wanted to test the effect of three different teaching methods (Traditional, Online, and Blended) on student performance, you would use a one-way ANOVA to see if there is a statistically significant difference in performance between the three teaching methods.

Explanation of Keywords

1. Researcher: A researcher is someone conducting a study to investigate a hypothesis or explore relationships between variables.

2. Independent Variables: Independent variables (IVs) are variables that are manipulated or categorized to observe their effect on the dependent variable (DV). In this question, the researcher has two independent variables.

3. Analysis of Variance (ANOVA): ANOVA is a statistical method used to compare means between groups to check for significant differences. It is applied when there are more than two groups or categories. The type of ANOVA used depends on the number of independent variables and their levels (categories).

4. Types of ANOVA:

A. One-Way ANOVA: One-way ANOVA involves only one independent variable with multiple levels. Since the researcher has two independent variables, One-way ANOVA is not applicable.

B. Factorial ANOVA: A Factorial ANOVA involves two or more independent variables.

The format "2 × 2 ANOVA" indicates:

- Two independent variables
- Each variable has two levels (e.g., Male/Female, Low/High)
- 2 × 2 ANOVA = 2 IVs with 2 levels each
- 4 × 3 ANOVA = 2 IVs, one with 4 levels and the other with 3 levels
- 3 × 2 × 2 ANOVA = 3 IVs (since the notation has 3 numbers)

31. Which of the following statements is true about personal space?

(A) It is silent and invisible.

(B) It is a geographic component of interpersonal relations.

(C) Invasions of personal space are a matter of degree.

(D) There are no across culture variations.

Correct Answer- A,B,C

(A) It is silent and invisible.

Personal space is silent and invisible since it is a psychological boundary that is not physically marked. People may react non-verbally when their space is invaded, through body language like stepping back, avoiding eye contact, or showing discomfort.

(B) It is a geographic component of interpersonal relations.

Personal space is considered a geographic or spatial component of how people relate to each other. How much space people prefer can vary based on interpersonal dynamics, culture, and social norms.

(C) Invasions of personal space are a matter of degree.

The level of discomfort caused by a personal space invasion depends on how close the invasion is, the relationship with the other person, and the context. A minor encroachment may cause slight discomfort, while a significant violation may lead to a strong reaction.

Explanation of other options

(D) There are no across culture variations.

Cultural variations in personal space are well-documented.

- Western cultures often prefer larger personal spaces.
- Latin American, Middle Eastern, and some Asian cultures may have smaller personal space norms and are more comfortable with close contact.
- Thus, personal space preferences differ significantly across cultures.

Explanation of Keywords:

1. Personal Space: It refers to the physical distance individuals maintain between themselves and others to feel comfortable. It is an invisible boundary that can vary depending on factors like relationships, culture, and environment. Violations of personal space can cause discomfort, anxiety, or even aggression.

2. Proxemics: The concept of personal space was introduced by Edward T. Hall through his study of proxemics (the study of how people use space in interpersonal interactions).

He identified four types of personal space zones:

- Intimate Space (0-18 inches): For close relationships.
- Personal Space (18 inches - 4 feet): For friends and family.
- Social Space (4-12 feet): For acquaintances and social settings.
- Public Space (12+ feet): For public speaking or large audiences.

32. If a person got a score of 75 on a test, which of the following distributions allow(s) for the most favourable interpretation of that score? (assuming higher values are more favourable)

(A) Mean = 55, Standard Deviation = 4

(B) Mean = 60, Standard Deviation = 3

(C) Mean = 65, Standard Deviation = 5

(D) Mean = 50, Standard Deviation = 10

Correct Answer- A,B

(A) Mean = 55, Standard Deviation = 4

Z score = Score- mean divided by standard deviation

- Z-Score = 75–55 divided by 4 =5.
- A z-score of 5.0 is exceptionally high, meaning the score of 75 is far above the average.

(B) Mean = 60, Standard Deviation = 3

- Z-Score = 75–60 divided by 3 =5.
- A z-score of 5.0 is also extremely favorable, as the score of 75 significantly exceeds the average.

Explanation of other options

(C) Mean = 65, Standard Deviation = 5

- Z-Score = 75–65 divided by 5 =2.0

- A z-score of 2.0 indicates that the person performed above average but not as exceptionally as in options A and B.This is moderately favorable but not the most favorable.

(D) Mean = 50, Standard Deviation = 10

- Z-Score = 75–50 divided by 10 =2.5
- A z-score of 2.5 is above average and suggests a good performance, but the spread of scores is wide, reducing the impact of the score of 75.This is somewhat favorable but not as much as options A and B.

Explanation of Keywords:

1. Score Interpretation: A score of 75 needs to be compared to the mean and the spread of scores (standard deviation) to determine how well the person performed.The more the score of 75 exceeds the mean, the more favorable the interpretation.

2. Mean: The mean represents the average score of the distribution. A score of 75 will be considered more favorable if the mean is lower, as it indicates the person performed better than most others.

3. Standard Deviation (SD): The standard deviation measures the spread of scores around the mean.

A smaller standard deviation indicates that scores are closely clustered around the mean, making a score of 75 even more exceptional. A larger standard deviation means scores are spread out, so the score of 75 may not stand out as much.

4. Z-Score: A z-score helps to understand how far the person's score is from the mean in units of the standard deviation using the formula:

- Z=X–Mean divided by Standard Deviation.
- Higher z-scores indicate a more favorable performance.

33.A man's wife is dying. She is in dire need of a drug. The only place to get the drug is at the store of a pharmacist who is known to overcharge people for drugs. The man can only pay ₹20000 but the pharmacist wants ₹50000, and refuses to sell it to him for less, or to let him pay later. What will the man do if he is at the conventional stage of morality as per Kohlberg's theory of moral reasoning?

(A) He would not steal the drug, as everyone will see him as a thief, and his wife would not approve of his stealing or accept the stolen drug.

(B) No matter what, he would obey the law because stealing is a crime.

(C) The man would not steal the drug, as he may get caught and go to jail.

(D) The man would steal the drug to cure his wife and then tell the authorities what he has done. He may have to pay a penalty, but at least he would have saved a human life.

Correct Answer- A,B

(A) He would not steal the drug, as everyone will see him as a thief, and his wife would not approve of his stealing or accept the stolen drug.

- This response reflects Stage 3 (Interpersonal Relationships).
- The man is concerned about how others will view him, seeking to maintain a good social image.
- He worries about being labeled as a thief and values his wife's disapproval more than the act of stealing.

(B) No matter what, he would obey the law because stealing is a crime.

- This response reflects Stage 4 (Maintaining Social Order).
- The man believes laws are necessary for social order and should be followed without exception.
- Even though his wife may die, he prioritizes respecting the legal system.

Explanation of other options

(C) The man would not steal the drug, as he may get caught and go to jail.

This response reflects Stage 1 (Obedience and Punishment), which is part of the pre-conventional level. The decision is based solely on fear of punishment, not societal rules or social approval.

(D) The man would steal the drug to cure his wife and then tell the authorities what he has done. He may have to pay a penalty, but at least he would have saved a human life.

This response reflects Post-conventional Morality (Stage 5 or 6).The man prioritizes saving a life over obeying the law and is willing to accept the consequences. It demonstrates an understanding of moral principles beyond legal rules.

Explanation of Keywords:

1. Conventional Stage of Morality (Kohlberg's Theory)

Lawrence Kohlberg proposed a theory of moral development with three levels, each containing two stages. The levels are:

- Pre-conventional (self-interest and avoiding punishment)
- Conventional (upholding social rules and seeking social approval)
- Post-conventional (based on abstract principles and justice)

The conventional stage (typically seen in adolescents and adults) is characterized by:

- Stage 3: Interpersonal Relationships – Acting to gain approval and maintain relationships.
- Stage 4: Maintaining Social Order – Following laws, rules, and authority to uphold social order.

2. Morality:It refers to principles and values that guide individuals in determining what is right or wrong. Kohlberg's theory focuses on the reasoning behind moral choices, not just the actions themselves.

3. Dire Need: Dire need means an urgent or desperate situation requiring immediate attention. In this case, the man's wife needs the drug to survive, creating a moral dilemma.

4. Overcharge: Overcharging means selling a product at an unreasonably high price. The pharmacist's refusal to lower the price or accept partial payment further complicates the moral dilemma.

5. Moral Dilemma: A moral dilemma is a situation where a person must choose between two or more conflicting moral principles. In this case, the man must choose between obeying the law (not stealing) or saving his wife's life (stealing the drug).

34. According to Erik Erikson, identity versus role confusion is the fifth stage of life span development. Which of the following outcomes may emerge as a result of identity crisis?

(A) Identity diffusion

(B) Identity moratorium

(C) Identity foreclosure

(D) Identity perception

Correct Answer- A,B

(A). Identity Diffusion

Definition: Identity diffusion is a state in which an individual has not yet explored or made any commitments regarding their personal identity, values, or beliefs. People in this status often lack a clear sense of direction in life and may feel unsure about who they are.

Key Characteristics:

- No exploration: They have not actively explored different roles, beliefs, or values.
- No commitment: They haven't made any decisions or commitments regarding their identity.
- This stage often occurs in adolescents, but can persist into adulthood if not addressed.

Example: A teenager who has not yet thought about their career, values, or beliefs, and has no clear goals or sense of self, would be in identity diffusion.

(B). Identity Moratorium

Definition: Identity moratorium is a status where an individual is in the process of exploring various identity options but has not yet made any final commitments. People in this stage are actively questioning and experimenting with different roles, beliefs, and values, but they haven't reached a conclusion or made stable decisions about their identity yet.

Key Characteristics:

- Active exploration: Individuals are exploring different aspects of themselves (e.g., career choices, values, beliefs).
- No commitment yet: They are still in the process of searching and have not yet made firm decisions about their identity.

Example: A college student who is exploring different career paths, trying out various activities, and questioning their personal beliefs but has not yet decided on a specific direction for their future is in identity moratorium.

Explanation of other options

(C). Identity Foreclosure

Definition: Identity foreclosure occurs when an individual has made a commitment to an identity without exploring other options. This often happens when someone accepts the identity prescribed by others (e.g., parents, society) without undergoing a period of self-exploration.

Key Characteristics:

- Commitment without exploration: Individuals make identity decisions prematurely, often because of pressure or influence from family, society, or other external sources.
- They are committed to a role, belief, or identity, but haven't explored other possibilities or considered alternatives.

Example: A person who has decided to follow their parents' career path (e.g., becoming a doctor) without considering other interests or options is in identity foreclosure.

(D). Identity Perception

Definition: Identity perception is not typically recognized as one of the core statuses in Marcia's Theory of Identity Statuses. This term may refer to an individual's perception of their own identity or how they see themselves in relation to others. However, it is not one of the established categories in Marcia's framework.

Key Characteristics:

- This could refer to how individuals perceive or understand their own identity, though it is not an identity "status" in the theoretical sense.
- It may involve personal reflection on self-concept, how one views their roles, or how they think others perceive them.

Example: Someone might have a certain self-perception of being a creative person, but this self-perception may not necessarily align with an identity status as per Marcia's model. It is more about how one sees themselves rather than their stage of identity development.

Explanation of Keywords

1. Erik Erikson

- Erik Erikson was a developmental psychologist known for his psychosocial theory of development.

- His theory consists of eight stages of life, each characterized by a specific conflict that individuals need to resolve for healthy psychological growth.

2. Identity Versus Role Confusion

- This is the fifth stage of Erikson's psychosocial development, typically occurring during adolescence (ages 12 to 18).
- During this stage, teenagers explore and develop their sense of self through experimenting with different roles, beliefs, and values.
- Successfully resolving this stage leads to identity formation — a clear sense of who they are.
- Failure to resolve this conflict results in role confusion — uncertainty about one's identity and future roles.

3. Identity Crisis

- An identity crisis is a period of intense self-exploration where adolescents struggle to define their personal values, beliefs, and career goals.
- It is a normal and often necessary process for forming a strong identity.
- The outcome of an identity crisis can lead to different identity statuses, as identified by James Marcia, who expanded on Erikson's work.

35. Life span experts argue that biological aging begins at birth. Which of the following is/are explanation/s of aging?

(A) Cells can divide to a maximum of about 75 to 80 times and that as people age, cells become less capable of dividing.

(B) People age because when cells metabolize energy, the by-products include unstable oxygen molecules known as free radicals.

(C) Aging is due to the decay of mitochondria.

(D) Cell division increases as people age.

Correct Answer- A,B,C

(A) Cells can divide to a maximum of about 75 to 80 times, and as people age, cells become less capable of dividing.

- This statement refers to the Hayflick limit.
- Leonard Hayflick discovered that human cells can divide approximately 75 to 80 times before they stop dividing.
- This limit is due to the gradual shortening of telomeres (protective caps at the ends of chromosomes) with each cell division.
- When telomeres become too short, the cell enters a state called senescence or undergoes apoptosis (programmed cell death).

(B) People age because when cells metabolize energy, the by-products include unstable oxygen molecules known as free radicals.

- This statement is based on the Free Radical Theory of Aging.
- During cellular metabolism, oxygen is used to produce energy, but a by-product of this process is the formation of free radicals.
- Free radicals are unstable molecules that damage cells, proteins, and DNA, contributing to aging and diseases like cancer and neurodegenerative disorders.

(C) Aging is due to the decay of mitochondria.

- This statement refers to the Mitochondrial Theory of Aging.
- Mitochondria are the energy-producing structures in cells.
- Over time, mitochondria suffer damage from free radicals and other stressors, leading to decreased energy production and cell damage.
- This decline in mitochondrial function is associated with muscle weakness, neurodegeneration, and other signs of aging.

Explanation of other options

(D) Cell division increases as people age.

- This statement is incorrect.
- As people age, the rate of cell division decreases, not increases.
- Due to telomere shortening, DNA damage, and reduced cellular repair mechanisms, older cells divide more slowly or stop dividing altogether.
- Increased cell division is more characteristic of cancerous growth, not normal aging.

Explanation of Keywords

Biological Aging: Biological aging refers to the gradual deterioration of cells, tissues, and organs over time, leading to functional decline. It is influenced by both genetic factors and environmental factors such as lifestyle, stress, and exposure to toxins. Various theories explain why and how biological aging occurs.

36. Which of the following are involved in sympathetic nervous system activation?

(A) Inhibited salivation

(B) Increased heart rate

(C) Inhibited digestion

(D) Constricted pupils

Correct Answer- A,B, C

(A) Inhibited Salivation

During sympathetic activation, salivation decreases as part of the body's effort to conserve energy for more critical functions. A dry mouth is often experienced in stressful or fearful situations.

(B) Increased Heart Rate

The SNS stimulates the heart, causing an increased heart rate (tachycardia) to pump more oxygen-rich blood to the muscles and brain. This ensures the body has the energy needed to respond to the threat.

(C) Inhibited Digestion

Digestive processes are inhibited during SNS activation. Blood flow is redirected away from the digestive system and toward the muscles, lungs, and heart, which are essential for immediate action.

Explanation of other options

(D) Constricted Pupils

The SNS actually causes pupil dilation (mydriasis) to allow more light into the eyes, improving vision and awareness during stressful situations.

Constricted pupils are associated with the parasympathetic nervous system (PNS), which is responsible for the "rest-and-digest" response.

Explanation of Keywords

Sympathetic Nervous System (SNS)

The SNS is a part of the autonomic nervous system (ANS), which controls involuntary bodily functions.

It is primarily responsible for the "fight-or-flight" response, preparing the body to respond to perceived threats or stressful situations. Activation of the SNS results in physiological changes that provide more oxygen, energy, and blood flow to essential organs like the heart and muscles.

37. How is/are genetic theories of psychopathology tested?

(A) Using twin studies

(B) Using family history studies

(C) Using adoption studies

(D) Using psychodynamic studies

Correct Answer- A, B , C

(A) Using Twin Studies

Definition: Twin studies are research designs used to examine the relative influence of genetics (nature) and environment (nurture) on behavior, traits, and disorders by comparing monozygotic (identical) twins and dizygotic (fraternal) twins. Monozygotic twins share 100% of their genetic material, while dizygotic twins share 50%. This allows researchers to assess the degree to which genetic factors influence the similarities and differences between twins.

Key Characteristics:

- Twin studies are particularly useful for examining the heritability of traits and disorders (e.g., intelligence, personality, mental health conditions).
- Researchers compare the concordance rates (how often both twins exhibit a trait) between identical and fraternal twins.
- High concordance rates in identical twins, compared to fraternal twins, suggest a genetic influence.

Example: A study comparing the rate of schizophrenia in identical and fraternal twins can help determine how much of the disorder is genetically inherited versus influenced by the environment.

(B) Using Family History Studies

Definition: Family history studies involve examining the patterns of behavior or traits within families to explore whether certain characteristics (such as mental health disorders, intelligence, or personality traits) tend to run in families. This method looks at first-degree relatives (parents, siblings) to assess the likelihood that a trait or condition is inherited.

Key Characteristics:

- Family history studies do not directly measure genetic inheritance but assess whether a trait or disorder appears more frequently in people who share genetic links.
- These studies can help researchers identify patterns or predispositions within families.
- However, they cannot isolate genetic factors from environmental ones, as family members often share both.

Example: If depression is more prevalent in the relatives of individuals with depression, researchers might hypothesize a genetic link. However, family history studies cannot distinguish genetic influence from shared environmental factors (e.g., family dynamics).

(C) Using Adoption Studies

Definition: Adoption studies examine individuals who were adopted at an early age and compare them to both their biological parents (genetic relatives) and their adoptive parents (environmental influences). These studies help isolate the effects of genetics and environment by comparing adopted children to their biological and adoptive families.

Key Characteristics:

- Adoption studies allow researchers to investigate the influence of genetics by comparing adopted children to their biological parents and environmental influences by comparing them to their adoptive parents.

- These studies are particularly helpful in understanding the genetic basis of behaviors or disorders, as they separate the genetic and environmental factors more clearly than twin or family studies.

Example: A researcher studying the heritability of intelligence might compare the IQ scores of adopted children to the IQ scores of their biological and adoptive parents. If the child's IQ is more similar to their biological parents, this suggests a genetic influence.

Explanation of other options

(D) Using Psychodynamic Studies

Definition: Psychodynamic studies focus on the exploration of unconscious processes, childhood experiences, and internal conflicts that influence an individual's behavior and mental health, often based on Sigmund Freud's psychoanalytic theory. These studies typically look at how early life experiences, unconscious drives, and repressed memories influence personality and behavior.

Key Characteristics:

- Psychodynamic studies tend to emphasize the role of early childhood experiences and unconscious motives.
- These studies are less focused on genetic or environmental influences but instead explore psychological forces within the individual that shape behavior, including defence mechanisms, transference, and unresolved conflicts.
- Research methods often involve case studies, therapy sessions, or projective tests (e.g., Rorschach inkblot test) to uncover unconscious thoughts and behaviors.

Example: A psychodynamic study might investigate how unresolved childhood trauma influences an adult's relationships or behavior. For instance, it might explore how a person's unconscious memories of early parental neglect affect their ability to form close relationships in adulthood.

Explanation of Keywords

1. Genetic Theories of Psychopathology

Genetic theories suggest that mental disorders or psychopathologies (e.g., depression, schizophrenia, bipolar disorder) can be inherited or influenced by genetic factors.

These theories explore how genes contribute to the development of psychological disorders.They are often tested by examining patterns of mental health across biological relatives.

2. Tested: The term "tested" refers to how researchers evaluate or investigate the validity of genetic theories.It involves using scientific methods to gather evidence that supports or refutes the role of genetics in psychopathology.

3. Twin Studies

Twin studies are a primary method to test genetic theories. They compare monozygotic twins (identical) who share 100% of their genes, and dizygotic twins (fraternal) who share about 50% of their genes.

4. Family History Studies

Family history studies examine the presence of psychological disorders across multiple generations within a family.They look for patterns of inheritance by identifying whether disorders are more frequent in biological relatives compared to the general population. This method helps researchers determine genetic predisposition to mental illnesses.

5. Adoption Studies

Adoption studies compare adopted individuals with their biological and adoptive families.If an adopted child resembles their biological parents in terms of psychopathology rather than their adoptive parents, it supports a genetic influence.

6. Psychodynamic Studies

Psychodynamic studies are based on Freud's psychoanalytic theory, which focuses on unconscious conflicts, childhood experiences, and internal drives. These studies do not test genetic theories.Instead, they explore how past experiences and unconscious motivations influence behavior and mental health.

38. An investigator approached college students who initially believed that water should be purified and asked them to compose and recite a videotaped speech against the use of water purifiers. To do this, some were offered large incentives and others were offered small incentives. Later their attitudes towards water purifiers were tested. Which of the following will be the expected finding(s)?

(A) The smaller the incentive, the greater will be the attitude change.

(B) All the students will change their attitudes towards water purifiers.

(C) All the students will continue to feel favourably about water purifiers.

(D) The larger the incentive, the greater will be the attitude change.

Correct Answer- (A): The smaller the incentive, the greater will be the attitude change.

According to cognitive dissonance theory, if students were offered a small incentive for acting against their beliefs, they would experience greater dissonance.

They cannot justify their behavior with the incentive alone, leading them to resolve the dissonance by changing their attitude to match their speech.They may convince themselves that water purifiers are not as beneficial as they initially thought.

Explanation of other options

(B)All the students will change their attitudes towards water purifiers.

Only students who received small incentives are likely to change their attitudes. Students who received large incentives will justify their behavior with the reward, reducing dissonance without needing to change their attitude.

(C) All the students will continue to feel favourably about water purifiers.

While some students may hold on to their initial beliefs, those with small incentives will likely change their attitudes.Therefore, it is incorrect to say that all students will continue to support water purifiers.

(D) The larger the incentive, the greater will be the attitude change.

Large incentives reduce dissonance because students can easily justify their behavior with the reward. They are more likely to think, "I did it for the money," and therefore experience less pressure to change their attitudes.

In contrast, smaller incentives create stronger dissonance, leading to a greater likelihood of attitude change.

Explanation of Keywords: Cognitive dissonance refers to the psychological discomfort that arises when a person holds two contradictory beliefs or attitudes or when their behavior conflicts with their beliefs. In this scenario, students believed water purifiers were good, but they were asked to speak against their own belief.

39. In which attachment style(s), do children tend to show clingy behaviour but then reject the attachment figure's attempt to interact with them?

(A) Resistant attachment

(B) Avoidant attachment

(C) Secure attachment

(D) Disorganized attachment

Correct Answer- (A) Resistant Attachment (also called Ambivalent Attachment)

Definition: Resistant attachment is characterized by infants who are very clingy and dependent on their caregivers but are also ambivalent or resistant when the caregiver tries to provide comfort. These children are often anxious and tend to have difficulty exploring their environment, even when their caregiver is present.

Key Characteristics:

○ Clinginess: The child is very attached to the caregiver and seeks comfort from them, but they are also wary or uncertain about the caregiver's responsiveness.

○ Anger and difficulty soothing: When the caregiver returns after a separation, the child may show mixed emotions, such as seeking comfort but also showing frustration, resistance, or anger.

○ Inconsistent caregiver behavior: This type of attachment is often linked to caregivers who are inconsistent in meeting the child's needs—sometimes attentive, sometimes neglectful, leading to confusion in the child.

Example: A child who is very upset when the mother leaves and, upon her return, might push her away while also reaching for her. The child feels anxious and unsure of whether the caregiver will meet their needs.

Explanation of other options

(B) Avoidant Attachment

Definition: Avoidant attachment occurs when infants avoid or ignore the caregiver, showing little emotional reaction to their departure or return. These children tend to suppress or hide their emotions, possibly due to caregivers being emotionally unavailable or unresponsive.

Key Characteristics:

- Independence: The child may appear independent and does not seek comfort from the caregiver during distress.
- Lack of emotional expression: When the caregiver leaves or returns, the child does not show distress or joy, possibly as a result of early experiences of rejection or emotional neglect.
- Dismissive caregiver behavior: This attachment style is often seen in children whose caregivers are emotionally distant or unavailable when needed.

Example:A child may not cry when the mother leaves, and when she returns, the child might avoid her or act indifferent. They do not seek comfort even when distressed.

(C) Secure Attachment

Definition: Secure attachment is the healthiest and most stable attachment style. Infants with this attachment feel safe and comfortable with their caregiver, allowing them to explore the environment while knowing that they can return to the caregiver for comfort when needed. Securely attached children trust that their caregivers will be responsive to their needs.

Key Characteristics:

- Comfort with exploration: The child feels confident to explore their surroundings and interact with others, knowing they can return to their caregiver for comfort if needed.
- Responsive to separation and reunion: When the caregiver leaves, the child may show distress, but they are quickly comforted when the caregiver returns.
- Consistent caregiver behavior: This attachment style is typically formed when caregivers are consistently responsive, attentive, and nurturing.

Example: A child who cries when the mother leaves the room but is easily comforted when she returns. The child seeks comfort from the caregiver and is then willing to continue exploring.

(D)Disorganized Attachment

- Definition: Disorganized attachment is characterized by inconsistent and confused behaviors in response to the caregiver. Children with this attachment style may exhibit contradictory actions, such as approaching the caregiver but then freezing or backing away. This type of attachment is often seen in children who experience abuse, neglect, or frightening behavior from their caregivers.
- Key Characteristics:

  - Confusion and fear: The child may display contradictory behaviors, like wanting to approach the caregiver but also feeling afraid of them, often because the caregiver is a source of both comfort and fear.
  - Lack of clear strategy: There is no clear, consistent behavior pattern like those seen in other attachment styles. The child may seem overwhelmed by conflicting feelings toward the caregiver.
  - Traumatic caregiver behavior: This attachment style is often associated with caregivers who are frightening, unpredictable, or abusive, causing the child to be unsure of how to react.

- Example:

  ○ A child may look towards the caregiver when distressed, but then suddenly freeze or avoid contact, possibly because the caregiver is abusive or emotionally unpredictable.

Explanation of Keywords

1. Attachment Style: Attachment refers to the emotional bond that forms between a child and their caregiver.

Attachment styles describe how children respond to their caregivers, especially during moments of stress or separation.These styles are often observed in the Strange Situation experiment by Mary Ainsworth.

2. Clingy Behavior: Clingy behavior refers to a child's excessive desire to stay close to their caregiver, seeking comfort and reassurance.

This often involves crying, holding onto the caregiver, or being unwilling to explore the environment. It is a sign of anxious attachment where the child fears separation.

4. Attachment Figure: An attachment figure is usually the primary caregiver (e.g., parent, guardian) who provides care, protection, and emotional support.The child relies on this figure for comfort and safety.

40. A study is conducted to see the effectiveness of volume levels of commercials. In the graph given below, values of mean effectiveness (dependent variable) are presented on the Y axis, and three levels of volume, namely, soft, medium and loud are presented on the X axis. The graph shows the relationship between volume and mean effectiveness for males in the continuous line and for females in the dashed line. Which of the following interpretation(s) is/are correct from the graph?

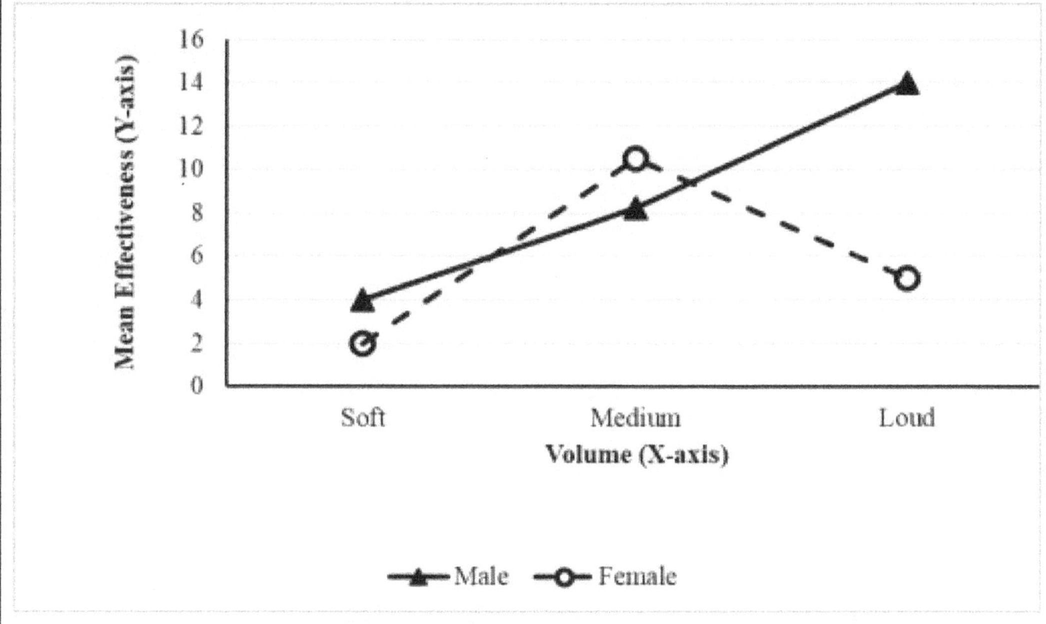

(A) A linear relationship exists for males and a nonlinear relationship for females.
(B) The effect of increasing volume on effectiveness depends on whether the participant is a male or a female.
(C) No interaction effect is seen.
(D) A linear relationship exists for both males and females.

Correct Answer – A and B

(A) A linear relationship exists for males and a nonlinear relationship for females.

- Males (Solid Line):

  ○ The solid line for males shows a consistent upward trend from soft to medium to loud volume.

- ◦ This suggests a linear relationship, where effectiveness increases steadily as the volume increases.

- Females (Dashed Line):

  - ◦ The dashed line for females increases from soft to medium volume, then drops sharply from medium to loud volume.
  - ◦ This indicates a nonlinear relationship since the effectiveness does not continue in one direction — it rises and then falls.

(B) The effect of increasing volume on effectiveness depends on whether the participant is a male or a female.

- The graph shows different patterns for males and females.
- For males, louder commercials lead to increased effectiveness.
- For females, effectiveness peaks at medium volume but declines at loud volume.
- This is a classic example of an interaction effect, where gender moderates the effect of volume on effectiveness.

Explanation of other options
(C) No interaction effect is seen.

- An interaction effect occurs when the effect of one variable (volume) on the dependent variable (effectiveness) differs depending on the level of another variable (gender).
- Here, the male and female lines cross, showing that the impact of volume is not the same for both genders.
- The effectiveness of loud volume is significantly different between males and females.

(D) A linear relationship exists for both males and females.

- While the relationship for males is linear, the relationship for females is not.
- The sharp decline in effectiveness at loud volume for females breaks the linearity.
- Therefore, it is inaccurate to claim that both relationships are linear.

Explanation of Keywords
Mean Effectiveness:The mean represents the average effectiveness score for each volume level across participants. It helps summarize the central tendency of responses for both males and females.

Linear Relationship: A linear relationship implies a consistent, straight-line increase or decrease in effectiveness as volume changes. In a linear relationship, effectiveness changes at a constant rate with each increase in volume.

Nonlinear Relationship: A nonlinear relationship means the change in effectiveness is not constant. It may show a curve, peak, or drop, indicating that the effect of volume on effectiveness varies at different levels.

Interaction Effect:An interaction effect occurs when the effect of one independent variable (volume) on the dependent variable (effectiveness) changes depending on the level of a second variable (gender). If males and females respond differently to the same volume levels, it suggests an interaction effect.

Dependent variable:It responds to the independent variable. It is called dependent because it "depends" on the independent variable.

Mock Paper 1

1.Which philosophical worldview emphasizes objective reality and measurement?

A. Constructivism

B. Pragmatism

C. Postpositivism

D. Behaviourism

2.Which research design integrates both numeric data and textual data?

A. Quantitative

B. Qualitative

C. Mixed methods

D. Cross-sectional

3.Which of the following are characteristics of qualitative research?MSQ

A. Emergent design

B. Deductive reasoning

C. Use of open-ended questions

D. Numerical analysis

4.In a mixed methods approach, which of the following is true?

A. Only qualitative methods are used

B. Data are always collected simultaneously

C. Integration of qualitative and quantitative data occurs

D. Only survey data is used

5.A good hypothesis should be:

A. Vague and open-ended

B. Non-testable

C. Testable and specific

D. Assumed true without evidence

6.Operational definition refers to:

A. The literal dictionary definition

B. The philosophical explanation

C. How a variable is measured in a study

D. The statistical summary

7.The population from which a sample is drawn is called:

A. Control group

B. Sampling frame

C. Experimental group

D. Variable group

8.Which of the following are types of sampling methods?MSQ

A. Simple random

B. Stratified

C. Quota

D. Thematic

9.A study using detailed life stories of participants is using:

A. Experimental method

B. Narrative research

C. Survey method

D. Ethnographic method

10.Field studies typically:

A. Are highly controlled

B. Take place in natural settings

C. Have no real-world applicability

D. Involve laboratory manipulation

11.A researcher conducts a group discussion with six adolescents. This is an example of:

A. Case study

B. Focus group

C. Structured interview

D. Content analysis

12.Which of the following are qualitative methods?MSQ

A. Case study

B. Ethnography

C. Experimental design

D. Survey questionnaire

13.Informed consent implies:

A. Participants must guess the purpose of the study

B. Participation must be voluntary and informed

C. Deception is always prohibited

D. Participants must always be paid

14.Which of the following are ethical concerns in research?MSQ

A. Confidentiality

B. Fabrication of data

C. Debriefing

D. Demand characteristics

15.Which measure is most affected by extreme scores?

A. Mean

B. Median

C. Mode

D. Range

16.In a normal distribution, approximately what percentage of scores fall within ± 1 SD?

A. 50%

B. 68%

C. 95%

D. 99.7%

17.Parametric tests require: MSQ

A. Normal distribution

B. Homogeneity of variance

C. Ordinal data

D. Interval/Ratio scale

18.Which test is non-parametric?

A. ANOVA

B. Chi-square

C. t-test

D. Pearson correlation

19. Effect size tells us:

A. Whether the hypothesis is true

B. The practical significance of results

C. Whether a test is valid

D. How random the sample is

20.A correlation of -0.80 indicates:

A. No relationship

B. Weak negative relationship

C. Strong negative relationship

D. Strong positive relationship

21.Point biserial correlation is used when:

A. Both variables are continuous

B. One is continuous, one is dichotomous

C. Both are dichotomous

D. None of the above

22.In multiple regression:

A. Only one predictor is used

B. One outcome is predicted from multiple variables

C. Several outcomes are predicted

D. It is not a statistical method

23.Which are types of special correlation methods?MSQ

A. Tetrachoric

B. Phi coefficient

C. Chi-square

D. Biserial

24. In a one-way ANOVA, the number of independent variables is:

A. 1

B. 2

C. 3

D. 0

25.Which design reduces order effects?

A. Between-subjects

B. Repeated measures

C. Latin square

D. Quasi-experimental

26. Repeated measures design involves: MSQ

A. Using different groups for each condition

B. The same participants across conditions

C. High risk of carryover effects

D. Between-group comparison

27.Which of the following designs involves analyzing more than one dependent variable?

A. MANOVA

B. ANOVA

C. Chi-square

D. ANCOVA

28.A cohort study is typically:

A. Experimental

B. Longitudinal

C. Cross-sectional

D. Laboratory-based

29.Single-subject designs are best suited for:

A. Studying group differences

B. Clinical interventions

C. Large-scale surveys

D. Ethnographic studies

30.Features of randomized block design include: MSQ

A. Random assignment within blocks

B. Matching participants

C. No control for variability

D. Reducing error variance

31. Psychometrics primarily deals with:

A. Personality theories

B. Measurement of psychological constructs

C. Clinical intervention

D. Learning theories

32.An item measuring arithmetic ability on an IQ test is an example of:

A. Projective test

B. Aptitude test

C. Performance test

D. Personality measure

33.Which are key components in test construction?MSQ

A. Item writing

B. Scaling

C. Sampling

D. Operationalization

34.Reliability refers to:

A. Accuracy of measurement

B. Consistency of measurement

C. Truthfulness of responses

D. Ethicality of testing

35.A test that predicts future performance has:

A. Content validity

B. Construct validity

C. Predictive validity

D. Concurrent validity

36.Split-half reliability estimates:

A. Test-retest consistency

B. Inter-rater agreement

C. Internal consistency

D. Face validity

37.Types of psychological tests include:MSQ

A. Achievement tests

B. Projective tests

C. Likert scales

D. Intelligence tests

38.Norms in psychological testing help in:

A. Creating test items

B. Validating hypotheses

C. Comparing individual performance to a group

D. Ensuring ethical standards

39.In item analysis, a good item should have:

A. High item-total correlation

B. Low discrimination index

C. Irrelevant content

D. Equal response choices

40.In test standardization, the goal is to:

A. Personalize each test

B. Ensure uniform administration and scoring

C. Increase subjectivity

D. Promote informal testing

41.Applications of psychological testing include: MSQ

A. Educational guidance

B. Clinical diagnosis

C. Organizational recruitment

D. Language translation

42.Validity differs from reliability in that:

A. Validity is consistency

B. Reliability is truthfulness

C. Validity is about accuracy

D. Reliability is about ethics

43.Cronbach's alpha is a measure of:

A. Predictive validity

B. Internal consistency

C. Test fairness

D. Item difficulty

44.The process of establishing test norms is called:

A. Scaling

B. Standardization

C. Sampling

D. Weighting

45.Aptitude tests are typically used in: MSQ

A. Counseling

B. Career guidance

C. Personality assessment

D. Educational settings

46.Which of the following is the primary goal of basic psychological research?

A. To solve practical problems

B. To evaluate interventions

C. To increase theoretical understanding

D. To improve therapy outcomes

47.In experimental research, random assignment is crucial because it:

A. Ensures participants know the hypothesis

B. Minimizes the impact of confounding variables

C. Increases the sample size

D. Allows researchers to generalize findings

48.Which of the following is an example of a non-experimental research design?

A. True experiment

B. Quasi-experiment

C. Correlational study

D. Repeated measures design

49. In psychological research, a variable that is manipulated to observe its effect on another variable is called the:

A. Dependent variable

B. Control variable

C. Confounding variable

D. Independent variable

50. Which of the following characteristics is essential for establishing causality in research?

A. High ecological validity

B. Random sampling

C. Temporal precedence

D. Use of surveys

Mock Paper 2

1. Which of the following neurotransmitters is primarily involved in mood regulation and implicated in depression?
a) Dopamine
b) Serotonin
c) Acetylcholine
d) GABA

2. The sympathetic nervous system is responsible for:
a) Stimulating digestion
b) Slowing heart rate
c) "Fight or flight" response
d) Deep sleep

3. Which structure in the brain is primarily involved in forming new memories?
a) Amygdala
b) Hippocampus
c) Thalamus
d) Cerebellum

4. Which of the following are invasive methods in physiological psychology? (MSQ)
a) EEG
b) Lesion techniques
c) Microelectrode studies
d) PET scan

5. The all-or-none principle applies to which of the following?
a) Hormonal secretion
b) Neural impulses
c) Muscle contraction
d) Synaptic cleft functioning

6. Hemispheric lateralisation refers to:
a) Equal functions of both brain hemispheres
b) Structural symmetry in brain lobes
c) Functional specialisation of the two hemispheres
d) Corpus callosum functioning

7. Which brain region regulates hunger and thirst?
a) Hippocampus
b) Thalamus
c) Hypothalamus
d) Medulla

8. Which chemical methods are used in invasive physiological psychology? (MSQ)
a) Hormone assays
b) Neurochemical lesioning
c) Neuroimaging
d) Microinjection

9. In which part of the neuron does the action potential typically begin?
a) Dendrite
b) Axon terminal
c) Cell body
d) Axon hillock

10. The endocrine system communicates using:

a) Electrical signals

b) Neurotransmitters

c) Hormones

d) Enzymes

11. Which chromosomal anomaly results in Down syndrome?

a) Trisomy 21

b) Monosomy X

c) Trisomy 18

d) XXY

12. EEG is primarily used to measure:

a) Brain structure

b) Hormone levels

c) Brain electrical activity

d) Blood flow

13. Degeneration techniques help in studying:

a) Muscle fatigue

b) Hormone interactions

c) Pathways of damaged neurons

d) EEG patterns

14. Twin studies help to understand: (MSQ)

a) Role of environment in behaviour

b) Neurotransmitter pathways

c) Heritability of traits

d) Impact of hormones on emotion

15. Which brain part is closely linked to emotional processing, especially fear?

a) Pons

b) Amygdala

c) Cerebellum

d) Occipital lobe

16. Which hormone directly affects the fight or flight response?

a) Cortisol

b) Insulin

c) Melatonin

d) Oxytocin

17. The vestibular sense is involved in:

a) Taste perception

b) Balance and spatial orientation

c) Touch Sensitivity

d) Color discrimination

18. Which of the following are the functions of glial cells? (MSQ)

a) Insulate neurons

b) Transmit action potentials

c) Remove waste

d) Form myelin

19. A microelectrode can be used to:

a) Map hormone pathways

b) Measure electrical activity in a single neuron

c) Detect neurotransmitter synthesis

d) Scan brain lobes

20. Which of the following methods are considered non-invasive? (MSQ)

a) PET

b) EEG

c) Lesion studies

d) fMRI

21. Which brain region is part of the limbic system?

a) Basal ganglia

b) Hippocampus

c) Occipital lobe

d) Cerebellum

22. Which neurotransmitter is most associated with reward pathways and addiction?

a) Dopamine

b) GABA

c) Serotonin

d) Norepinephrine

23. Hormonal regulation of behaviour can influence: (MSQ)

a) Sexual motivation

b) Sleep-wake cycle

c) Language acquisition

d) Aggression

24. Which of the following is NOT a function of the hypothalamus?

a) Regulating body temperature

b) Coordinating voluntary movement

c) Controlling appetite

d) Hormonal regulation

25. Which two factors are involved in the nature-nurture controversy?

a) Endocrine vs exocrine

b) Neural vs hormonal

c) Genetic inheritance vs environmental influence

d) Brain vs spinal cord

MCQs and MSQs

26. The minimum stimulation required to detect a stimulus 50% of the time is known as:

a) Sensory adaptation

b) Absolute threshold

c) Difference threshold

d) Sensory threshold

27. Which of the following is an example of classical conditioning?

a) A rat learning to press a lever for food

b) A dog salivating at the sound of a bell

c) A child modelling behaviour after a parent

d) Memorizing a list through rehearsal

28. In operant conditioning, a reinforcement is most effective when it is:

a) Delayed and random

b) Immediate and consistent

c) Punitive and repetitive

d) Paired with a neutral stimulus

29. Which theory emphasises mental processes in learning, such as insight and latent learning?

a) Classical conditioning

b) Operant conditioning

c) Social learning theory

d) Cognitive learning theory

30. Gestalt psychologists emphasised:

a) The most minor units of sensation

b) That perception is the sum of sensations

c) That perception is organised and whole

d) That behaviour is solely based on reinforcement

31. Which of the following senses detects body position and movement changes? (MSQ)

a) Vestibular

b) Olfactory

c) Kinesthetic

d) Auditory

32. Which of the following are monocular cues for depth perception? (MSQ)

a) Retinal disparity

b) Linear perspective

c) Texture gradient

d) Interposition

33. The role of attention in perception is to:

a) Increase threshold levels

b) Filter and prioritise sensory input

c) Equalize all sensory modalities

d) Reduce memory load

34. Which process is involved in long-term memory retrieval? (MSQ)

a) Cue-dependent recall

b) Reconstructive processing

c) Sensory registration

d) Contextual encoding

35. The forgetting curve was first demonstrated by:

a) Skinner

b) Ebbinghaus

c) Piaget

d) Bandura

36. Which of the following best defines sensory adaptation?

a) The process of selective attention

b) The decrease in sensitivity to a constant stimulus

c) The increase in perception after exposure

d) The transformation of stimulus energy

37. The organ of Corti is located in the:

a) Cochlea

b) Semicircular canal

c) Eustachian tube

d) Auditory nerve

38. Which sensory modality is processed directly by the limbic system without passing through the thalamus?
a) Audition
b) Touch
c) Olfaction
d) Vision

39. According to the interference theory of forgetting, forgetting occurs because:
a) Memory decays with time
b) Information is blocked by similar information
c) Retrieval cues are absent
d) Encoding was shallow

40. Which of the following statements about operant conditioning is true? (MSQ)
a) It involves voluntary responses
b) Pavlov first studied it
c) Reinforcement increases behaviour likelihood
d) Punishment permanently eliminates behaviour

41. The physical trace of memory in the brain is referred to as a:
a) Schema
b) Mnemonic
c) Engram
d) Cue

42. The vestibular system contributes to: (MSQ)
a) Detecting body movement
b) Coordinating eye movement
c) Interpreting taste
d) Maintaining balance

43. Which of the following describes a gestalt principle of perception?
a) Bottom-up processing
b) Law of effect
c) Figure-ground organisation
d) Serial position effect

44. Social learning theory emphasises the role of:
a) Trial-and-error learning
b) Insight learning
c) Observation and modelling
d) Reflexive responses

45. Which memory store has the shortest duration?
a) Sensory memory
b) Short-term memory
c) Long-term memory
d) Working memory

46. The decay theory of forgetting postulates that:
a) Interference causes forgetting
b) Memories fade over time due to disuse
c) Information retrieval is context-dependent
d) Emotional trauma blocks encoding

47. What is the function of the amygdala in memory?
a) Encodes verbal memories
b) Stores procedural memory

c) Tags emotional content in Memories

d) Stores spatial information

48. Which of the following is true about sensory thresholds? (MSQ)

a) They vary across individuals

b) They can change due to fatigue

c) They are fixed for all stimuli

d) They are used to define just noticeable differences

49. In memory, the serial position effect refers to:

a) Tendency to remember information based on emotional value

b) Better recall of items at the beginning and end of a list

c) Rehearsing items based on semantic content

d) Errors during memory reconstruction

50. Which of the following processes is associated with the encoding phase of memory?

a) Long-term potentiation

b) Retroactive interference

c) Retrieval failure

d) Consolidation

Mock Paper 3

1.Which of the following best illustrates the concept of a "prototype"?

A. A mental image of your own pet dog

B. The idea of "dog" that includes all breeds

C. A golden retriever when thinking of the concept "dog"

D. A list of dog characteristics

2.Which of the following is NOT a component of the information processing model in cognitive psychology?

A. Sensory memory

B. Long-term memory

C. Drive reduction

D. Working memory

3.Which theory emphasizes the role of environmental interaction in shaping cognitive processes?

A. Information-processing approach

B. Psychodynamic theory

C. Ecological approach

D. Dual-process theory

4.Heuristics in problem-solving can be described as:

A. Guaranteed methods to solve problems

B. Mental shortcuts that may lead to errors

C. Step-by-step procedures

D. Random strategies

5.Which of the following best explains "functional fixedness"?

A. Failure to see new uses for a familiar object

B. A tendency to overuse heuristics

C. Selective attention in decision-making

D. Focusing only on emotional aspects of a problem

6.Metacognitive processing involves:

A. Automatic processing

B. Thinking about one's own thinking

C. Memorizing facts

D. Use of reflexive actions

7.The representativeness heuristic leads individuals to:

A. Choose the most statistically probable answer

B. Rely on how typical something seems

C. Avoid decision-making

D. Always use logic over intuition

8.According to Gardner, musical intelligence is an example of:

A. Interpersonal intelligence

B. Spatial intelligence

C. Specialized intelligence

D. Multiple intelligence

9.Sternberg's triarchic theory of intelligence does NOT include:

A. Analytical intelligence

B. Practical intelligence

C. Creative intelligence

D. Emotional intelligence

10.Cattell differentiated intelligence into:

A. Logical and verbal intelligence

B. Creative and practical intelligence

C. Crystallized and fluid intelligence

D. Componential and experiential intelligence

11.Which of the following theorists proposed a two-factor theory of intelligence?

A. Thurstone

B. Gardner

C. Spearman

D. Jensen

12.Emotional intelligence includes all EXCEPT:

A. Managing emotions

B. Identifying others' emotions

C. Solving arithmetic problems

D. Using emotions constructively

13.The main difference between intelligence and aptitude is that:

A. Aptitude is broader than intelligence

B. Intelligence refers to specific abilities

C. Aptitude refers to potential for learning

D. Intelligence cannot be measured

14.Imagery is most closely associated with which cognitive activity?

A. Language acquisition

B. Problem-solving

C. Mental rotation

D. Logical reasoning

15.Which of the following is a common obstacle in decision-making?

A. Functional fixedness

B. Overconfidence bias

C. Fluid intelligence

D. Spearman's law

(MSQ)

16.Which of the following are part of Sternberg's triarchic theory?

A. Analytical intelligence

B. Interpersonal intelligence

C. Practical intelligence

D. Creative intelligence

17.Which are common problem-solving strategies?

A. Algorithm

B. Insight

C. Heuristic

D. Daydreaming

18.Examples of heuristics include:

A. Availability heuristic

B. Representativeness heuristic

C. Serial positioning

D. Mental set

19.The ecological approach in cognitive psychology emphasizes:

A. The use of laboratory-based studies

B. Real-world tasks

C. Naturalistic observation

D. Computer simulations

20.Imagery helps in:

A. Enhancing memory

B. Solving spatial tasks

C. Impairing language skills

D. Representing concepts

(MCQ)

21.Which of the following is NOT part of Freud's structural model?

A. Ego

B. Self

C. Superego

D. Id

22.In the five-factor model of personality, "Openness" refers to:

A. Warmth in social situations

B. Imaginative and creative tendencies

C. Conscientious behavior

D. Desire to be around people

23.Which psychologist is most associated with the social cognitive view of personality?

A. Carl Jung

B. Albert Bandura

C. Carl Rogers

D. Hans Eysenck

24.The MMPI is primarily used to assess:

A. Intelligence

B. Psychopathology

C. Motivation

D. Interests

25.Which trait is part of Eysenck's model?

A. Neuroticism

B. Agreeableness

C. Self-esteem

D. Locus of control

26.According to Carl Rogers, a well-adjusted person experiences:

A. Congruence between self and experience

B. Unconditional negative regard

C. Anxiety due to unconscious conflict

D. Detachment from social relationships

27.A key feature of the trait perspective is:

A. Emphasis on unconscious drives

B. Emphasis on consistent behavior patterns

C. Rejection of empirical methods

D. Focus on stages of development

28.Biological approaches to personality often examine:

A. Early childhood trauma

B. Conditioned reflexes

C. Genetic influences

D. Defense mechanisms

29.Which of the following is a projective technique?

A. WAIS

B. TAT

C. MMPI

D. BDI

30.Which defense mechanism involves attributing one's own unacceptable thoughts to others?

A. Denial

B. Rationalization

C. Projection

D. Repression

(MSQ)

31.Freud's psychosexual stages include

A. Oral

B. Anal

C. Phallic

D. Conscientious

32.According to Bandura, personality is shaped by:

A. Observational learning

B. Reinforcement

C. Reciprocal determinism

D. Self-actualization

33.Assessment of personality using inventories includes:

A. 16 PF

B. NEO-PI-R

C. Rorschach

D. MMPI

34.Humanistic theories emphasize:

A. Free will

B. Self-concept

C. Unconscious motives

D. Personal growth

35.Common criticisms of trait theories include:

A. Lack of explanatory depth

B. Ignoring situational factors

C. Over-reliance on biological factors

D. Poor reliability of measures

(MCQ)

36.Which type of concept is based on specific rules and features?

A. Natural concept

B. Prototype concept

C. Formal concept

D. Fuzzy concept

37.In the dual-process theory, System 1 is typically characterized as:

A. Logical and effortful

B. Fast and intuitive

C. Statistical and rational

D. Slow and analytical

38.Which theorist argued that intelligence is largely genetically determined?

A. Gardner

B. Jensen

C. Thurstone

D. Sternberg

39.Which method is most effective for solving well-defined problems?

A. Incubation

B. Algorithm

C. Brainstorming

D. Insight

40.Which component is shared by both intelligence and creativity?

A. Divergent thinking

B. Working memory

C. Fluid reasoning

D. Motivation

(MSQ)

41.Features of fluid intelligence include:

A. Problem-solving in novel situations

B. Use of accumulated knowledge

C. Independent of education

D. Declines with age

42.Obstacles to problem-solving can include:

A. Confirmation bias

B. Functional fixedness

C. Mental set

D. Algorithm use

43.Cognitive psychologists are interested in studying:

A. Language comprehension

B. Sensation thresholds

C. Problem-solving behavior

D. Mental imagery

44.Which of the following are subtests of standard intelligence scales like the WAIS?

A. Vocabulary

B. Block Design

C. Thematic Apperception

D. Arithmetic

45.Differences between aptitude and intelligence tests include:

A. Aptitude tests predict future performance

B. Intelligence tests measure global capacity

C. Intelligence tests are always verbal

D. Aptitude tests are more specific

(MCQ)

46.Which of the following statements best reflects the behaviorist view of personality?

A. Personality is a result of unconscious conflicts

B. Personality is learned through environmental reinforcement

C. Personality traits are inherited

D. Personality is shaped by cognitive schemas

47.Which theory focuses most on self-concept and unconditional positive regard?

A. Psychoanalytic theory

B. Trait theory

C. Humanistic theory

D. Social learning theory

48.In Jung's theory, the 'persona' represents:

A. The inner self

B. The repressed memory

C. The social mask we wear

D. The shadow side of personality

49.The term "reciprocal determinism" is most associated with:

A. Freud

B. Bandura

C. Skinner

D. Maslow

50.Which of the following is a biological basis for personality differences?

A. Childhood attachment

B. Neurotransmitter activity

C. Social modeling

D. Self-actualization needs

Mock Paper 4

1.Which theory of motivation suggests behavior is driven by a desire to maintain an optimal level of arousal?

A. Instinct Theory

B. Drive Reduction Theory

C. Arousal Theory

D. Incentive Theory

2.Which of the following best explains the concept of achievement motivation?

A. Desire to engage in novel experiences

B. Striving to meet internal standards of excellence

C. Drive to reduce physiological needs

D. Effort to maintain homeostasis

3.The Schachter-Singer theory of emotion emphasizes:

A. Physiological arousal followed by emotional labeling

B. Cognitive appraisal before arousal

C. Simultaneous arousal and emotion

D. Emotion arises from instinctual drives

4.According to Lazarus' cognitive-mediational theory, which comes first in the emotional process?

A. Physiological arousal

B. Emotional expression

C. Cognitive appraisal

D. Hormonal changes

5.Which stage of the General Adaptation Syndrome is characterized by the depletion of body resources?

A. Alarm

B. Resistance

C. Exhaustion

D. Recovery

6.Problem-focused coping involves:

A. Avoiding the problem

B. Engaging in distraction techniques

C. Directly addressing the source of stress

D. Reappraising the emotional meaning

7.Which of the following is a key idea in Rational Emotive Behavior Therapy (REBT)?

A. Behavior is the result of unconscious drives

B. Changing irrational beliefs can change emotions

C. Stress is a result of environmental triggers alone

D. Emotional catharsis leads to insight

8.Incentive theory of motivation suggests that:

A. Behavior is internally driven

B. External rewards guide behavior

C. Humans are passive recipients of stimuli

D. Motivation arises solely from instincts

9.The biological basis of emotion involves all EXCEPT:

A. Amygdala

B. Hypothalamus

C. Pituitary gland

D. Hippocampus

10.Curiosity-driven behavior is an example of:

A. Drive-reduction

B. Intrinsic motivation

C. Extrinsic motivation

D. Incentive motivation

(MSQ)

11.Which of the following are theories of emotion?

A. Drive-Reduction Theory

B. Cannon-Bard Theory

C. James-Lange Theory

D. Schachter-Singer Theory

12.Stressors can be:

A. External events

B. Internal thoughts

C. Physiological needs

D. All of the above

13.Emotion-focused coping strategies may include:

A. Meditation

B. Denial

C. Reframing

D. Solving the problem directly

14.Intrinsic motivation is characterized by:

A. Desire for external rewards

B. Internal satisfaction

C. Curiosity-driven behavior

D. Social praise

15.Which of the following are biological components involved in emotion processing?

A. Amygdala

B. Prefrontal cortex

C. Medulla oblongata

D. Hippocampus

(MCQ)

16.According to Heider's Attribution Theory, attributing someone's behavior to their personality is called:

A. External attribution

B. Situational attribution

C. Dispositional attribution

D. Defensive attribution

17.The tendency to comply with a request made by someone of higher authority is known as:

A. Conformity

B. Obedience

C. Compliance

D. Suggestibility

18.Which of the following theories explains attitude change due to inconsistency among beliefs and behaviors?

A. Attribution Theory

B. Cognitive Dissonance Theory

C. Reinforcement Theory

D. Balance Theory

19.Which of the following is NOT part of social perception?

A. Attribution

B. Impression formation

C. Problem-solving

D. Implicit personality theories

20.A key component of prosocial behavior is:

A. Seeking reward

B. Aggression

C. Helping others

D. Asserting dominance

21.Which leadership style is characterized by shared decision-making and collaboration?

A. Authoritarian

B. Laissez-faire

C. Democratic

D. Autocratic

22.Prejudice differs from discrimination in that prejudice is:

A. A behavior

B. A legal term

C. An attitude

D. Always visible

23.According to Sherif's Realistic Conflict Theory, intergroup conflict arises from:

A. Personality clashes

B. Communication breakdown

C. Competition over limited resources

D. Cultural differences

24.Social categorization helps individuals to:

A. Create stereotypes

B. Organize information

C. Promote group conflict

D. Avoid ambiguity

25.In Milgram's obedience study, participants were willing to administer shocks because of:

A. Aggressive traits

B. Peer pressure

C. Obedience to authority

D. Group conformity

(MSQ)

26.Which of the following are elements of attitude?

A. Affective component

B. Behavioral component

C. Cognitive component

D. Situational component

27.Implicit personality theories involve:

A. Beliefs about trait associations

B. Awareness of one's biases

C. Stereotyping

D. Logical deduction of personality traits

28.Factors influencing conformity include:

A. Group size

B. Unanimity

C. Personal confidence

D. Normative influence

29.Theories of intergroup conflict include:

A. Social Identity Theory

B. Drive-Reduction Theory

C. Realistic Conflict Theory

D. Equity Theory

30.Effective persuasion includes which of the following components?

A. Source credibility

B. Message clarity

C. Audience involvement

D. Punishment

MCQs

31.Which hormone is primarily associated with the stress response in the body?

A. Oxytocin

B. Cortisol

C. Insulin

D. Dopamine

32.Which approach to motivation is most associated with Maslow's hierarchy of needs?

A. Drive theory

B. Humanistic approach

C. Arousal theory

D. Instinct theory

33.Which of the following is least likely to be classified as a stressor?

A. Loss of a loved one

B. Daily traffic jam

C. Winning a lottery

D. Taking a nap

34.Which technique is central to meditation as a stress reduction tool?

A. Logical reasoning

B. Focused attention

C. Behavioral reinforcement

D. Emotional repression

35.The 'alarm' stage of the General Adaptation Syndrome corresponds with:

A. Relaxation and recovery

B. Activation of the sympathetic nervous system

C. Long-term immune suppression

D. Exhaustion and collapse

MSQs

36.Which of the following are classified as intrinsic motivators?

A. Enjoyment of a task

B. Curiosity

C. Receiving a trophy

D. Sense of accomplishment

37.Features of emotional states include:
A. Short duration
B. Triggered by identifiable causes
C. No physiological arousal
D. Subjective experience

38.Which of the following are associated with emotional regulation?
A. Prefrontal cortex
B. Amygdala
C. Hippocampus
D. Cerebellum
39.REBT focuses on:
A. Identifying irrational beliefs
B. Replacing distorted thoughts
C. Exploring unconscious conflicts
D. Learning relaxation techniques
40.Which of the following are consequences of prolonged stress?
A. Impaired immunity
B. Cardiovascular disease
C. Improved working memory
D. Anxiety disorders
MCQs
41.Which concept refers to our tendency to attribute others' behavior to their disposition rather than situational factors?
A. Fundamental attribution error
B. Actor-observer bias
C. Defensive attribution
D. Self-serving bias
42.Which of the following is an example of compliance?
A. Changing belief due to group pressure
B. Obeying orders from authority
C. Agreeing to a request without being forced
D. Following personal conviction
43.Prosocial behavior is most likely influenced by:
A. Empathy
B. Fear
C. Narcissism
D. Bystander apathy
44.Which of the following best describes prejudice?
A. A behavior toward a group
B. A generalization applied to all members of a group
C. A positive or negative evaluation of a group
D. An objective perception of social differences
45.Which of the following experiments is associated with conformity?
A. Asch's line judgment study
B. Milgram's obedience study
C. Zimbardo's prison study
D. Harlow's monkey experiment

MSQs

46.Which of the following factors influence obedience?

A. Presence of authority figure

B. Physical proximity of victim

C. Group unanimity

D. Legitimacy of authority

47.Group dynamics can be influenced by:

A. Leadership style

B. Social loafing

C. Groupthink

D. Aggression

48.Which of the following are methods of attitude change?

A. Persuasion

B. Fear appeals

C. Meditation

D. Role playing

49.According to Social Identity Theory, individuals derive self-esteem from:

A. Group memberships

B. Personal achievements only

C. Social comparisons

D. Private self-concept alone

50.Belief systems are shaped by:

A. Culture

B. Religion

C. Early experiences

D. Genetic factors only

Mock Paper 5

MCQs

1.Which of the following best exemplifies the 'nature' component in the nature vs nurture debate?

A. Parenting style

B. Educational background

C. Genetic inheritance

D. Peer influence

2.Which stage of Piaget's cognitive development is characterized by object permanence?

A. Sensorimotor

B. Preoperational

C. Concrete operational

D. Formal operational

3.Which of the following best defines teratogens?

A. Genetic mutations

B. Agents causing prenatal harm

C. Stress hormones in pregnancy

D. Dietary supplements

4.Which psychologist proposed the psychosocial theory of development?

A. Piaget

B. Vygotsky

C. Erikson

D. Freud

5.According to Kohlberg, which level of moral development involves adherence to rules to gain social approval?

A. Pre-conventional

B. Conventional

C. Post-conventional

D. None of the above

6.Which of the following prenatal stages occurs first?

A. Embryonic

B. Germinal

C. Fetal

D. Zygotic

7.The Flynn effect primarily refers to:

A. Increased physical growth over generations

B. The increase in average IQ scores over time

C. Delays in language acquisition

D. Reduced attention spans in children

8.Which part of development is associated with Erikson's stage of "identity vs role confusion"?

A. Infancy

B. Early childhood

C. Adolescence

D. Late adulthood

9.In Vygotsky's theory, the Zone of Proximal Development refers to:

A. The difference between what a learner can do without help and with help

B. The area of brain activation during learning

C. Social norms of learning environments

D. Reward zones in reinforcement learning

10. According to the programmed theories of aging, aging is due to:

A. Random cell damage

B. Pre-set biological timeline

C. Exposure to carcinogens

D. Stress accumulation

MSQs

11. Which of the following are physical changes during adolescence?

A. Puberty

B. Growth spurts

C. Object permanence

D. Menopause

12. Which of the following are components of DNA?

A. Nucleotides

B. Ribosomes

C. Adenine

D. Lysosomes

13. Cognitive decline in late adulthood is often associated with:

A. Alzheimer's disease

B. Reduced sensory input

C. Increased creativity

D. Decreased processing speed

14. Which developmental stages are associated with moral reasoning according to Kohlberg?

A. Pre-conventional

B. Pre-operational

C. Conventional

D. Post-conventional

15. Infants typically show which of the following behaviors in psychosocial development?

A. Stranger anxiety

B. Attachment formation

C. Self-concept clarity

D. Basic trust development

16. Which of the following factors influence gene expression in prenatal development?

A. Teratogens

B. Nutrition

C. Social class

D. Hormonal levels

17. Which are primary characteristics of adolescence?

A. Increased independence

B. Identity exploration

C. Senescence

D. Egocentrism

18. Which of the following are cognitive developments during childhood?

A. Conservation of quantity

B. Abstract reasoning

C. Language acquisition

D. Imaginary audience

19. Theories of aging include:

A. Wear-and-tear theory

B. Activity theory

C. Socio-emotional selectivity theory

D. Reinforcement theory

20.Which of the following are considered teratogenic effects?

A. Birth defects

B. Cognitive impairments

C. Accelerated development

D. Premature birth

MCQs

21.The DSM is primarily used for:

A. Personality assessment

B. Intelligence testing

C. Diagnosis of mental disorders

D. Behavior modification

22.Which therapy focuses on unconscious conflicts and childhood experiences?

A. Behavioral

B. Psychodynamic

C. Cognitive

D. Humanistic

23.Which psychological disorder is most strongly linked to trauma exposure?

A. OCD

B. PTSD

C. Bipolar disorder

D. Schizophrenia

24.Albert Ellis is most associated with which therapy type?

A. Client-centered therapy

B. Rational emotive behavior therapy

C. Behavior therapy

D. Gestalt therapy

25.Which psychological concept is most applicable in resolving workplace conflicts?

A. Defense mechanisms

B. Group dynamics

C. Classical conditioning

D. Self-actualization

26.Which of the following best describes 'territoriality' in environmental psychology?

A. Competition for mates

B. Personal claim over space

C. Overcrowding

D. Noise control

27.Which technique is often used in cognitive therapy?

A. Dream analysis

B. Free association

C. Thought restructuring

D. Aversion therapy

28.Which educational strategy is rooted in Skinner's operant conditioning?

A. Free writing

B. Positive reinforcement

C. Free association

D. Classical conditioning

29.Which component is most critical in person-centered therapy?

A. Free will

B. Transference

C. Unconditional positive regard

D. Exposure hierarchy

30.Which of the following is a biological therapy?

A. Electroconvulsive therapy

B. Exposure therapy

C. Rational emotive therapy

D. Cognitive rehearsal

MSQs

31.Factors contributing to educational achievement include:

A. Socioeconomic status

B. Emotional intelligence

C. Peer relationships

D. Defense mechanisms

32.PTSD symptoms may include:

A. Hypervigilance

B. Flashbacks

C. Delusions

D. Avoidance behavior

33.Phenomenological therapies emphasize:

A. Self-awareness

B. Rational thinking

C. Subjective experience

D. Behavioral change

34.DSM classifications are based on:

A. Symptoms

B. Causes

C. Functional impairments

D. Personality styles

35.Group dynamics in organizational settings involve:

A. Norms

B. Roles

C. Self-actualization

D. Group cohesiveness

36.Common assessment tools in clinical psychology include:

A. MMPI

B. Beck Depression Inventory

C. Stanford-Binet Test

D. EEG

37.Applications of motivation theories in schools include:

A. Goal-setting strategies

B. Use of punishments

C. Praise for effort

D. Peer comparison

38.Leadership styles in organizational settings include:

A. Democratic

B. Authoritarian

C. Reflective

D. Laissez-faire

39.Issues caused by crowding include:

A. Reduced privacy

B. Increased aggression

C. Enhanced learning

D. Anxiety

40.Biological therapies for mental disorders include:

A. Antipsychotic medication

B. Psychosurgery

C. Systematic desensitization

D. rTMS

MCQs

41.In prenatal development, which structure facilitates nutrient and waste exchange between mother and fetus?

A. Amniotic sac

B. Placenta

C. Umbilical cord

D. Ovary

42.The ability to think hypothetically and reason abstractly is developed during which of Piaget's stages?

A. Concrete operational

B. Preoperational

C. Sensorimotor

D. Formal operational

MSQs

43.Which of the following influence psychosocial development in adolescence?

A. Peer group influence

B. Identity formation

C. Hormonal changes

D. Reflexive motor skills

44.According to Erikson's theory, which stages occur during adulthood?

A. Identity vs role confusion

B. Intimacy vs isolation

C. Generativity vs stagnation

D. Integrity vs despair

45.Which of the following are common milestones in infancy?

A. Crawling

B. Stranger anxiety

C. Hypothetical thinking

D. Babbling

MCQs

46.Which of the following best characterizes behavior therapy?

A. Focus on past trauma

B. Exploration of unconscious conflict

C. Use of reinforcement and punishment

D. Focus on existential meaning

47.Which concept is most relevant to understanding spacing in interpersonal communication?

A. Crowding

B. Proxemics

C. Conformity

D. Locus of control

MSQs

48.Which of the following are techniques used in cognitive-behavioral therapy (CBT)?

A. Cognitive restructuring

B. Thought diaries

C. Free association

D. Exposure therapy

49.Applications of psychology in organizational settings may involve:

A. Enhancing leadership skills

B. Reducing employee stress

C. Treating eating disorders

D. Promoting teamwork

50.School counselling interventions may focus on:

A. Career guidance

B. Learning difficulties

C. Corporate training

D. Social skills development

Anwer Key 1

1. Answer: C
2. Answer: C
3. Answer: A, C
4. Answer: C
5. Answer: C
6. Answer: C
7. Answer: B
8. Answer: A, B, C
9. Answer: B
10. Answer: B
11. Answer: B
12. Answer: A, B
13. Answer: B
14. Answer: A, B, C
15. Answer: A
16. Answer: B
17. Answer: A, B, D
18. Answer: B
19. Answer: B
20. Answer: C
21. Answer: B
22. Answer: B
23. Answer: A, B, D
24. Answer: A
25. Answer: C
26. Answer: B, C
27. Answer: A
28. Answer: B
29. Answer: B
30. Answer: A, B, D
31. Answer: B
32. Answer: C
33. Answer: A, B
34. Answer: B
35. Answer: C
36. Answer: C
37. Answer: A, B, D
38. Answer: C
39. Answer: A
40. Answer: B
41. Answer: A, B, C
42. Answer: C
43. Answer: B
44. Answer: B

45. Answer: A, B, D
46. Answer: C
47. Answer: B
48. Answer: C
49. Answer: D
50. Answer: C

1. B
2. C
3. B
4. B, C
5. B
6. C
7. C
8. B, D
9. D
10. C
11. A
12. C
13. C
14. A, C
15. B
16. A
17. B
18. A, C, D
19. B
20. A, B, D
21. B
22. A
23. A, B, D
24. B
25. C
26. B
27. B
28. B
29. D
30. C
31. A, C
32. B, C, D
33. B
34. A, B, D
35. B
36. B
37. A
38. C
39. B
40. A, C
41. C
42. A, B, D
43. C
44. C

45. A
46. B
47. C
48. A, B, D
49. B
50. A

Answer Key 3

1. C
2. C
3. C
4. B
5. A
6. B
7. B
8. D
9. D
10. C
11. C
12. C
13. C
14. C
15. B
16. A, C, D
17. A, B, C
18. A, B
19. B, C
20. A, B, D
21. B
22. B
23. B
24. B
25. A
26. A
27. B
28. C
29. B
30. C
31. A, B, C
32. A, B, C
33. A, B, D
34. A, B, D
35. A, B
36. C
37. B
38. B
39. B
40. C
41. A, C, D
42. A, B, C
43. A, C, D
44. A, B, D

45. A, B, D
46. B
47. C
48. C
49. B
50. B

1. C
2. B
3. A
4. C
5. C
6. C
7. B
8. B
9. C
10. B
11. B, C, D
12. D
13. A, B, C
14. B, C
15. A, B, D
16. C
17. B
18. B
19. C
20. C
21. C
22. C
23. C
24. B
25. C
26. A, B, C
27. A, C
28. A, B, D
29. A, C
30. A, B, C
31. B
32. B
33. D
34. B
35. B
36. A, B, D
37. A, B, D
38. A, B, C
39. A, B
40. A, B, D
41. A
42. C
43. A
44. C

45. A
46. A, B, D
47. A, B, C
48. A, B, D
49. A, C
50. A, B, C

Answer Key 5

1. C
2. A
3. B
4. C
5. B
6. B
7. B
8. C
9. A
10. B
11. A, B
12. A, C
13. A, B, D
14. A, C, D
15. A, B, D
16. A, B, D
17. A, B, D
18. A, C
19. A, B, C
20. A, B, D
21. C
22. B
23. B
24. B
25. B
26. B
27. C
28. B
29. C
30. A
31. A, B, C
32. A, B, D
33. A, C
34. A, C
35. A, B, D
36. A, B
37. A, C
38. A, B, D
39. A, B, D
40. A, B, D
41. B
42. D
43. A, B, C
44. B, C, D

45. A, B, D
46. C
47. B
48. A, B, D
49. A, B, D
50. A, B, D